UML Toolkit

Hans-Erik Eriksson
Magnus Penker

WILEY COMPUTER PUBLISHING

JOHN WILEY & SONS, INC.

New York • Chichester • Weinheim • Brisbane • Singapore • Toronto

Publisher: Robert Ipsen

Editor: Theresa Hudson

Managing Editor: Micheline Frederick

Text Design & Composition: SunCliff Graphic Productions

Designations used by companies to distinguish their products are often claimed as trademarks. In all instances where John Wiley & Sons, Inc. is aware of a claim, the product names appear in initial capital or all capital letters. Readers, however, should contact the appropriate companies for more complete information regarding trademarks and registration.

This text is printed on acid-free paper.

Copyright © 1998 by Hans-Erik Eriksson and Magnus Penker
Published by John Wiley & Sons, Inc.

This publication is designed to provide accurate and authoritative information in regard to the subject matter covered. It is sold with the understanding that the publisher is not engaged in rendering legal, accounting, or other professional service. If legal advice or other expert assistance is required, the services of a competent professional person should be sought.

Library of Congress Cataloging-in-Publication Data

Eriksson, Hans-Erik, 1961–
    UML toolkit / Hans-Erik Eriksson, Magnus Penker.
        p.   cm.
    Includes index.
    ISBN: 0-471-19161-2 (pbk./CD-ROM : alk. paper)
    1. Object-oriented methods (Computer science)   2. Computer
software--Development.   3. UML (Computer science)   I. Penker,
Magnus, 1968- .   II. Title.
QA76.64.E75   1998
005.1'17--dc21   97-35768
                                                                          CIP

Printed in the United States of America
10 9 8 7 6 5

To my parents
—Hans-Erik

To my beloved Maria
—Magnus

Contents

Use-Case Modeling   **45**

Chapter 4

Classes, Objects, and Their Relationships   65

CHAPTER 5

Dynamic Modeling 119

CHAPTER 6

Advanced Dynamic Modeling: Real–Time Systems 161

CHAPTER 7

Physical Architecture 197

CHAPTER 8

Extending the UML 217

CHAPTER 9

Design Patterns and UML 255

CHAPTER 10

A Process for Using UML 269

CHAPTER 11

Getting Started 295

CHAPTER 12

Case Study 319

Preface

From training and consulting in the object-oriented field, it has become apparent that the lack of standardization for object-oriented modeling is a serious problem. Every method, tool, and practice has its own set of symbols and terminology, resulting in a lot of confusion and frustration, especially for those trying to learn object-oriented technology, whose focus should not be on remembering in which direction the arrows are drawn in a specific tool or notation, but on creating high-quality models to help them build better and more effective software systems.

When the Unified Modeling Language (UML) was first announced, many in the object-oriented community greeted it with enthusiasm because it was the type of effort that many had been waiting for. By establishing a common modeling language that can be used for all kinds of systems, all phases of development, all scales of size, and with many different processes, object-oriented technology can take one step further to infiltrating the mainstream marketplace. This is most evident in the emerging new generation of CASE and visual modeling tools based on UML but it is also apparent in the further development of existing or new processes/methods.

UML is more than just a standardization and discovery of a "unified" notation. It also contains new and interesting concepts not generally found in the object-oriented community, such as how to describe and use patterns in a modeling language, how to use the concept of stereotypes to extend and adapt the language, how to provide complete traceability from conceptual models of a system to the executable components in the physical architecture, and more. Therefore, understanding UML means not only learning the symbols and their meaning; it means learning object-oriented modeling in a state-of-the-art mode.

UML was designed by Grady Booch, James Rumbaugh, and Ivar Jacobson; known as the three amigos. Their work is impressive not just because UML is an excellent modeling language, but because they were able to put aside their own methods and notations in order to achieve this standardization effort. Thanks to their work, methodologists, toolmakers, trainers, and practitioners can now concentrate on locating and establishing appropriate ways of putting UML to real use, rather than discussing which notation is best.

Structure of the Book

The purpose of this book is to provide a comprehensive, nuts-and-bolts guide to the UML. While the reference works by OMG (Object Management Group, the leading organization for standards within the object-oriented field), Booch, Rumbaugh, and Jacobson are based on the final definition of the UML, our book attempts to present the language in a complete yet practical manner, covering all the defined diagrams and concepts. We have tried to avoid theoretical discussions as much as possible, but have included numerous examples and figures in the text—after all, this is a book on a visual modeling language. However, presenting UML is impossible without discussing object-oriented modeling and technology in general, so the book also contains a lot of material on these topics. We also cover real-time systems, design patterns, and process, topics that e feel are important enough to devote entire chapters. The book concludes with a case study that demonstrates the use of the UML in a small application. followed by some exercises for the reader to extend the case study in different ways.

The first chapter contains the background of the Unified Modeling Language: where it comes from, how it can be used, and what the goals are for it. It presents the context in which UML is used, and contains a description of the structure of the book.

Chapter 2 provides an overview of UML to give the reader a feel for the language. The most common elements and their relationships are described, supplemented by the different diagrams that make up the views of a system. The chapter ends with a discussion about modeling with UML.

Use-case modeling is a well-established technique for capturing the requirements of a system, from the viewpoint of an external user (*actor*). In Chapter 3 use cases are described, along with how they are represented in UML.

Chapter 4 contains a description of classes and objects. The main diagram for describing them is the class diagram, which is the most extensive diagram in UML. The representation of classes and objects, the different relationships they may have, and the different variations that are applied to them are all areas discussed in this chapter. The chapter closes with a discussion about model quality, what it is and how to achieve maximum quality in a model.

A class diagram captures most of the static structure and relationships of classes and objects. However, there is also behavior that is dynamic; it happens at a specific point in the life of a system, changes over time, or contains complex interactions between objects. Chapter 5 deals with dynamic modeling. In UML, this is described with a number of diagrams: state, activity, sequence, and collaboration.

Real-time systems are software systems with very high timing requirements, and where the system consists of a number of concurrently executing processes (*active objects*). The specific problems with real-time systems and how they are modeled in UML is the focus of Chapter 6.

Chapter 7 deals with the physical architecture. In the previous chapters, we dealt with the logical architecture. The physical architecture is the code and executable software components of which the system is made, as well as the hardware components such as computers, devices, and their connections. This physical architecture, also known as the *system topology*, and the distribution of software components are modeled in UML.

Chapter 8 describes how UML is extended and adapted. The concept of stereotypes is used heavily in the language and allows users to create their own "types" of elements with specific semantics. This makes it possible to extend or adapt UML to fit a particular process or architectural standard.

One very interesting research area in object-oriented programming and design is the concept of design patterns. Patterns describe good, reusable, and well-proven design solutions to common problems. Chapter 9 describes how patterns are documented and expressed using UML.

Since UML is only a modeling language without a process, it is necessary to create or adapt processes for use with the language. Chapter 10 describes the characteristics of a process and what is needed to define it. It also describes the main criteria of a process that the authors of UML had in mind when designing the language. A description is made of the Unified Process, which is a follow-up work from that concluded at Rational Software Corporation in an attempt to define a process for UML, along with an example process of how the UML is used. Finally, the use of CASE tools is discussed along with an overview of the most popular of these tools.

Chapter 11 describes how to get started with UML. Since most readers probably are converting to UML from other modeling languages, the process of upgrading from other methods such as Booch, OMT, or OOSE/Objectory is discussed. There is also a description of how to perform and lead a modeling session, with several tips on how to achieve efficient and productive sessions.

The book concludes with a case study, where the use of UML is illustrated in an example. The work of transforming the requirements of a system to the final code is illustrated by a set of UML models. This is followed by two appendixes containing a visual glossary of all the model elements in UML and a short explanation, and a text glossary with short descriptions of all common terminology used in UML.

Every chapter ends with a summary and some exercises for the reader. Throughout the book, the Java programming language is used to show the corresponding Java code for different UML concepts and constructions. Even though UML is much more than a visual representation of program code, the translation of models to code is often lacking in books and papers though it's very important that this is done correctly. Java was chosen for these samples because it's a modern object-oriented language that can be used on any platform. Since Java has the same style as C++, a C++ programmer should have no problem in reading and understanding this code.

We've also included a CD-ROM with the book. It contains:

- The demo version of Rational Rose 4.0 for Windows 95 and WindowsNT
- The models and the Java code in the case study

Acknowledgments

We would like to acknowledge the work of some of the people who helped us in this effort. First and foremost, Mikael Fernström and Mona Larsson, who did a tremendous job of proofreading and reviewing all the chapters in detail. Other reviewers who gave us valuable opinions on the text are Martin Sjöblom, Magnus Rådbo, Mats Henricsson, and Anders Engström. Many thanks to Terri Hudson, Micheline Frederick, Sandy Bontemps, Janice Borzendowski, and all the staff at Wiley for their support and work done to produce this book.

Any remaining mistakes or errors in the text are the responsibility of the authors. Readers who would like to contact us to pose a question or just discuss parts of the UML may feel free to do so at the addresses listed here.

Stockholm, September 1997

Hans-Erik Eriksson
Objekt Teknik AB
Odengatan 24, 6 tr.
113 51 STOCKHOLM
SWEDEN
E-mail: hanserik@objektteknik.se

Magnus Penker
Astrakan Strategisk Utbildning AB
Karlavägen 2
112 56 STOCKHOLM
SWEDEN
E-mail: magnus.penker@astrakan.se

1 *What Is the Unified Modeling Language?*

The importance of models has been evident in all engineering disciplines for a long time. Whenever something is built, drawings are made that describe the look and behavior of that "thing." The thing under development may be a house, a machine, or a new department within a company. The drawings work as a specification of how we want the finished product to look. The drawings are handed over to subcontractors, or they are broken down into more detailed drawings necessary for the actual construction work. Plans for cost and time estimation, work distribution, and resource allocation are made based on the information contained in the drawings.

Again, the drawings are models of some thing. A model is a description of some thing. This thing may exist, be in the development stage, or still be in the planning stage. During the work of making a model (modeling), the model designers must investigate the requirements for the finished product. The requirements include areas such as functionality, appearance, performance, and reliability. The designers must then create a model that describes all the different aspects of the product. The model is often broken down into a number of views, each of which describes a specific aspect of the product or system under construction. The model can go through a number of phases where each phase adds detail to the model.

Creating models is highly creative work. There is no final solution, no correct answer that is checked at the end of the work. The model designers, through iterative work, assure that their models achieve the goals and the requirements of the project under construction. But a model is not final; it's typically changed and updated throughout a project to reflect new insights and experiences of the designers. During the modeling, the best solutions are often achieved by allowing a high degree of brainstorming during which different solutions and views are modeled and

1

tested. By iterating different possibilities, the designers reach a deeper understanding of the system, and can finally create models of the systems that achieve the goals and requirements of the system and its users.

Models are usually described in a visual language, which means that most of the information in the models is expressed by graphical symbols and connections. The old saying that "a picture speaks a thousand words" is also relevant in modeling. Using visual descriptions is necessary to communicate complex relationships; it also makes the practical modeling work easier. Not everything is suitable for a visual description, however, some information in models is best expressed in ordinary text. Usable models are:

- *Accurate*: They correctly describe the system to be built.

- *Consistent*: Different views don't express things that are in conflict with each other.

- Easy to communicate to others.

- Easy to change.

- *Understandable*: As simple as possible, but not simpler.

For a long time, there has been talk in the software industry about the so-called software crisis. These crisis discussions are based on the fact that not only do many software projects fail to produce systems that meet the customers' requirements and needs, but also end up exceeding budgets and time schedules. New techniques such as object-oriented programming, visual programming, and advanced development environments have helped to increase productivity. However, they are in many cases directed at the lowest level of system development: the programming. One of the main problems with today's software development is that many projects start programming too soon and concentrate too much effort on writing code. This is partly because managers lack the understanding of the software development process and become anxious when their programming team is not producing code. It's also because the programmers themselves feel more secure when they're programming—a task with which they are very familiar—than when they're building abstract models of the system they are to create.

Certain methods have been around for some time which attempt to prevent the urge to view system development as a "small matter of programming." This multitude of different methods, all with their own unique notation and tools, have left many developers confused. The lack of a well-established notation upon which many methods and tools can agree has also made it more difficult to learn how to use a good method. Furthermore, the quality of many of the early object-oriented methods must be called into question, as many of them were best suited for small systems with limited functionality, and hence didn't have the capability to scale up to the larger systems that are now prevalent.

The trends of the software industry all point to the need for creating models of the systems we intend to build. Visual programming is a technique by which programs are constructed by visually manipulating and connecting symbols; modeling and programming are highly integrated. Systems are becoming larger and distributed over many computers through client/server architectures (with the Internet as the ultimate client/server architecture). The need to integrate complex systems in distributed environments requires that systems have some common models. Business engineering, where the business processes of a company are modeled and improved, requires computer systems that support these processes to implement the business models. Building models of systems before implementing them will become as normal and accepted in the software engineering community as it is in other engineering disciplines.

The Unified Modeling Language

The Unified Modeling Language (UML) is an attempt to solve some of the problems just described. The UML has the potential to become both the formal and de facto standard for making models.

The Method Wars

One of the initial concepts behind UML was to put an end to the "method wars" within the object-oriented community. Object orientation was initially spawned by the programming language Simula, but it didn't become popular until the late '80s with the advent of programming languages such as C++ and Smalltalk. When object-oriented programming became a success, the need for methods to support software development followed. Some of the object-oriented methods that became popular in the early '90s are:

- *Booch*: Grady Booch's method for object-oriented development is available in a number of versions. Booch defined the notion that a system is analyzed as a number of views, where each view is described by a number of model diagrams. The Booch method of notation was very extensive, and some users found some of the symbols (the infamous *clouds*) very hard to draw manually. The method also contained a process by which the system was analyzed from both a macro- and micro-development view, and was based on a highly incremental and iterative process.

- *OMT*: The Object Modeling Technique (OMT) is a method developed at General Electric where James Rumbaugh previously worked. It's a rather straightforward process for tests, based on a requirements specification. The system is described by a number of models: the object model, the dynamic model, the functional model, and the use-case model, which complement each other to give the complete description of the system. The OMT method (J. Rumbaugh et al., 1991) also contained a lot of practical descriptions on how to make a system design, taking into account concurrency and mapping to relational databases.

- *OOSE/Objectory*: The OOSE and Objectory methods both build on the same basic viewpoint formed by Ivar Jacobson. The OOSE method (I. Jacobson et al., 1994) is Jacobson's vision of an object-oriented method; the Objectory method is used for building a number of systems, as diverse as telecommunication systems for Ericsson and financial systems for Wall Street companies. Both methods are based on use cases, which define the initial requirements on the system as seen by an external actor. The use cases are then implemented in all phases of the development, all the way to system testing, where they are used to verify the system. Objectory has also been adapted for business engineering, where the ideas are used to model and improve business processes.

- *Fusion*: The Fusion method comes from Hewlett-Packard (D. Coleman, 1994). It's called a second-generation method, because it's based on the experiences of many of the initial methods. Fusion has enhanced a number of important previous ideas, including techniques for the specification of operations and interactions between objects. The method has a large number of model diagrams.

- *Coad/Yourdon*: The Coad/Yourdon method, also known as OOA/OOD, was one of the first methods used for object-oriented analysis and design. The method was rather simple and easy to learn, and as such, it worked well for introducing novices to the ideas and terminology of object-oriented technology. However, the notation and method could not scale up to handle anything but very limited systems. Consequently, the method is seldom used today.

Each of these methods had its own notation (the symbols used to draw object-oriented models), process (which activities to perform in different parts of the development), and tools (the CASE tools that support the notation and the process). This made the choice of method a very important decision, and often led to heated discussions and debates about which method was "the best," "most advanced," and "the right" method to use in a specific project. As with any such discussions there seldom was a good answer, because all the methods had their own strengths and weaknesses. Experienced developers often took one method as a base, and then borrowed good ideas and solutions from others. In practice, the differences between the methods weren't really that significant, and as time passed and the methods developed, they grew to resemble each other. This was recognized by several of the method gurus, who began to seek ways to cooperate.

The UML

Grady Booch and James Rumbaugh at Rational Software Corporation started the work on UML in 1994. Their goal was to create a new method, the "Unified Method," that would unite the Booch method and the OMT-2 method of which Rumbaugh was the leading developer. In 1995, Ivar Jacobson—the man behind the OOSE and the Objectory methods—joined them. Rational Software also bought Objective Systems, the Swedish company that developed and distributed Objectory. At this point, the future developers of UML also realized that their work was aimed more directly at creating a standard modeling language, and renamed their work the "Unified Modeling Language." To succeed in establishing a standard modeling language is a much simpler task than doing the same thing for a process, since a process differs substantially between different companies and cultures. It's doubtful whether it's at all possible to create a standard process that can be used by everybody.

Booch, Rumbaugh, and Jacobson released a number of preliminary versions of UML to the object-oriented community. Feedback from this gave them a lot of ideas and suggestions to incorporate to improve the language. Version 1.0 of the Unified Modeling Language was released in January 1997.

Even though the main parts of UML are based on the Booch, OMT, and OOSE methods, these designers also included concepts from other methods. For example, the work of David Harel on state charts has been adopted in the UML state diagrams; parts of the Fusion notation for numbering operations has been included in collaboration diagrams; and the work of Gamma-Helm-Johnson-Vlissides on patterns and how to document them has inspired details of class diagrams.

The goals of UML, as stated by the designers, are:

- To model systems (and not just software) using object-oriented concepts.
- To establish an explicit coupling to conceptual as well as executable artifacts.
- To address the issues of scale inherent in complex, mission-critical systems.
- To create a modeling language usable by both humans and machines.

UML is destined to be the dominant, common modeling language used by the industry. It has a broad range of usage, it's built on well-established and proven techniques for modeling systems, and it has industry support necessary to establish a standard in the real world. The UML is also very well documented with metamodels of the language, and with a formal specification of the semantics of the language.

Acceptance of UML

To establish UML, the developers and Rational realized that the language had to be made available to everyone. Therefore, the language is nonproprietary and open to all. Companies are free to use it with their own methods; tool vendors are free to create CASE tools for it; and authors are encouraged to write books about it.

During 1996, a number of organizations joined Rational to form the UML Partners consortium. These organizations regarded UML as strategic to their business and were willing to contribute to the definition of UML. Naturally, they were interested in getting their own areas of expertise into the definition. The different companies, as of January 1997, were Digital Equipment Corporation, HP, I-Logix, Intellicorp, IBM, ICON Computing, MCI Systemhouse, Microsoft, Oracle, Texas Instruments, Unisys, and of course Rational. The companies also supported the proposal to adapt UML as the Object Management Group (OMG) standard for modeling languages.

Rational also made an agreement with Microsoft stating that the companies will jointly develop and market enterprise development tools. This means that they will cross-license technologies from each other, so that their products will easily integrate with each other. For example, Rational Rose will be an integrated high-end CASE tool to low-end development environments such as Microsoft Visual C++ or Visual Basic. The companies will codevelop and comarket their integrated solutions. Rational has also acquired Microsoft Visual Test for broadening its product base to other support environments for the software engineering process.

OMG Standardization

When the work with UML started, it was intended to establish itself as a de facto standard, which means that through practical use by many developers it would become recognized as the premier modeling language. However, when OMG made a request for a standard modeling language, the UML developers realized that they could also get UML accepted as a formal standard. This placed a higher demand on a more precise and formal definition of the UML and improved the quality of the language. A formal standardization is important for many industries before they are willing to use a new technology, such as the developers of military systems. At this book's writing, OMG has decided to use UML as their standard and is working on the final details of the specification. A vote will take place among OMG members in late 1997 to decide on the specification's final standard.

Methods and Modeling Languages

There are important differences between a method and a modeling language. A *method* is an explicit way of structuring one's thinking and actions. A method tells the user what to do, how to do it, when to do it, and why it's done (the purpose of a specific activity). Methods contain models, and these models are used to describe something and to communicate the results of the use of a method. The main difference between a method and a modeling language is that the modeling language lacks a process or the instructions for what to do, how to do it, when to do it, and why it's done.

When we build models, we also structure our thoughts. A model is always a model of something and it has a purpose. If the model does not have an explicit purpose, it will cause problems, because no one will know how or why to use it. A model is expressed in a *modeling language*. A modeling language consists of notation—the symbols used in the models—and a set of rules directing how to use it. The rules are syntactic, semantic, and pragmatic.

The syntax tells us how the symbols should look and how the symbols in the modeling language are combined. The syntax is compared to words in natural language; it is important to know how to spell them correctly and how to put different words together to form a sentence. The semantic rules tell us what each symbol means and how it should be interpreted by itself and in the context of other symbols; they are compared to the meanings of words in a natural language.

The pragmatic rules define the intentions of the symbols through which the purpose of a model is achieved and becomes understandable for others. This corresponds in natural language to the rules for constructing sentences that are clear and understandable. For example, books about writing style are referred to as pragmatic in that sense.

To use a modeling language well, it's necessary to learn all of these rules. The good news is that the UML is a lot easier to comprehend than a natural language. Most modeling languages cover only syntax and semantics. Pragmatics is a bit difficult to describe since it can't be formalized; it can only act as a guideline.

Naturally, even when the language is mastered, there is no guarantee that the models produced will be good. Just like writing a story in a natural language, the language is just a tool that the author must master. It's still up to the author to write a good story.

Object-Oriented Software Development

As an object-oriented modeling language, all the elements and diagrams in UML are based on the object-oriented paradigm. As described in this book, definitions are made of different object-oriented concepts. Any reader totally unfamiliar with object orientation and its terminology should read some introductory text (such as (D. Taylor 1991)). The primary views of the authors on object orientation are:

- Object orientation is a technology for producing models that reflect a domain, such as a business domain or a machine domain, in a natural way, using the terminology of the domain.

- Object-oriented models, when constructed correctly, are easy to communicate, change, expand, validate, and verify.

- When done correctly, systems built using object-oriented technology are flexible to change, have well-defined architectures, and provide the opportunity to create and implement reusable components. Requirements on the system are traceable to code in the system.

- Object-oriented models are conveniently implemented in software using object-oriented programming languages. Using programming languages that are not object-oriented to implement object-oriented systems is not recommended. However, it's important to realize that object-oriented software engineering is much more than just a couple of mechanisms in a programming language.

- Object orientation is not just a theory, but a well-proven technology used in a large number of projects and for building many different types of systems. The field still lacks standardization to show the way to an industrialization of object technology. The work provided by OMG strives to achieve such standardization.

- Object orientation requires a method that integrates a development process and a modeling language with suitable construction techniques and tools.

Use of UML

The UML is used to model systems, the range of which is very broad; many different types of systems can be described. UML can also be used in the different phases in the development of a system, from the requirements specification to the test of a finished system.

Different Types of Systems

The goal of UML is to describe any type of system, in terms of object-oriented diagrams. Naturally, the most common use is to create models of software systems, but UML is also used to describe mechanical systems without any software or the

Programming

In the programming, or construction, phase, the classes from the design phase are converted to actual code in an object-oriented programming language (using a procedural language is *not* recommended). Depending on the capability of the language used, this can either be a difficult or an easy task. When creating analysis and design models in UML, it is best to avoid trying to mentally translate the models into code. In the early phases, the models are a means to understand and structure a system; thus, jumping to early conclusions about the code can be counterproductive to creating simple and correct models. The programming is a separate phase during which the models are converted into code.

Test

A system is normally tried in unit tests, integration tests, system tests, and acceptance tests. The unit tests are of individual classes or a group of classes, and are typically performed by the programmer. The integration test integrates components and classes in order to verify that they cooperate as specified. The system test views the system as a "black box" and validates that the system has the end functionality expected by an end user. The acceptance test conducted by the customer to verify that the system satisfies the requirements is similar to the system test. The different test teams use different UML diagrams as the basis for their work: unit tests use class diagrams and class specifications, integration tests typically use component diagrams and collaboration diagrams, and the system tests implement use-case diagrams to validate that the system behaves as initially defined in these diagrams.

2 An Overview of UML

The Unified Modeling Language has a broad spectrum of usage. It can be used for business modeling, software modeling in all phases of development and for all types of systems, and general modeling of any construction that has both a static structure and a dynamic behavior. In order to achieve these wide-ranging capabilities, the language is defined to be extensive and generic enough to allow for the modeling of such diverse systems, avoiding the too specialized and too complex.

This chapter provides an overview of UML to demonstrate its scope and structure. The elements of the language are described only briefly here; more in-depth explanations and details are included in later chapters. Because of this organization, not all the pieces may fall into place at once, but they will gradually. The reader is not expected to fully understand the diagrams shown in this chapter, but rather to just get a glimpse of UML and its possibilities.

The overview describes the different parts of UML:

- *Views*: Views show different aspects of the system that are modeled. A view is not a graph, but an abstraction consisting of a number of diagrams. Only by defining a number of views, each showing a particular aspect of the system, can a complete picture of the system be constructed. The views also link the modeling language to the method/process chosen for development.

- *Diagrams*: Diagrams are the graphs that describe the contents in a view. UML has nine different diagram types that are used in combination to provide all views of the system.

- *Model elements*: The concepts used in the diagrams are model elements that represent common object-oriented concepts such as classes, objects, and messages, and the relationships among these concepts including association, dependency, and generalization. A model element is used in several different diagrams, but it always has the same meaning and symbol.

- *General mechanisms*: General mechanisms provide extra comments, information, or semantics about a model element; they also provide extension mechanisms to adapt or extend the UML to a specific method/process, organization, or user.

Views

Modeling a complex system is an extensive task. Ideally, the entire system is described in a single graph that defines the entire system unambiguously, and is easy to communicate and understand. However, this is usually impossible. A single graph cannot capture all the information needed to describe a system. A system is described with a number of different aspects: functional (its static structure and dynamic interactions), nonfunctional (timing requirements, reliability, deployment, etc.), and organizational aspects (work organization, mapping to code modules, etc.). Thus a system is described in a number of views, where each view represents a projection of the complete system description, showing a particular aspect of the system.

Each view is described in a number of diagrams that contain information that emphasizes a particular aspect of the system. There is a slight overlap, so that a diagram can actually be a part of more than one view. By looking at the system from different views, it is possible to concentrate on one aspect of the system at a time. A diagram in a particular view should be simple enough to be easily communicated, yet coherent with the other diagrams and views so that the complete picture of the system is described by all the views together (through their respective diagrams). A diagram contains graphical symbols that represent the model elements of the system. Figure 2.1 shows the views of UML. They are:

- *Use-case view*: A view showing the functionality of the system as perceived by external actors.
- *Logical view*: A view showing how the functionality is designed inside the system, in terms of the system's static structure and dynamic behavior.
- *Component view*: A view showing the organization of the code components.
- *Concurrency view*: A view showing concurrency in the system, addressing the problems with communication and synchronization that are present in a concurrent system.
- *Deployment view*: A view showing the deployment of the system into the physical architecture with computers and devices called *nodes*.

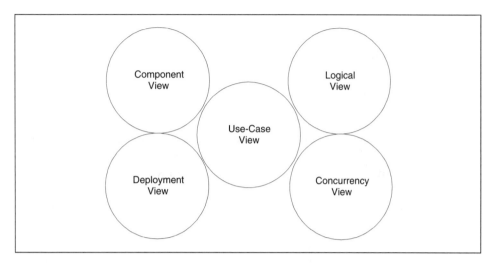

Figure 2.1 *The views in UML.*

When you choose a tool to draw the diagrams, make sure it's one that makes it easy to navigate from one view to another. In addition, in order to see how a function is designed to work within a diagram, the tool should make it easy to switch to either the use-case view to see how the function is described by an external user or to the deployment view to see how the function is distributed in the physical structure. In other words, find out which computers it is available in.

Note that other views can be used including static-dynamic, logical-physical, workflow, and others. UML doesn't require that these views be used, but they are those that the designers of UML had in mind, so it's likely that most tools will be based on these views.

Use-Case View

The use-case view describes the functionality the system should deliver, as perceived by external actors. An actor interacts with the system; it can be a user or another system. The use-case view is for customers, designers, developers, and testers; it is described in use-case diagrams and occasionally in activity diagrams. The desired usage of the system is described as a number of use cases in the use-case view, where a use case is a generic description of a usage of the system (a function requested).

The use-case view is central, since its contents drive the development of the other views. The final goal of the system is to provide the functionality described in this view—along with some nonfunctional properties—hence this view affects all the others. This view is also used to validate and finally verify the system by testing the use-case view against the customers (asking "Is this what you want?") and against the finished system (asking "Does the system work as specified?").

Logical View

The logical view describes how the system functionality is provided. It is mainly for designers and developers. In contrast to the use-case view, the logical view looks inside the system. It describes both the static structure (classes, objects, and relationships) and the dynamic collaborations that occur when the objects send messages to each other to provide a given function. Properties such as persistence and concurrency are also defined, as well as the interfaces and internal structure of classes.

The static structure is described in class and object diagrams. The dynamic modeling is described in state, sequence, collaboration, and activity diagrams.

Component View

The component view is a description of the implementation modules and their dependencies. It is mainly for developers, and consists of the component diagram. The components, which are different types of code modules, are shown with their structure and dependencies. Additional information about the components, such as resource allocation (responsibility for a component), or other administrative information, such as a progress report for the development work, can also be added.

Concurrency View

The concurrency view deals with the division of the system into processes and processors. This aspect, which is a nonfunctional property of the system, allows for efficient resource usage, parallel execution, and the handling of asynchronous events from the environment. Besides dividing the system into concurrently executing threads of control, the view must also deal with communication and synchronization of these threads.

The concurrency view is for developers and integrators of the system, and it consists of dynamic diagrams (state, sequence, collaboration, and activity diagrams) and implementation diagrams (component and deployment diagrams).

Deployment View

Finally, the deployment view shows the physical deployment of the system, such as the computers and devices (nodes) and how they connect to each other. The deployment view is for developers, integrators, and testers, and is represented by the deployment diagram. This view also includes a mapping that shows how the components are deployed in the physical architecture; for example, which programs or objects execute on each respective computer.

Diagrams

The diagrams are the actual graphs that show model element symbols arranged to illustrate a particular part or aspect of the system. A system model typically has several diagrams of each type. A diagram is part of a specific view; and when it is drawn, it is usually allocated to a view. Some diagram types can be part of several views, depending on the contents of the diagram.

This section describes the basic concepts behind each diagram. All details about the diagrams, their syntax, their exact meaning, and how they interact are described in the later chapters. The diagrams are taken from different types of systems to show the diversity of UML.

Use-Case Diagram

A use-case diagram shows a number of external actors and their connection to the use cases that the system provides (see Figure 2.2). A use case is a description of a functionality (a specific usage of the system) that the system provides. The descrip-

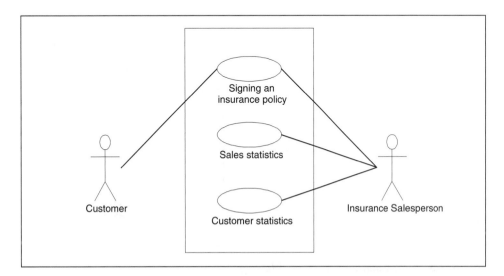

Figure 2.2 *Use-case diagram for an insurance business.*

tion of the actual use case is normally done in plain text as a documentation property of the use-case symbol, but it can also be described using an activity diagram. The use cases are described only as viewed externally by the actor (the system behavior as the user perceives it), and do not describe how the functionality is provided inside the system. Use cases define the functionality requirements of the system; use-case diagrams are described in greater detail in Chapter 3.

Class Diagram

A class diagram shows the static structure of classes in the system (see Figure 2.3). The classes represent the "things" that are handled in the system. Classes can be related to each other in a number of ways: associated (connected to each other), dependent (one class depends/uses another class), specialized (one class is a specialization of another class), or packaged (grouped together as a unit). All these relationships are shown in a class diagram along with the internal structure of the classes in terms of attributes and operations. The diagram is considered static in that the structure described is always valid at any point in the system's life cycle.

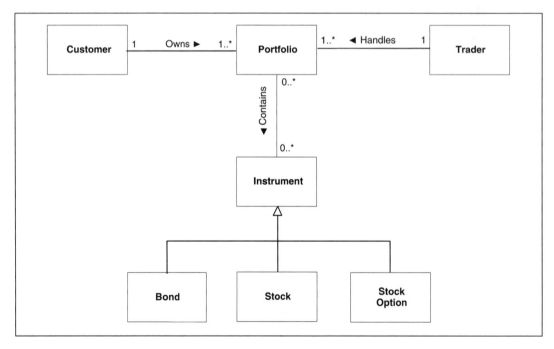

Figure 2.3 *A class diagram for financial trading.*

A system typically has a number of class diagrams—not all classes are inserted into a single class diagram—and a class can participate in several class diagrams. Class diagrams are described in Chapter 4.

Object Diagram

An object diagram is a variant of a class diagram and uses almost identical notation. The difference between the two is that an object diagram shows a number of object instances of classes, instead of the actual classes. An object diagram is thus an example of a class diagram that shows a possible snapshot of the system's execution—what the system could look like at some point in time. The same notation as for class diagrams is used, with two exceptions: objects are written with their names underlined and all instances in a relationship are shown (see Figure 2.4).

Object diagrams are not as important as class diagrams, but they can be used to exemplify a complex class diagram by showing what the actual instances and the relationships could look like. Object diagrams are also used as part of collaboration diagrams, in which the dynamic collaboration between a set of objects is shown.

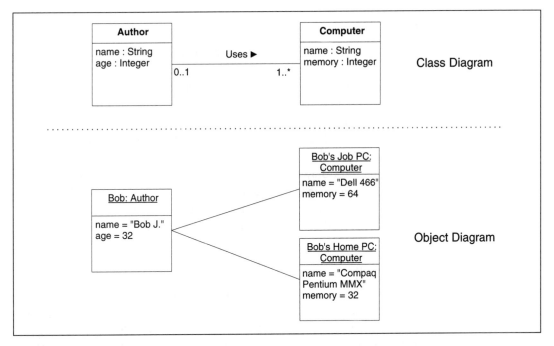

Figure 2.4 *A class diagram showing classes and an object diagram showing instances of the classes.*

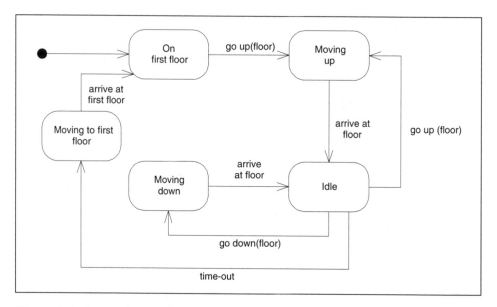

Figure 2.5 *A state diagram for an elevator.*

State Diagram

A state diagram is typically a complement to the description of a class. It shows all the possible states that objects of the class can have, and which events cause the state to change (see Figure 2.5). An event can be another object that sends a message to it—for example, that a specified time has elapsed—or that some condition has been fulfilled. A change of state is called a *transition*. A transition can also have an action connected to it that specifies what should be done in connection with the state transition.

State diagrams are not drawn for all classes, only for those that have a number of well-defined states and where the behavior of the class is affected and changed by the different states. State diagrams can also be drawn for the system as a whole. State diagrams are described in more detail in Chapters 5 and 6.

Sequence Diagram

A sequence diagram shows a dynamic collaboration between a number of objects, as shown in Figure 2.6. The important aspect of this diagram is to show a sequence of messages sent between the objects. It also shows an interaction between objects, something that will happen at one specific point in the execution of the system. The diagram consists of a number of objects shown with vertical lines. Time passes

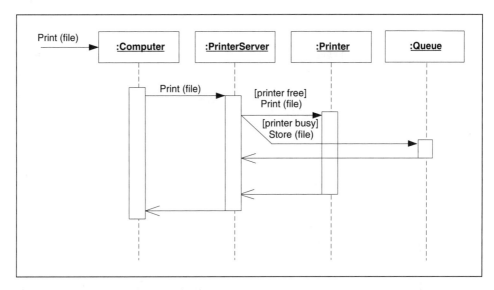

Figure 2.6 *A sequence diagram for a print server.*

downward in the diagram, and the diagram shows the exchange of messages between the objects as time passes in the sequence or function. Messages are shown as lines with message arrows between the vertical object lines. Time specifications and other comments are added in a script in the margin of the diagram. Sequence diagrams are described in Chapters 5 and 6.

Collaboration Diagram

A collaboration diagram shows a dynamic collaboration, just like the sequence diagram. It is often a choice between showing a collaboration as either a sequence diagram or as a collaboration diagram. In addition to showing the exchange of messages (called the *interaction*), the collaboration diagram shows the objects and their relationships (sometimes referred to as the *context*). Whether you use a sequence diagram or a collaboration diagram can often be decided by: If time or sequence is the most important aspect to emphasize, choose sequence diagram; if the context is important to emphasize, choose collaboration diagram. The interaction between the objects is shown in both diagrams.

The collaboration diagram is drawn as an object diagram, where a number of objects are shown along with their relationships (using the notation in the class/object diagram). Message arrows are drawn between the objects to show the flow of messages between the objects. Labels are placed on the messages, which

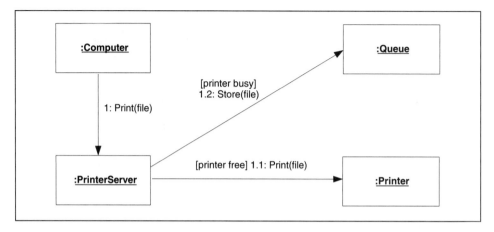

Figure 2.7 *A collaboration diagram for a printer server.*

among other things, show the order in which the messages are sent. It can also show conditions, iterations, return values, and so on. When familiar with the message label syntax, a developer can read the collaboration and follow the execution flow and the exchange of messages. A collaboration diagram can also contain active objects, those that execute concurrently with other active objects (see Figure 2.7). Collaboration diagrams are described in Chapters 5 and 6.

Activity Diagram

An activity diagram shows a sequential flow of activities, as shown in Figure 2.8. The activity diagram is typically used to describe the activities performed in an operation, though it can also be used to describe other activity flows, such as a use case or an interaction. The activity diagram consists of action states, which contain a specification of an activity to be performed (an action). An action state will leave the state when the action has been performed (a state in a state diagram needs an explicit event before it leaves the state). Thus the control flows among the action states, which are connected to each other. Decisions and conditions, as well as parallel execution of action states, can also be shown in the diagram. The diagram can also contain specifications of messages being sent or received as part of the actions performed. Activity diagrams are described in Chapter 5.

Component Diagram

A component diagram shows the physical structure of the code in terms of code components. A component can be a source code component, a binary compo-

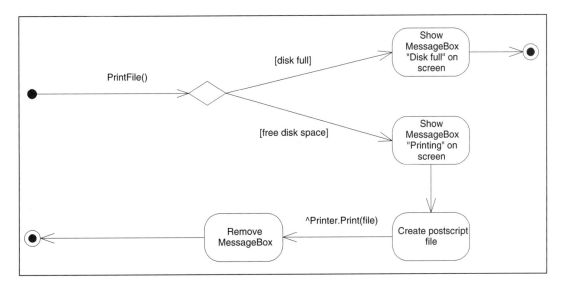

Figure 2.8 *An activity diagram for a printer server.*

nent, or an executable component. A component contains information about the logical class or classes it implements, thus creating a mapping from the logical view to the component view. Dependencies between the components are shown, making it easy to analyze how other components are affected by a change in one component. Components can also be shown with any of the interfaces that they expose, such as OLE/COM interfaces; and they can be grouped together in packages. The component diagram is used in practical programming work (see Figure 2.9). Component diagrams are described in more detail in Chapter 7.

Deployment Diagram

The deployment diagram shows the physical architecture of the hardware and software in the system. You can show the actual computers and devices (nodes), along with the connections they have to each other; you can also show the type of connections. Inside the nodes, executable components and objects are allocated to show which software units are executed on which nodes. You can also show dependencies between the components.

As we stated previously, the deployment diagram, showing the deployment view, describes the actual physical architecture of the system. This is far from the functional description in the use-case view. However, with a well-defined model, it's possible to navigate all the way from a node in the physical architecture to its components to the class it implements to the interactions that objects of the class

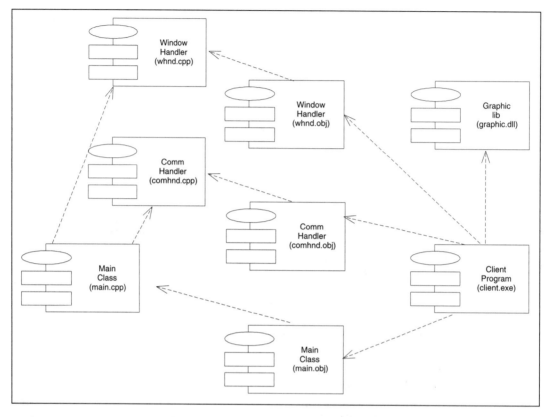

Figure 2.9 *A component diagram showing dependencies between code components.*

participate in and finally to a use case. Different views of the system are used to give a coherent description of the system as a whole (see Figure 2.10). Deployment diagrams are described in Chapter 7.

Model Elements

The concepts used in the diagrams are called model elements. A model element is defined with semantics, a formal definition of the element or the exact meaning of what it represents in unambiguous statements. A model element also has a corresponding view element, which is the graphical representation of the element or the graphical symbol used to represent the element in diagrams. An element can exist in several different types of diagrams, but there are rules for which elements can be shown in each type of diagram. Some example model elements are class, object, state, node, package, and component, as shown in Figure 2.11.

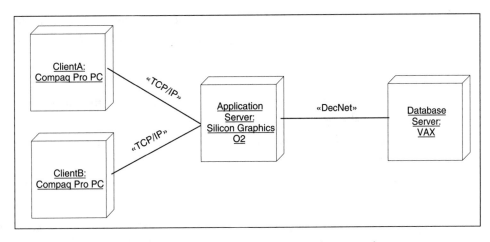

Figure 2.10 *A deployment diagram shows the physical architecture of a system.*

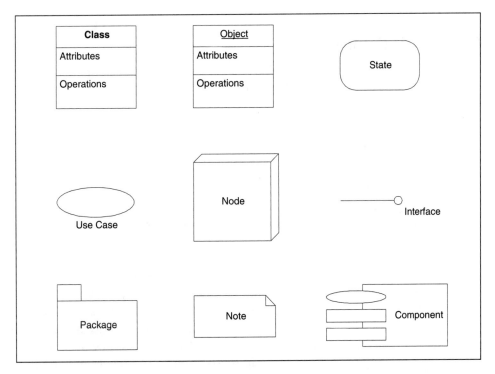

Figure 2.11 *Some common model elements.*

Figure 2.12 shows examples of relationships, which are also model elements, and are used to connect other model elements with each other. Some different relationships are:

- *Association*: Connects elements and links instances.
- *Generalization*: Also called inheritance, it means that an element can be a specialization of another element.
- *Dependency*: Shows that one element depends in some way on another element.
- *Aggregation*: A form of association in which an element contains other elements.

Other model elements besides those described include messages, actions, and stereotypes. All model elements, their meaning, and allowed usage are explained in the later chapters, their semantics are described using more informal practical descriptions rather than the formal definitions used in the UML reference manual. A discussion about the semantic framework behind the UML is contained in Chapter 8.

General Mechanisms

UML utilizes some general mechanisms in all diagrams, for additional information in a diagram, typically that which cannot be represented using the basic abilities of the model elements.

Adornments

Graphical adornments can be attached to the model elements in diagrams. The adornments add semantics to the element. An example of an adornment is the technique used to separate a type from an instance. When an element represents a type, its name is displayed in boldface type. When the same element represents an instance of the type, its name is underlined and may specify both the name of the instance as well as the name of the type. A class rectangle, with the name in bold representing a class and the name underlined representing an object, is an example of this. The same goes for nodes, where the node symbol can be either a type in boldface, such as **Printer**, or an instance of a node type, such as John's HP 5MP-printer. Other adornments are specifications of multiplicity of relationships, where the multiplicity is a number or a range that indicates how many instances of connected types can be involved in the relation. Adornments are written close to the

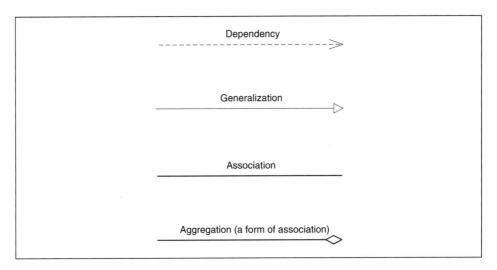

Figure 2.12 *Examples of some relationships.*

element to which they add information. All the adornments are described in conjunction with the description of the element that they affect (see Figure 2.13).

Notes

Not everything can be defined in a modeling language, no matter how extensive the language. To enable adding information to a model that otherwise cannot be represented, UML provides a notes capability. A note can be placed anywhere in any diagram, and it can contain any type of information. Its information type is a string that is not interpreted by the UML. The note is typically attached to some element in the diagram with a dashed line that specifies which element is explained or detailed, along with the information in the note (see Figure 2.14).

A note often contains comments or questions from the modeler as a reminder to resolve a dilemma at a later time. Notes can also have stereotypes that describe

Figure 2.13 *Adornments add information to an element symbol. In this example, the boldface and underlining specifies whether the symbol represents a class or an object.*

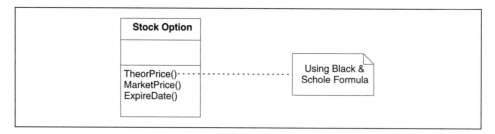

Figure 2.14 *A note contains any additional information such as a simple comment.*

the note type. Stereotypes are described in more detail in the next section, Extending UML.

Specifications

Model elements have properties that hold data values about the element. A property is defined with a name and a value called a *tagged value*, which is of a specified type like an integer or a string. There are a number of predefined properties such as Documentation, Responsibility, Persistence, and Concurrency.

Properties are used to add additional specifications about element instances that are not normally shown in the diagram. Typically a class is described with some text that more informally itemizes the responsibilities and capabilities of the class. This type of specification is not normally shown in the diagram itself, but is available in a tool usually accessed by double-clicking on an element that brings up a specification window with all of the properties (see Figure 2.15).

Extending UML

UML can be extended or adapted to a specific method, organization, or user. We'll touch on three extension mechanisms here: stereotypes, tagged values, and constraints. These mechanisms are described in more detail in Chapter 8.

Stereotypes

A stereotype extension mechanism defines a new kind of model element based on an existing model element. Thus, a stereotype is "just like" an existing element, plus some extra semantics that are not present in the former. A stereotype of an element can be used in the same situations in which the original element is used. Stereotypes are based on all types of elements—classes, nodes, components, and notes, as well as relationships such as associations, generalizations, and dependen-

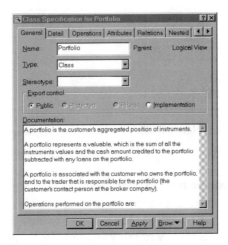

Figure 2.15 *A specification window in a CASE tool that shows properties of the class.*

cies. A number of stereotypes are predefined in the UML, and they are used to adjust an existing model element instead of defining a new one. This keeps the basic UML language simple.

A stereotype is described by placing its name as a string—for example, «StereotypeName»—around the name of the element, as shown in Figure 2.16. The angle brackets are called *guillemets*. A stereotype can also have its own graphical representation, such as an icon, connected to it. An element of a specific stereotype may be shown in its normal representation with the stereotype name in front of the name, as a graphical icon representing the stereotype, or as a combination of both. Whenever an element has a stereotype name or icon connected to it, it's read as an element type of the specified stereotype. For example, a class with the stereotype «Window» is read as "a class of the Window stereotype," meaning it is a window type of class. The particular characteristics a Window class must have are defined when the stereotype is defined.

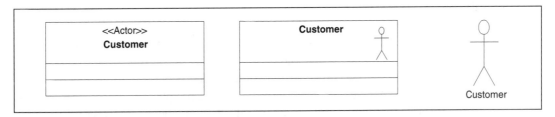

Figure 2.16 *The customer is a class with the stereotype «Actor». The stereotype adds extra semantics to the class; in this case, that the class represents an external user of the system.*

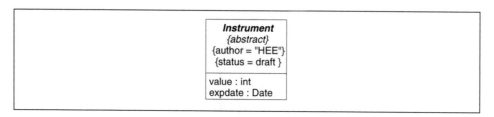

Figure 2.17 *Properties on an Instrument class. Abstract is a predefined property; author and status are user-defined tagged values.*

As we stated previously, a stereotype is an excellent extension mechanism, and one that prevents the UML from becoming overly complex, yet enables the necessary extensions and adaptations to be performed. Most requested new model elements have a basic prototype in the UML. A stereotype can then be used to add the necessary semantics required in order to define the missing model element.

Tagged Values

As described earlier, elements can have properties that contain name-value pairs of information about them (see Figure 2.17). These properties are also called *tagged values*. A number of properties are predefined in UML, but properties can also be defined by the user to hold additional information about elements. Any type of information can be attached to elements: method-specific information, administrative information about the progress of modeling, information used by other tools, such as code generation tools, or any other kind of information that the user wants to attach to elements.

Constraints

A constraint is a restriction on an element that limits the usage of the element or the semantics (meaning) of the element. A constraint is either declared in the tool and repeatedly used in several diagrams, or it's defined and applied as needed in a diagram.

Figure 2.18 shows an association between the Senior Citizen Group class and the Person class, indicating that the group may have persons associated to it. However, to express that only people older than 60 years of age may be attached to it, a constraint is defined that limits participation to only persons whose age attribute is greater than 60. This definition constrains which people are used in the association. Without it, there could be a misunderstanding when interpreting the diagram. In a worst-case scenario, it could lead to an incorrect implementation of the system.

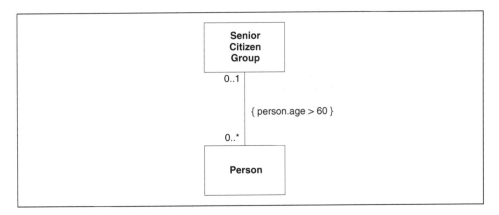

Figure 2.18 *A constraint restricts which Person objects may participate in the association.*

In this case, the constraint is defined and applied directly to the diagram in which it is used, but it could also be defined as a constraint with a name and a specification such as "Senior Citizen" and "Person.Age > 60" and used in several diagrams. There are a number of predefined constraints that can be used, and they are all described in Chapter 8.

Modeling with UML

When building systems with UML, not just a single model is built. There are distinct models in different phases of development, and the purposes of the models are separate. In the analysis phase, the purpose of the model is to capture the requirements of the system and to model the basic "real-world" classes and collaborations. In the design phase, the purpose of the model is to expand the analysis model into a working technical solution with consideration for the implementation environment. In the implementation phase, the model is the actual source code that is programmed and compiled into programs. And finally, in the deployment model, a description explains how the system is deployed in the physical architecture. The tracking between the phases and models is maintained through properties or refinement relationships.

Although the models are different, they are normally built by expanding the contents of earlier models. Because of this, all models should be saved so that it's easy to go back and redo or expand the initial analysis model, and then gradually introduce the change into the design and implementation models (see Figure 2.19).

UML is phase independent, which means the same generic language and the same diagrams are used to model different things in different phases. It's up to the

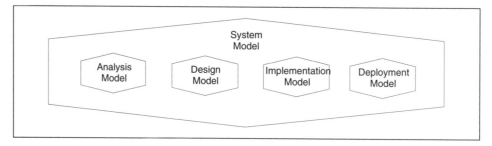

Figure 2.19 *A system is described in several models.*

modeler to decide the purpose and scope that a model should cover. The modeling language only provides the ability to create models in an expressive and consistent manner.

When modeling with the UML, the work should be governed by a method or process that outlines the different steps to take and how these steps are implemented. Such a process typically divides the work in successive iterations of requirement analysis/analysis/design/implementation/deployment phases. (Chapter 10 offers object-oriented software development processes and examples.) However, there is also a smaller process that concerns the actual modeling work. Normally, when producing a model or a single diagram, the work is started by collecting a suitable group of people who present the problem and the goals; they engage in an informal brainstorming and sketching session during which ideas about a possible model are exchanged. The tools used are very informal—usually Post-it notes and a whiteboard. This session continues until the participants feel they have a practical suggestion for the basis of a model (an early hypothesis). The result is then put into a tool; the hypothesis model is organized, and an actual diagram is constructed according to the rules of the modeling language. Next, the model is detailed through iterative work, through which more details about the solution are discovered and documented. As more information is acquired about the problem and its solution, the hypothesis gradually becomes a diagnosis for a usable model. When the model is almost finished, an integration and verification step is taken, which leads to the model or diagram being integrated with other diagrams or models in the same project to ensure that no inconsistencies exist. The model is also validated to verify that it solves the right problem (see Figure 2.20).

Finally, the model is implemented into some kind of prototype that is evaluated for any deficiencies in the actual solution. Deficiencies include such things as missing functionality, bad performance, or high development costs. The deficiencies should lead the developers back to the respective step(s) in order to remove them. If the problems are major, the developers may have to go all the way back to the

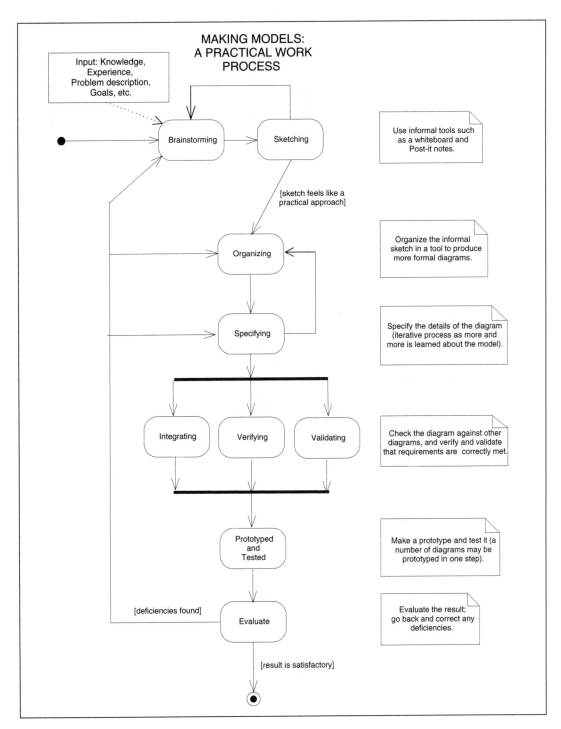

Figure 2.20 *A practical modeling work process.*

brainstorming/sketching phase. If the problems are minor, the developers probably will just have to change parts of the organization or specification of the model. Note that the prototype step cannot be performed immediately after the diagram is finished; it should be taken when a number of diagrams can be prototyped together. The prototype can be a throwaway, constructed just for evaluation, or if the prototype step is successful it becomes an iteration in the real development process.

Probably we are not aware of all the possibilities of UML. Traditionally, designers of programming or macro languages are surprised at what their languages are used for. For example, James Gosling told us that his macro language is used in the Emacs editor to write satellite navigation systems or basic compilers! Given the versatility of UML, we can be sure it has a similar destiny.

Tools

Using a modeling language as complex and extensive as UML requires the support of tools. Even if the first sketches of a model are done using a whiteboard (drawing the models manually), the work of maintaining, synchronizing, and providing consistency in a number of diagrams is almost impossible without a tool.

The modeling tool or CASE tool market remains surprisingly immature since the release of the first visions of programs used to produce programs. Many tools are little more than drawing tools, with few consistency checks or knowledge of the method or modeling language present. Still, there have been improvements, and today the tools are closing in on the initial vision, as shown in Figure 2.21. But many tools remain unpolished, with bugs or peculiarities that ordinary application software doesn't have, such as problems with cut and paste. These tools also are limited by the fact that they all have their own modeling language, or at least their own definitions of the language. With the release of UML, tool vendors can now spend more time improving on the tools and less time on defining new methods and languages.

A modern CASE tool should provide these functions:

- *Draw diagrams*: The tool must support easy rendering of the diagrams in the modeling language. The tool should be intelligent enough to understand the purpose of the diagrams and know simple semantics and rules so that it can warn or prohibit inappropriate or incorrect use of the model elements.

- *Act as a repository*: The tool must support a common repository so that the collected information about the model is stored in one place. If the name of a class is changed in one diagram, the change must be reflected in all other diagrams in which the class is used.

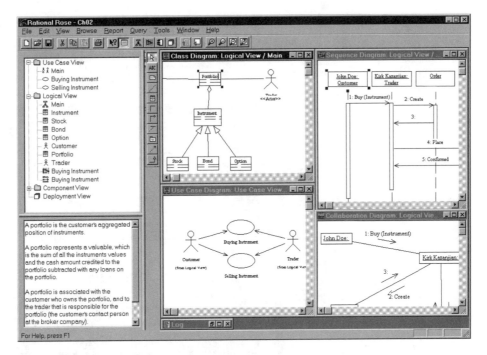

Figure 2.21 *A modern modeling tool: Rational Rose.*

- *Support navigation*: The tool should make it easy to navigate the model, to trace an element from one diagram to another, or to expand the description of an element.

- *Provide multiuser support*: The tool should support multiple users, and enable them to work on a model without interfering or disturbing each other.

- *Generate code*: An advanced tool should be able to generate code, where all the information in the model is translated into code skeletons that are used as a base for the implementation phase.

- *Reverse engineer*: An advanced tool should be able to read existing code and produce models from it. Thus, a model could be made from existing code; or a developer could iterate between working in the modeling tool and programming.

- *Integrate with other tools*: A tool should be able to integrate with other tools, both with development environments such as an editor, compiler, and debugger, and with other enterprise tools such as configuration management and version control systems.

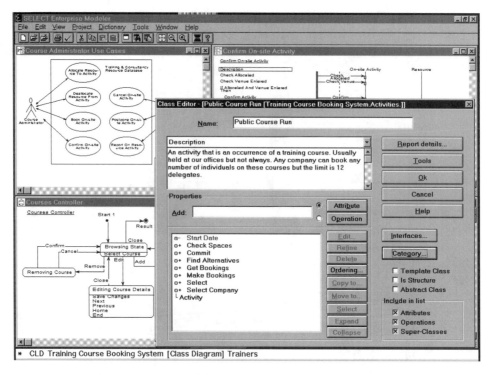

Figure 2.22 *Select Enterprise Modeler.*

- *Cover the model at all abstraction levels*: The tool should be easy to navigate from the top-level description of the system (as a number of packages) down to the code level. Then, to access the code for a specific operation in a class, you would click on the operation name in a diagram.
- *Interchange models*: A model or individual diagrams from a model should be able to export from one tool and then import into another tool, like Java code is produced in one tool and then used in another tool. The same interchange should apply to models in a well-defined language (see Figure 2.22).

Drawing Support

A tool must make the drawing of diagrams easy and fun. The time is long gone when an advanced drawing tool can call itself a CASE tool, for not only must the tool provide excellent mechanisms for selecting, placing, connecting, and defining the elements in a diagram, there must also be support to assist the modeler in rendering a *correct* diagram. The tool should "have an understanding" of the semantics of the elements so that it can issue a warning if an element is incorrectly used or if a specific operation is inconsistent with some other operation. For example, if a proposed change in one diagram conflicts with another diagram in the same model.

The tool should also have support for layout design for the diagrams. This should include allowing the modeler to rearrange the elements and for automatically rearranging message lines so that they don't cross each other. Many CAD systems have very elegant algorithms for doing this, and many modeling tool vendors could learn a lot by looking at those systems.

Model Repository

The CASE tool must maintain a model repository that provides a database with all information about the elements used in a model, regardless of which diagram the information comes from. This repository should contain the base information about the entire model, which is then viewed through a number of diagrams, as shown in Figure 2.23.

Some tasks that the tool can perform with the help of a repository are:

- *Checking for inconsistency*: If an element is used inconsistently in different diagrams, the tool must warn or prohibit this. If the modeler tries to delete an element in one diagram and it is used in other diagrams, the developer must be warned about this. If the developer insists in deleting the element, it must be deleted from all diagrams where it is referenced, and the developer must go back and update these diagrams to make them valid.

- *Critiquing*: Using the information in a repository, a tool can critique the model, pointing out parts that haven't been specified or applying model heuristics that show possible mistakes or inappropriate solutions.

- *Reporting*: The tool can automatically generate complete and extensive documentation about all elements, such as classes or diagrams in a model, similar to term catalogs of all data.

- *Reusing elements or diagrams*: A repository can support reuse so that modeling solutions or parts of a solution in one project can be easily reused in another project. Components in a UML model are directly connected to the source code so that both the model and the actual code are reused in different projects.

Navigation

When several views and diagrams are used together to describe a system, it's very important that it be easy to navigate between them. Therefore the tool must sup-

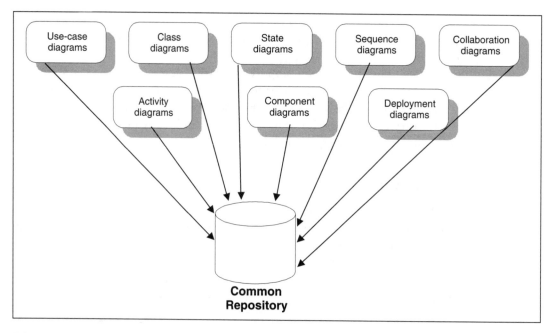

Figure 2.23 *A repository contains all the information from all the diagrams necessary to make sure the model is consistent and enables generic tools for documentation and reuse.*

port easy navigation, both in terms of scale and browsing. It must be easy to browse the different diagrams, and to perform searches for model elements.

An element should have hyperlinks, links that are not visible when looking at the printed diagrams, but that are accessible only through the tool. It should be possible to click on an element with the right mouse button and get a pop-up menu that displays common operations and gives navigation possibilities, such as looking at other diagrams where the element is present or accessing detailed information about the element. Parts of a diagram should be expandable or collapsible. It should be easy to expand and view the contents of the package, and collapse to view the surrounding package.

Another way to handle a complex diagram is to define filters, which can separate or highlight some interesting aspect of the diagram; for example, to show only one type of relationship or class. Modelers should have control over what is shown, so that they may study only the part that is important at a given moment.

Multiuser Support

A tool should enable several users to work cooperatively on the same model; that is, without disturbing or interfering with each other. Typically, a user working on a diagram should lock it so that no one else can change it at the same time. Furthermore, any changes made to shared elements in the repository should be identified by the tool. But decisions about which change is valid must be resolved by the users.

Code Generation

Modern tools have support for code generation, so that those parts of the work worth saving from the modeling phase don't have to be re-created when the implementation phase begins. These tools typically generate *code skeletons* in a target language and transfer the information from the models into code in that language. The type of code generated usually is static information, such as class declarations, including attributes and method declarations. The bodies of the methods containing the actual code are normally left blank, to be filled in by the programmer—though it is theoretically possible that parts of dynamic models can be translated into body code. The code generation can be parameterized by the users, in that they give instructions about how the generated code should look (see Figure 2.24).

Different types of target languages are used. Naturally, object-oriented programming languages such as C++ or Java are used, but languages such as SQL (for

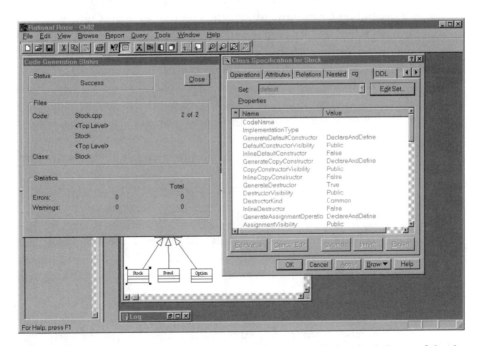

Figure 2.24 *A tool with code-generation capability can produce code skeletons of the classes.*

the schema definition of a relational database) or IDL (for interfaces in a CORBA-compliant system) can also be generated. Therefore a tool should have the capability to plug in different code generators for different languages.

What happens if you generate code from a model, start coding the bodies of the methods, and then make a change in the model? Is the code work lost when you generate the code skeleton from the updated model? Luckily, that is not the case. The generated code contains marks that show which sections of the code are generated from the model and which are manually coded. When the code is generated anew, the sections that contain manual code will not be touched by the code generator.

Reverse Engineering

A reverse-engineering functionality is almost the opposite of the code-generation functionality. Code is read and analyzed by the tool, and diagrams are created that show the structure of the code. Typically, only static structure diagrams such as class diagrams are constructed from the code: No dynamic information is extracted from the code. The reverse-engineering function is used for both unknown code that is bought or coded manually and for code generated with the code-generation function. When applied to unknown code, the result is either uplifting or depressing depending on the structure of the code. Code that is unstructured is inevitably unveiled when reverse-engineered into a diagram. When buying class libraries, reverse engineering is often used to get a diagram that represents the structure of the library, so that the classes in the library can be used in diagrams.

When code generation and reverse engineering are combined, it's commonly referred to as *round-trip engineering*. Using round-trip engineering, a developer can iterate between modeling and implementation, so that a model is defined; code is generated, explored, and changed in the development environment, and then reverse-engineered back to a model. The development process then truly becomes iterative.

Integration

Traditional modeling tools are (finally!) becoming more integrated with other tools used in system development (see Figure 2.25). Since the modeling tool actually stores a model of the entire system, it's really the natural hub for all the other tools, such as these:

- *Development environment*: With these tools, it's possible to go directly from a model element in a diagram to a development environment, where the code is edited, compiled, and debugged. The opposite is also true. The tool

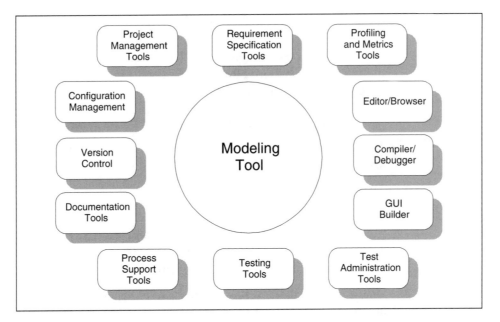

Figure 2.25 *Tools integrated with a modeling tool.*

should go directly from editing a code module to determine its location in the logical and physical models of the system.

- *Configuration and version control*: These are tools for handling several different configurations of the system and different versions of both the system and individual elements. The version-control should be of both the models and of the code.

- *Documentation tools*: These tools can automatically generate documentation from the model repository. The tool should also be able to generate statistics based on the information found there.

- *Testing tools*: Testing tools are mainly for the administration of the test process—collecting and maintaining test reports. Testing is really the validation (Did we build the right system?) and verification (Did we build the system the right way?) of the development process. As such, the models contain a lot of information to the testing process that should transfer to the testing tools.

- *GUI builders*: A good idea is to have associations from classes in the model to their GUI representations in a GUI builder, where the organization of the user interface is stored. It should also be possible to automatically generate GUI forms for classes in the model. For example, if the attributes in a class are read, the fields of appropriate types in a form are generated for those attributes.

- *Requirement specification tools*: UML has use cases to capture the functional requirements of a system. However, there are also nonfunctional aspects of the system, and these could be described using requirement specification tools. Some methods prefer techniques other than use cases for requirement engineering, and therefore need other tools.

- *Project management and process support tools*: A project management tool is devised to help the project manager define time schedules and resource allocation plans and perform follow-ups on the progress. Since the production of models is a large part of a project, it's beneficial when the project manager can easily check the progress of the modeling work. The integration with process support tools is probably not a top priority. Process support tools support the usage of a specific method or process; and, naturally, the production of models is a substantial part of any method or process.

Note that not all of these tools need to be used in every project; nor is there a modeling tool on the market today that is integrated in this manner. The integration possibilities described are more of a vision.

Interchange of Models

It used to be impossible to create a model in one tool and then export it to another tool. One prerequisite is a standardized format for storing a model. Work on defining such a format for the UML is in progress, though that format will not be part of the OMG standard. When models are interchangeable between tools, it will be easier to provide simple modeling tools built into the development environments, where models can then be transferred and integrated into a more advanced tool. Naturally, another advantage is that users will not have to rely on just one CASE vendor, but will be able to move their models to another product if they feel like it. With a common format, other independent tools such as documentation, report, and database-generation tools can be more easily developed.

Summary

UML organizes a model in a number of views that present different aspects of a system. Only by combining all the views can a complete picture of a system be achieved. A view is not a graph; its contents are described in diagrams that are graphs with model elements. A diagram typically shows only a part of the contents in a view, and a view is defined with many diagrams. A diagram contains model elements such as classes, objects, nodes, components, and relationships such as association, generalization, and dependency. The elements have semantics—a meaning—and graphical symbols to represent them.

The UML diagrams are: class, object, use case, state, sequence, collaboration, activity, component, and deployment. The purpose of the diagrams and the rules for drawing them are described in the chapters to come.

UML has some general mechanisms with which to add information not visible in the diagram drawings. These include adornments placed next to elements, notes that can hold any type of information, and specification properties. There are also extension mechanisms, including tagged values, constraints on elements, and stereotypes that define a new kind of model element based on an existing model element.

A system is described in several different model types, each with a different purpose. The analysis model describes the functional requirements and the modeling of real-world classes. The design transforms the analysis result into a technical solution in terms of a complete working software design. The implementation model implements the system by coding it in an object-oriented programming language. And, finally, the deployment model places the programs constructed in a physical architecture with computers and devices (called nodes). The work is done iteratively and not in sequence. The development process is explained in Chapter 10.

You'll need a tool to use UML seriously in real-life projects. A modern tool has the capability to draw the diagrams, store the overall information in a common repository, allow easy navigation in the model between different views and diagrams, create reports and documentation, generate code skeletons from the model, read unknown code and produce models, and easily integrate with other development tools.

3 *Use-Case Modeling*

A *use case* is a modeling technique used to describe what a new system should do or what an existing system already does. A use-case model is built through an iterative process during which discussions between the system developers and the customers (and/or end users) lead to a requirement specification on which all agree. Use-case modeling was created by Ivar Jacobson (I. Jacobson, 1994) based on his experiences developing the AXE system at Ericsson, specifically, the OOSE and Objectory methods. Use cases have received a lot of interest from the object-oriented community and have affected many object-oriented methods.

The primary components of a use-case model are use cases, actors, and the system modeled. The boundaries of the system are defined by the functionality that is handled by the system. The functionality is represented by a number of use cases, and each use case specifies a complete functionality. When the functionality is complete, the use case must handle the entire function, from its initiation by an external actor until it has performed the requested functionality. A use case must always deliver some value to an actor, the value being whatever the actor wants from the system. The actor is any external entity that has an interest in interacting with the system. Often, it is a human user of the system, but it can also be another system or some kind of hardware device that needs to interact with the system.

In use-case modeling, the system is looked upon as a "black box" that provides use cases. How the system does this, how the use cases are implemented, and how they work internally is not important. In fact, when the use-case modeling is done early in the project, the developers have no idea how the use cases will be implemented. The primary purposes for use cases are:

- To decide and describe the functional requirements of the system, resulting in an agreement between the customer (and/or end user) and the software developers who are building the system.

- To give a clear and consistent description of what the system should do, so that the model is used throughout the development process to communicate to all developers those requirements, and to provide the basis for further design modeling that delivers the requested functionality.

- To provide a basis for performing system tests that verify the system. For example, asking, does the final system actually perform the functionality initially requested?

- To provide the ability to trace functional requirements into actual classes and operations in the system. To simplify changes and extensions to the system by altering the use-case model and then tracing the use cases affected into the system design and implementation.

The actual work required to create a use-case model involves defining the system, finding the actors and the use cases, describing the use cases, defining the relationships between use cases, and finally validating the model. It is a highly interactive format that should include discussions with the customer and the people representing the actors. The use-case model consists of use-case diagrams showing the actors, the use cases, and their relationships. These diagrams give an overview of the model, but the actual descriptions of the use cases are typically textual. Visual models can't provide all the information necessary in a use-case model, so both use-case diagrams and text descriptions are used.

A number of different people have an interest in the use-case models. The customer (and/or end user) is interested because the use-case models specify the functionality of the system and describe how the system can and will be used. It is helpful when the customer plays an active role in the use-case modeling because then models can be adapted in detail to the customer's wishes. The use cases are described in the language and terminology of the customer/user. The developers need the use-case models to understand what the system should do, and to provide them with the foundation for future work (other models, architecture design, and implementation). The integration and system test teams need the use cases to test the system to ensure that it performs the functionality specified in the use cases. And, finally, anyone involved in activities connected to the functionality of the system may have an interest in the use-case models; this may include marketing, sales, support, and documentation teams.

The use-case model represents the use-case view of the system. This view is very important, as it affects all other views of the system. Both the logical and

physical architecture are influenced by the use cases, because the functions specified in the use-case model are implemented in those architectures. A solution is
designed that satisfies the requirements.

Use-case modeling is used not only to capture requirements of new systems; it
is also used when new generations of systems are developed. When a new generation (version) of a system is developed, the new functionality is added to the extant
use-case model by inserting new actors and use cases, or by modifying the specifications of current use cases. When adding to an extant use-case model, be careful
not to remove any functionality that still is needed.

Use-Case Diagram

A use-case model is described in UML as a *use-case diagram*, and a use-case model
can be divided into a number of use-case diagrams. A use-case diagram contains
model elements for the system, the actors, and the use cases, and shows the different relationships such as generalization, association, and dependency between these
elements, as shown in Figure 3.1. Each of the elements is described in more detail
in the sections that follow.

The actual description of the use-case contents is usually given in plain text. In
UML, the description is treated as the documentation property for the use-case el-

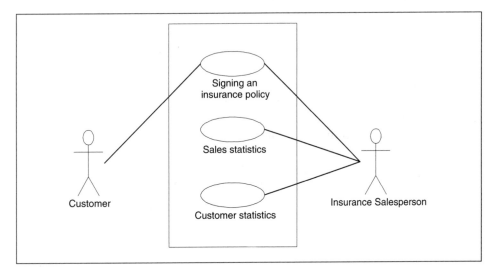

Figure 3.1 *A use-case diagram shows actors, use cases, and their relationships. The system
is defined through system boundaries.*

ement. This description contains vital information for defining the actual requirements and functionality. As an alternative to describing the use case in text, you can draw an activity diagram. (Activity diagrams are described in more detail in Chapter 5.) However, it's important to remember that a use case should be easy to communicate to an end user, and a more formal structure, such as an activity diagram, can be intimidating to people not used to interpreting them.

System

As part of use-case modeling, the boundaries of the system developed are defined. Note that a system does not necessarily have to be a software system; it can be a business or a machine. Defining the boundaries and the overall responsibility of the system is not always easy, because it's not always obvious which tasks are best automated by the system and which are best handled manually or by other systems. Another consideration is how large the system should be in its first generation. It's tempting to be ambitious for the first release, but such lofty goals can make the system too large and the time to delivery much longer. A better idea is to identify the basic functionality and concentrate on defining a stable and well-defined system architecture to which more functionality can be added in future generations of the system.

It is essential to compile a catalog of central concepts (entities) with suitable terms and definitions at an early stage. This is not a domain object model, but rather an attempt to describe the terminology of the system or the business modeled. The terminology then describes the use cases. The catalog can also be used to begin the domain analysis that follows later. The extent of this catalog can vary; it can be a conceptual model showing simple relationships or just a text catalog containing terms and a short description of what it is in the real world.

A system in a use-case diagram is described as a box; the name of the system appears above or inside the box. The box also contains symbols for the use cases in the system, as shown in Figure 3.2.

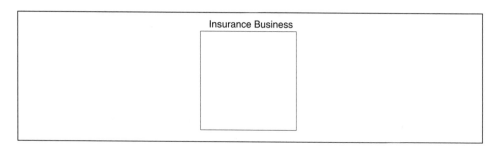

Figure 3.2 *A system in a use-case model.*

Actors

An *actor* is someone or something that interacts with the system; it's who or what uses the system. By "interacts with the system," we mean that the actor sends or receives messages to and from the system, or exchanges information with the system. In short, actors carry out use cases. Again, an actor can be a human being or another system (such as another computer to which the system is connected or some kind of hardware device that communicates with the system).

An actor is a type (a class), not an instance. The actor represents a role, not an individual user of the system. If John Doe wants to get auto insurance from an insurance company, it is his *role* as the insurance buyer or policyholder that we want to model, not John Doe. In fact, one person may be different actors in the system, depending on his or her role in the system. And the roles a person may have in the system can be restricted. For example, the same person can be prohibited from both entering an invoice and approving the invoice. An actor has a name, and the name should reflect the actor's role. The name should not reflect a specific instance of an actor, nor reflect the functionality of the actor.

The actor communicates with the system by sending and receiving messages, which are similar to those found in object-oriented programming, though they are not as formally specified in a use case. A use case is always initiated by an actor that sends a message to it. This is sometimes called a *stimulus*. When a use case is performed, the use case might send messages to one or more actors. These messages may also go to other actors in addition to the one that initiated the use case.

Actors can be ranked. A *primary actor* is one that uses the system's primary functions, such as the main functionality. For example, in an insurance system, a primary actor might be one that handles the registration and management of insurance. A *secondary actor* is one that uses the secondary functions of the system, those functions that maintain the system, such as managing databases, communications, backups, and other administration tasks. An example of a secondary actor might be a manager or a board member using functions in the system to retrieve statistics about the business or the company. Both types of actors are modeled to ensure that the entire functionality of the system is described, even though the primary functions are those that are of most interest to the customer.

Actors can also be defined as active or passive. An *active actor* is one that initiates a use case, while a *passive actor* never initiates a use case, but only participates in one or more use cases.

Finding Actors

By identifying the actors, we establish those entities interested in using and interacting with the system. It is then possible to take the position of the actor to try to identify the actor's requirements on the system and which use cases the actor needs. The actors can be identified by answering a number of questions:

- Who will use the main functionality of the system (primary actors)?
- Who will need support from the system to do their daily tasks?
- Who will need to maintain, administrate, and keep the system working (secondary actors)?
- Which hardware devices does the system need to handle?
- With which other systems does the system need to interact? This could be divided into systems that initiate contact with the system and the systems that this system will contact. Systems include other computer systems as well as other applications in the computer in which this system will operate.
- Who or what has an interest in the results (the value) that the system produces?

When looking for the users of the system, don't consider only individuals sitting in front of a computer screen. Remember, the user can be anyone or anything that directly or indirectly interacts with the system and uses the services of the system to achieve something. Keep in mind that use-case modeling is done to model a business; therefore the actors usually are the customers of that business. Thus they are not users in the computer sense of the term.

As a means of identifying different actors, conduct a study of users of the current system (a manual system or an existing system), asking what different roles they play when they perform their daily work with the system. The same user may perform several roles at different times, depending on which functions in the system are currently in use.

To repeat, an actor is a role (a class), not an individual instance. However, by providing examples of a couple of instances of an actor, you can validate that the actor really exists. An actor must have some association with one or more use cases. Although that actor might not initiate a use case, that actor will at some point communicate with one. The actor is given a name that reflects the role in the system.

Actors in UML

Keeping in mind that actors in UML are classes with the stereotype «actor», and that the name of the class is the actor name (reflecting the role of the actor), an actor class can have both attributes and behavior as well as a documentation property describing the actor. An actor class has a standard stereotype icon, the "stickman" figure, with the name of the actor beneath the figure, as shown in Figure 3.3.

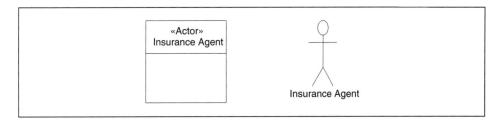

Figure 3.3 *An actor is a class, and is shown as a class rectangle with the stereotype «actor». The standard stereotype icon of a stickman is normally shown in use-case diagrams. The stickman icon has the actor name below the figure.*

Relationships between Actors

Since actors are classes, they can have the same relationships as classes. In use-case diagrams, only generalization relationships are used to describe common behavior between a number of actors.

Generalization

When several actors, as part of their roles, also play a more generalized role, it is described as a *generalization*. This occurs when the behavior of the general role is described in an actor superclass. The specialized actors inherit the behavior of the superclass, then extend that behavior in some way. Generalization between actors is shown as a line with a hollow triangle at the end of the more general superclass, as shown in Figure 3.4. This is the same notation used for generalization between any classes in UML.

Use Cases

A use case represents a complete functionality as perceived by an actor. A use case in UML is defined as *a set of sequences of actions a system performs that yield an observable result of value to a particular actor.* The actions can involve communicating with a number of actors (users and other systems) as well as performing calculations and work inside the system. The characteristics of a use case are:

- *A use case is always initiated by an actor.* A use case is always performed on behalf of an actor. The actor must directly or indirectly order the system to perform the use case. Occasionally the actor may not be aware of initiating a use case.

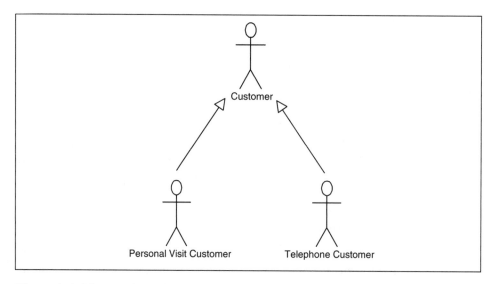

Figure 3.4 *The actor base class Customer describes the general role played by Telephone Customer, which calls in by phone, and by Personal Visit Customer, which makes a personal visit. Use cases that don't consider how the customer contacts the system can work with the generalized actor, while use cases that emphasize the importance of how contact occurs must work with the actual actor subclass.*

- *A use case provides value to an actor*: A use case must deliver some kind of tangible value to the user. The value doesn't always have to be salient, but it must be discernible.

- *A use case is complete*: A use case must be a complete description. A common mistake is to divide a use case into smaller use cases that implement each other much as functions call each other in a programming language. A use case is not complete until the end value is produced, even if several communications (such as user dialogs) occur along the way.

Use cases are connected to actors through associations, which are sometimes referred to as *communication associations*. Associations show which actors the use case communicates with, including the actor that initiates the execution of the use case. The association is normally a one-to-one relationship with no direction. This means that one actor instance communicates with one use-case instance, and that they can communicate in both directions. A use case is named for which instance the use case performs, such as Signing Insurance Policy, Updating Register, and so on, and is often a phrase rather than a one-word label.

A use case is a class, not an instance. It describes the functionality as a whole, including possible alternatives, errors, and exceptions that can occur during the execution of the use case. An instantiation of a use case is called a *scenario*, and it represents an actual usage of the system (a specific execution path through the system). For example, a scenario instance of the use case Signing Insurance could be "John Doe contacts the system by telephone and signs for car insurance for the Toyota Corolla he just bought."

Finding Use Cases

The process for finding use cases starts with the actors previously defined. For each of the actors identified, ask the following questions:

- Which functions does the actor require from the system? What does the actor need to do?
- Does the actor need to read, create, destroy, modify, or store some kind of information in the system?
- Does the actor have to be notified about events in the system, or does the actor need to notify the system about something? What do those events represent in terms of functionality?
- Could the actor's daily work be simplified or made more efficient through new functions in the system (typically functions currently not automated in the system)?

Other questions to ask that don't involve one of the current actors are:

- What input/output does the system need? Where does this input/output come from or go to?
- What are the major problems with the current implementation of this system (perhaps a manual system instead of an automated system)?

The last questions are not meant to infer that the use cases identified don't have an actor, just that the actors are recognized first by identifying the use case and then the actor(s) involved. A use case must always be connected to at least one actor.

Use Cases in UML

A use case is represented in UML as an ellipsis containing the name of the use case, or with the name of the use case below it. A use case is normally placed inside the boundaries of a system, and can be connected to an actor with an association or a

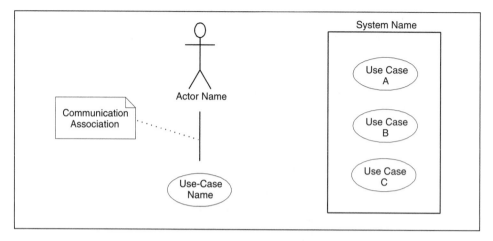

Figure 3.5 *Use cases in UML are represented as ellipses inside a system boundary and can have associations to actors.*

communication association that shows how the use case and the actor interact (see Figure 3.5).

Relationships between Use Cases

There are three types of relationships between use cases: extends, uses, and grouping. The extends and uses relationships are different forms of inheritance. Grouping is a way of placing related use cases together in a package. The relationship definitions are as follows:

- *Extends relationship*: A generalization relationship where one use case extends another use case by adding actions to a general use case. The extending use case may include behavior from the use case being extended, depending on conditions on the extension.

- *Uses relationship*: A generalization relationship where one use case uses another use case, indicating that as part of the specialized use case, the behavior of the general use case will also be included.

- *Grouping*: When a number of use cases handle similar functionality or are in some way related to each other, they can be bundled in a UML package. The package mechanism is described in more detail in Chapter 4. A package groups related model elements, and can be expanded or collapsed into an icon, allowing the developer to view one package at a time. The package has no other semantical meaning.

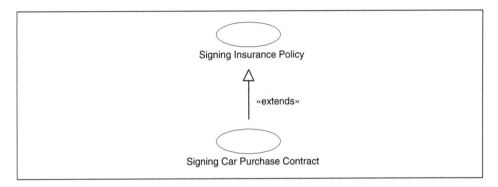

Figure 3.6 *An extends relationship shows how one use case extends another use case, where the extending use case may include the behavior of the use case extended.*

Extends Relationship

When a use case extends another use case, it means that first may include some of the behavior of the use case it extends. It doesn't have to include the entire behavior; it can choose which parts of the behavior from the generalized use case it wants to reuse. The use case being extended must be complete. Since use cases normally are described in plain text, it can be hard to define which parts in an extended use case are reused from the generalized use case, which are redefined, and which are added to the generalized use case.

An extended use case can handle exceptions that are specific cases of the general use case that are not easily described in the general use case, or that are made as the system progresses in development. An extends relationship between use cases is shown as a generalization (a line with a hollow triangle pointing at the use case being extended) with the stereotype «extends», as shown in Figure 3.6.

Uses Relationship

When a number of use cases have common behavior, this behavior can be modeled in a single use case that is used by the other use cases. When a use case uses another, the entire use case must be used (though the activities in the used use case don't have to be in the same sequence; they can be intermixed with the activities of the using use case). If the use case being used is never used by itself, it is called an *abstract use case*.

A uses relationship is shown through the generalization relationship (a line with a hollow triangle pointing at the use case being used) with the stereotype «uses», as shown in Figure 3.7.

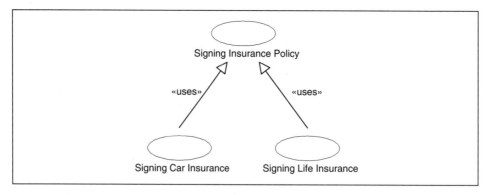

Figure 3.7 *A uses relationship shows how common behavior in a number of use cases can be described in a general use case that is used by the use cases.*

Describing Use Cases

As we've noted several times, the description of the use case is normally done through a text description. This is a simple and consistent specification about how the actors and the use cases (the system) interact. It concentrates on the external behavior of the system and ignores how things are actually performed inside the system. The language and terminology used in the description is the same as that used by the customer/user of the system.

The text description should include:

- *Objective for the use case*: What are the ultimate objectives of this use case? What is it trying to achieve? Use cases are goal-oriented, and the goal of each use case should be apparent.

- *How the use case is initiated*: Which actor initiates the execution of the use case, and in which situations?

- *The flow of messages between actors and the use case*: Which messages or events does the use case and the actor exchange to notify each other, update or retrieve information, and help each other with decisions? What should describe the main flow of messages between the system and the actors, and which entities in the system are used or modified?

- *Alternative flow in the use case*: A use case can have alternative executions depending on conditions or exceptions. Mention these, but be cautious not to describe them in too much detail as they might "hide" the main flow of actions in the general case. Specific error-handling is described as scenarios.

- *How the use case finishes with a value to the actor*: Describe when the use case is considered finished and the kind of value delivered to the actor.

Remember that the description identifies what is done in relevance to the external actor, not how things are done inside the system. The text should be clear and consistent so that a customer can understand and validate it (agree that it represents what he or she wants from the system). Avoid complicated sentences that are hard to interpret and easy to misunderstand.

A use case can also be described through an *activity diagram*, as shown in Figure 3.8. The activity diagram (described in more detail in Chapter 5) shows a sequence of activities, their ordering, and optional decisions that are made to indicate which activity performs next. Keep in mind that a use-case model must be easy to communicate to a user, and should not be described too formally.

As a complement to a use-case description that contains the complete and general description, a number of actual scenarios are used to illustrate what happens when the use case is instantiated. The scenario description illustrates a specific case, with both the actors and the use cases involved as actual instances. Customers can better understand a complex use case when a more practical scenario describes the behavior of the system. But note, a scenario description is a complement to, not a substitution for, the use case description.

After the use cases are described, a specific activity reveals whether the relationships previously described are identified. Not until all use cases are described do the developers have the complete knowledge to identify suitable relationships, and it can be dangerous to try otherwise. During this activity, answer the following questions:

- Do all actors involved in a use case have a communication association to it?

- Are there similarities between a number of actors that represent a common role and thus could be described as a *base class actor*?

- Do similarities exist between a number of use cases that represent a common flow of activities and could be described as a uses relation to a use case?

- Do special cases of a use case exist that could be described as an extends relation?

- Are there any actors or use cases without communication associations? If so, something is wrong: Why are the actors there?

- Are any functional requirements known, but not handled by any use case? If so, create a use case for that requirement.

Testing Use Cases

The use cases also have a purpose in testing. Two very different types of tests are performed: *verification* and *validation*. Verification confirms that the system is developed correctly or according to the specifications made. Validation assures that the system under development is one that the customer or end user really needs.

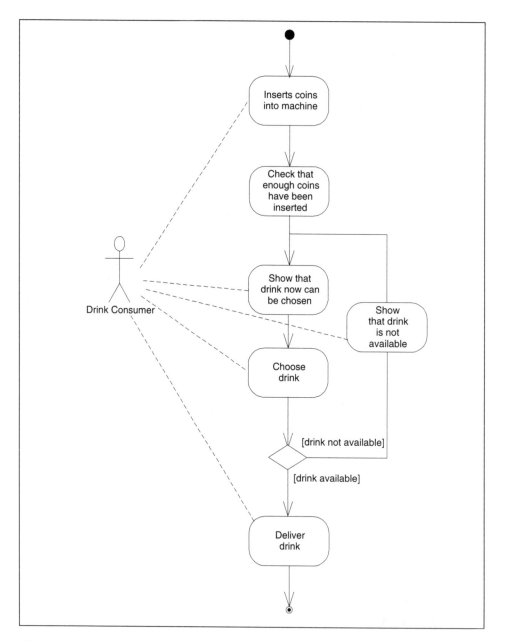

Figure 3.8 *An activity diagram used to describe the interaction between the actor and the use case.*

Validation is done up front in the development process. As soon as there is a finished use-case model (or perhaps during the development of the use-case model), the model is presented to and discussed with customers and end users. They must validate that this model correctly and completely meets their expectations of the system; specifically, the way the system provides the functionality for them. To do this, the developer must ensure that the customers really understand the model and its meaning, to preclude approval for something that is not acceptable. During this process, questions and ideas will no doubt arise that will need to be added to the use-case model before final validation. Validation can also be done at system test time, but the problem with this is that if the system doesn't meet the correct user requirements, the whole project may have to be reworked from scratch.

Verification of the system tests that it works according to the specifications. Thus it can't be carried out until there are working parts of the system. Then it is possible to test that the system behaves as specified by the users, that the use cases described in the use-case model perform, and that they behave as described in the use-case description.

Walking the Use Case

A good technique implemented during both the definition and the testing of use cases is called *walking the use case.* In this technique, different people in the model group role play the actors and the system in a specific use case. The person playing the role of an actor starts out by saying what the actor does with the system. This results in the system executing a specific use case that is started by this action; the person playing the role of the system then says what he does when the use cases executes. The developers not involved in the role-playing take notes and try to find deficiencies in the use cases described by the players. Typically, you find that some alternatives are not described at all and some actions are not described in enough detail.

The more insight into the usage of the system the role players have, the better the test of the use cases will be. So switching who plays the different roles will result in varying interpretations and views, giving the modelers input on how to make the use-case description less ambiguous and pointing out things they missed. When the roles of all the actors are played out and all use cases are executed in this manner, an entire test of the use-case model is complete.

Realizing Use Cases

Use cases are implementation-independent descriptions of system functionality of the system. This means that the use cases are *realized* in the system, that the responsibilities to perform the actions described in the use-case descriptions are allocated to collaborating objects that implement the functionality.

The UML principles for realizing use cases are:

- *A use case is realized in a collaboration*: A collaboration shows an internal implementation-dependent solution of a use case in terms of classes/objects and their relationships (called the *context* of the collaboration) and their interaction to achieve the desired functionality (called the *interaction* of the collaboration). The symbol for a collaboration is an ellipsis containing the name of the collaboration.

- *A collaboration is represented in UML as a number of diagrams showing both the context and the interaction between the participants in the collaboration*: Participating in a collaboration are a number of classes (and in a collaboration instance: objects). The diagrams are collaboration, sequence, and activity. The type of diagram to use to give a complete picture of the collaboration depends on the actual case. In some cases, one collaboration diagram may be sufficient; in other cases, a combination of different diagrams may be necessary.

- *A scenario is an instance of a use case or a collaboration*: The scenario is a specific execution path (a specific flow of events) that represents a specific instantiation of the use case (one usage of the system). When a scenario is viewed as a use case, only the external behavior toward the actors is described. When a scenario is viewed as an instance of a collaboration, the internal implementation of the involved classes, their operations, and their communication is described.

The task of realizing a use case is to transform the different steps and actions in the use-case description (as described in text or an activity diagram) to classes, operations in these classes, and relationships between them. This is described as allocating the responsibility of each step in the use case to the classes participating in the collaboration that realizes the use case. At this stage, a solution is found that gives the external behavior the use case has specified; it is described in terms of a collaboration inside the system (see Figure 3.9).

Each step in the use-case description is transformed into operations on the classes that participate in the collaboration realizing the use case. A step in the use case is transformed to a number of operations on the classes; it is unlikely that there is a one-to-one relationship between an action in the use case and an operation in the interaction between objects of the participating classes. Also note that a class can participate in many use cases. The total responsibility of the class is the integration of all roles it plays in the use cases.

The relationship between a use case and its implementation in terms of a collaboration is shown either through a *refinement relationship* (a dotted line with an ar-

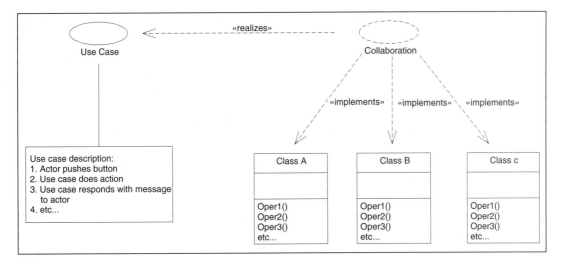

Figure 3.9 *A use case is realized in a collaboration, and a number of classes participate in the collaboration. To realize a use case, the responsibility of each step in the use case (typically described in text) must be transformed to collaborations between the classes in terms of relationships and operations.*

row) or through, for example, an invisible hyperlink in a tool. A hyperlink in a tool makes it possible to switch from watching a use case in a use-case diagram to the actual collaboration that implements it. Hyperlinks are also used to switch from a use case to a scenario (typically any of the dynamic models: activity diagram, sequence diagram, or a collaboration diagram) that describes a specific execution of the use case (an instantiation of the use case).

Allocating responsibilities to classes successfully is a task that requires some experience. As always, when object orientation is involved, it is highly iterative work. The developer tries different possibilities, gradually improving on his or her solution until he or she has a model that performs the functionality and that is flexible enough to allow for future changes (model quality is discussed in Chapter 4).

Jacobson uses a method of defining three types of stereotype object types (i.e., classes): boundary objects (previously called interface objects), control objects, and entity objects. For each use case, these objects are used to describe a collaboration that implements the use case. The responsibility for each of these stereotypes is as follows:

- *Boundary objects*: This object type lies close to the boundary of the system (though still within it). It interacts with the actors outside the system and passes messages to and from them to the other object types inside the system.
- *Control objects*: This object type controls interactions between a group of objects. Such an object could be the "controller" for a complete use case, or it

could implement a common sequence of several use cases. Often such an object exists only during the execution of the use case.

- *Entity objects*: This object type represents a domain entity in the area the system handles. It is typically passive in that it doesn't initiate interactions on its own. In information systems, entity objects are normally persistent and stored in a database. Entity objects typically participate in many use cases.

The stereotypes for these classes have their own icons (similar to the symbols used in the Objectory method), and can be used when drawing the diagrams that describe a collaboration or in a class diagram. After defining the different types of objects and specifying the collaboration, a specific activity can be made to look for similarities between them so that some classes can be used in a number of use cases. Applying the use cases in this way can also be the basis for analysis and design of the system; the development process is what Jacobson calls use case-driven.

Different methods suggest variably when to allocate responsibilities to classes from the use cases. Some methods suggest that a domain analysis be made, showing all the domain classes with their relationships. Then the developer takes each use case and allocates responsibility to classes in the analysis model, sometimes modifying it or adding new classes. Other methods suggest that the use cases become the basis for finding the classes, so that during the allocation of responsibilities, the domain analysis model is gradually established.

It is important to again emphasize that the work is iterative. When responsibility is allocated to classes, errors and omissions in the class diagrams may be discovered and lead to modification of the class diagrams. New classes will surely be identified in order to support the use cases. In some cases, it might even be necessary to modify the use-case diagrams because a deeper understanding of the system has made the developer recognize that a use case is incorrectly described. Use cases help us to focus on the functionality of the system, so that it is correctly described and correctly implemented in the system. One problem with several object-oriented methods that don't have use cases is that they concentrate on the static structures of classes and objects (sometimes called conceptual modeling) while ignoring the functional and dynamic aspects of the system being developed.

Summary

Use-case modeling is a technique used to describe the functional requirements of a system. Use cases are described in terms of external actors, use cases, and the system modeled. Actors represent a role that an external entity such as a user, hardware, or another system plays in interacting with the system. Actors initiate and communicate with use cases, where a use case is a set of sequences of actions performed in the system. A use case must deliver a tangible value to the actor, and is normally described through text documentation. Actors and use cases are classes. An actor is connected to one or more use cases through associations, and both actors and use cases can have generalization relationships that describe common behavior in superclasses inherited by one or more specialized subclasses. A use-case model is described in one or more UML use-case diagrams.

Use cases are realized in collaborations, where a collaboration is a description of a context showing classes/objects and their relationships and an interaction showing how the classes/objects interact to perform a specific functionality. A collaboration is described with activity diagrams, collaboration diagrams, and interac-

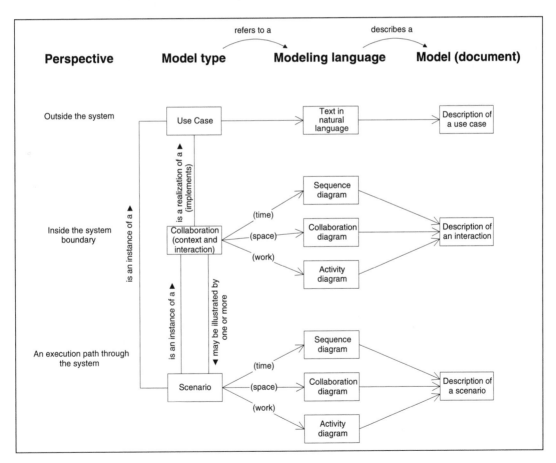

Figure 3.10 *The relationships between use case, collaboration, and scenario.*

tion diagrams (as described in Chapter 5). When a use case is implemented, the responsibility of each of the action steps in the use case must be allocated to classes participating in the collaboration, typically by specifying operations on these classes, along with how they interact. A scenario is an instance of a use case, or a collaboration, showing a specific execution path. As such, a scenario is an illustration or an example of a use case or a collaboration. When viewed as an instance of a use case, only the interaction between the use case and the external actor is described, but when viewed as an instance of a collaboration, the interaction between the classes/objects inside the system, which implement the system, is described (see Figure 3.10).

4 Classes, Objects, and Their Relationships

In object-oriented modeling, classes, objects, and their relationships are the primary modeling elements. Classes and objects model what it is in the system we are trying to describe, and the relationships between them reveals how they are structured in terms of each other. Classification has been used for thousands of years to simplify descriptions of complex systems, so that we can more easily understand them. When using object-oriented programming to build software systems, classes and relationships become the actual code.

Classes and Objects

An object is an item we can talk about and manipulate. An object exists in the real world (or more precisely, our understanding of the real world). It could be a part of any type of system, for example, a machine, an organization, or a business. There are objects (such as implementation objects in a software system) that do not directly exist in the real world, but that can be viewed as derivatives as concluded from studying the structure and behavior of objects in the real world. Thus objects, in one way or another, relate to our understanding of the real world.

A class is a description of an object type. All objects are instances of a class, where the class describes the properties and behavior of one type of object. Objects can be instantiated from the class (instances created of the class type). An object relates to a class similarly to a variable relating to a type in an ordinary programming language. We use classes to discuss systems and to classify the objects we identify in the real world. Consider Darwin, who used classes to describe the human race. He combined his classes via inheritance to describe his theory of evolution. The technique with inheritance between classes is also used in object orientation.

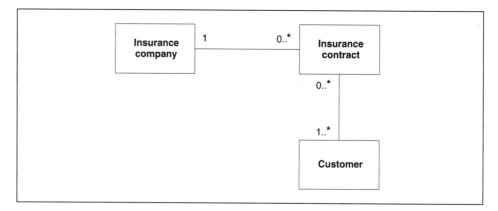

Figure 4.1 *A simple model of an insurance business. One insurance company has many (zero-to-many) insurance contracts. An insurance customer has many (zero-to-many) insurance contracts. An insurance contract is related to one insurance company. The insurance contract is related to many (one-to-many) insurance customers. The entities shown in the model are classes.*

When we model and build business systems, information systems, machines, or other systems, concepts from the problem domain should be used to make the models understandable and easy to communicate. If we build a system for an insurance company, it should be based on the concepts in the insurance business. If we build a system for the military, the concepts from that world should be used to model the system. A system based on the primary concepts of a business can easily be redesigned to fit new laws, strategies, rules, and so on, because we just have to adjust the differences between the old business and the new business. When machines are modeled, it is useful to mimic as closely as possible their real-world appearance, to make them easier to understand and to discuss with the customer. It is important then, that models be easy to discuss, easy to verify against functional requirements, and easy to maintain. When models are built based on how their real-world counterparts look and are based on the concepts in the problem domain, object orientation fits perfectly. The bases of object orientation are classes, objects, and the relationships between them (see Figure 4.1).

A class could be a description of an object in any type of system—information, technical, embedded real-time, distributed, software, and business. Artifacts in a business, information that should be stored or analyzed and roles that the actors in the business play often turn into classes in information and business systems. Examples of classes in business and information systems (an information system could be seen as a part of a business system) are:

Customer
Agreement
Invoice
Debt
Asset
Quotation

Classes in technical systems often involve technical objects such as devices used in the systems. Examples of classes in technical systems are:

Sensor
Display
I/O card
Engine
Button
Control class

System software often has classes representing software entities in an operating system. Examples of classes in system software are:

File
Executable program
Device
Icon
Window
Scrollbar

Class Diagram

A class diagram is a model type, specifically a static model type. A class diagram describes the static view of a system in terms of classes and relationships among the classes. Although it has similarities to data models, remember that the classes not only show the structures of our information but describe behavior as well. One purpose of the class diagram is to define a foundation for other diagrams where other aspects of the system are shown (such as the states of the objects and the collaboration between objects shown in the dynamic diagrams). A class in a class diagram can be directly implemented in an object-oriented programming language that has direct support for the class construct. A class diagram shows only classes, but there a variant identifies where actual object instances of the classes are shown (an object diagram).

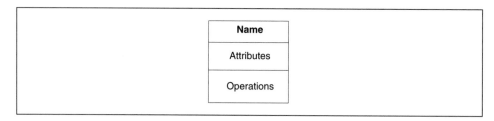

Figure 4.2 *A class in UML.*

To create a class diagram, the classes have to be identified and described; and when a number of classes exist, they can be related to each other by using a number of relationships. A class is drawn with a rectangle, divided into three compartments, the name compartment, the attribute compartment, and the operation compartment, as shown in Figure 4.2. The syntax used for the compartments is independent of programming languages, although another syntax could be used (C++, Java, etc.).

Finding Classes

Looking for classes is a creative endeavor, and it should be done with experts in the problem domain. The classes should be from the problem domain, and named for what they represent there (our understanding of the real world or business). When we are looking for classes, there are some questions that can help us to identify them:

- Do we have information that should be stored or analyzed? If there is any information that has to be stored, transformed, analyzed, or handled in some other way, then it is a possible candidate for a class. The information might be concepts that must always be registered in the system or events or transactions that occur at a specific moment.

- Do we have external systems? If so, they are normally of interest when we model. The external system might be seen as classes that our system contains or should interact with.

- Do we have any patterns, class libraries, components, and so on? If we have patterns, class libraries, or components from earlier projects, colleagues, or manufacturers, they normally contain class candidates.

- Are there devices that the system must handle? Any technical devices connected to the system turn into class candidates that handle these devices.

- Do we have organizational parts? Representing an organization is done with classes, especially in business models.

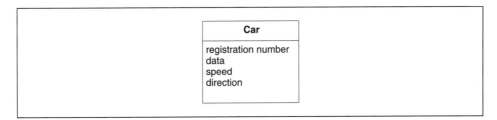

Figure 4.3 *A class Car with the attributes registration number, data, speed, and direction. Attribute names typically begin with a lowercase letter.*

- Which roles do the actors in the business play? These roles can be seen as classes; for example, user, system operator, customer, and so on.

If we have a requirement specification or a business analysis, it should be used as a basis for finding the classes.

Name Compartment

The top compartment of the class rectangle contains the name of the class; it is typed in boldface and centered. Again, the name should be derived from the problem domain and should be as unambiguous as possible. Therefore it should be a noun; for instance, invoice or debt. The class name should not have a prefix or a suffix.

Attribute Compartment

Classes have attributes that describe the characteristics of the objects. Figure 4.3 shows the class Car with attributes of registration number, data, speed, and direction. The correct class attributes capture the information that describes and identifies a specific instance of the class. However, only the attributes that are interesting within the system being modeled should be included. Furthermore, the purpose of the system also influences which attributes should be used.

An attribute has a type, which tells us what kind of attribute it is, as shown in Figure 4.4. Typical attribute types are integer, Boolean, real, point, area, and enumeration, which are called *primitive types*. They can be specific for a certain programming language; however, any type can be used, including other classes.

The attributes can have different *visibility*. Visibility describes whether the attribute is visible and can be referenced from classes other than the one in which they are defined. If an attribute has the visibility public, it can be used and viewed outside that class. If an attribute has the visibility private, you cannot access it from other classes. Another visibility attribute is protected, which is used together with

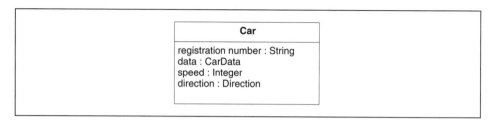

Figure 4.4 A class with typed attributes.

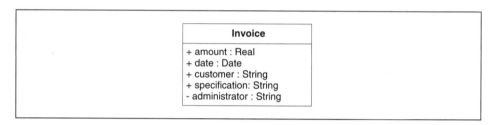

Figure 4.5 A class with public and private attributes.

generalization and specialization. Additional kinds of visibility might be defined for a particular programming language, but public and private are normally all that are necessary to express your class diagrams. Public is expressed with a plus sign (+) and private is expressed with a minus sign (–), as shown in Figure 4.5. If neither sign is displayed, it means that the visibility is undefined (there is no default visibility). Figure 4.6 shows an attribute with a default value. It's assigned at the same time an object of the class is created.

An attribute could also be defined as a class-scope attribute, as shown in Figure 4.7. This means that the attribute is shared between all objects of a certain class (sometimes called a *class variable*). A class-scope attribute is underlined.

A property-string can be used to identify explicitly which values are allowed for an attribute. It's used to specify enumeration types such as color, status, direc-

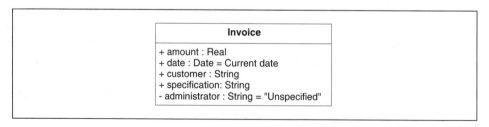

Figure 4.6 A class with attributes and their default values.

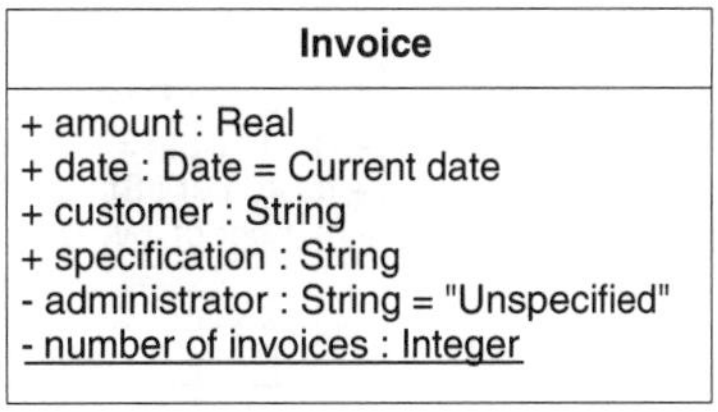

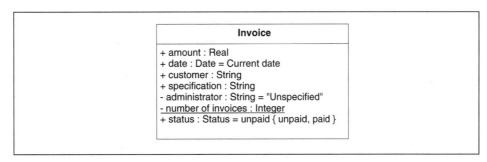

Invoice

+ amount : Real
+ date : Date = Current date
+ customer : String
+ specification : String
- administrator : String = "Unspecified"
- <u>number of invoices : Integer</u>

Figure 4.7 *A class with a class-scope attribute. The attribute number_of_invoices is used to count the invoices; the value of this attribute is the same in all objects because the attribute is shared between them.*

tion, and so on, as shown in Figure 4.8. A property-string is written within curly braces; it is a comma-separated list of all possible values of the enumeration attribute.

The formal syntax for describing an attribute is:

```
visibility name : type-expression = initial-value { property-
string }
```

Only the name and the type are mandatory; all other parts are optional. The property-string can also be used to specify other information about the attribute, such as that the attribute should be persistent (see Chapter 8).

Java Implementation

A class can be implemented directly into an object-oriented language such as Java. All object-oriented programming languages have support for classes and objects. It's a rather straightforward process to translate the model class into code, as shown in Figure 4.9.

Invoice

+ amount : Real
+ date : Date = Current date
+ customer : String
+ specification : String
- administrator : String = "Unspecified"
- <u>number of invoices : Integer</u>
+ status : Status = unpaid { unpaid, paid }

Figure 4.8 *An attribute with an enumeration type status. The property-list is {unpaid, paid}.*

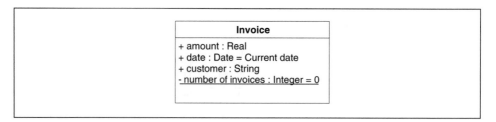

Figure 4.9 *An Invoice class.*

```
public class Invoice
{
    public double amount;
    public Date date = new Date();
    public String customer;
    static private int number_of_invoices = 0;

    // Constructor, called every time an objects is created
    public Invoice ()
    {
        // Other initialization

        number_of_invoices++; // Increment the class attribute
    }
    // Other methods go here
};
```

Operation Compartment

Figure 4.10 demonstrates that a class has both attributes and operations. Attributes are values that characterize objects of the class; sometimes the values of the attributes are a way to describe the state of the object. Operations are used to manipulate the attributes or to perform other actions. Operations are normally called functions, but they are inside a class and can be applied only to objects of that class. An operation is described with a return-type, a name, and zero or more parameters. Together, the return-type, name, and parameters are called the *signature of the operation*. The signature describes everything needed to use the operation. To perform an operation, an operation is applied to an object of that class (is called on an object). The operations in a class describe what the class can do, that is, what services it offers, thus they could be seen as the interface to the class. Just like an attribute, an operation can have visibility and scope.

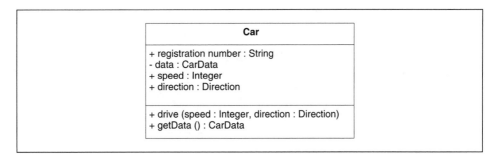

Figure 4.10 *The class Car has attributes and operations. The operation drive has two pa-rameters,* speed *and* direction. *The operation getData has a return type, CarData.*

A class can also have class-scope operations, as shown in Figure 4.11. A class-scope operation can be called without having an object of the class, but it is restricted to access only class-scope attributes. Class-scope operations are defined to carry out generic operations such as creating objects and finding objects where a specific object is not involved (except as possibly the result of the operation).

The formal syntax for an operation is:

```
visibility name ( parameter-list ): return-type-expression
{ property-string }
```

where parameter-list is a comma-separated list of formal parameters, each specified using the syntax:

```
name : type-expression = default-value
```

Visibility is the same as for attributes (+ for public, - for private). Not all operations need to have a return-type, parameters, or a property-string, but they must always have a unique signature (= return type, name, parameters) (see Figure 4.12).

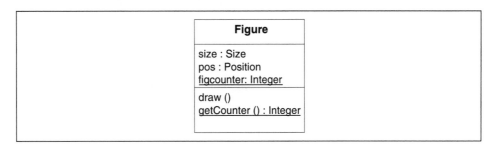

Figure 4.11 *Class-scope operation getCounter.*

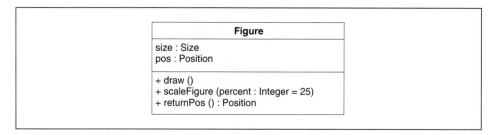

Figure 4.12 *Operation signatures.*

It's possible to have default values on parameters, which means that if the caller of the operation doesn't provide a parameter, the parameter will use the specified default value, as shown in Figure 4.13.

The operation is a part of the interface for a class; the implementation of an operation is called a *method*. An operation is specified with a signature (return-type, name, parameter-list) or with precondition, postcondition, algorithm, and the affect it has on a object. A precondition is one that must be true before the operation can execute. It might be that a figure must be drawn before the resize operation can be called. A postcondition is one that must be true after the operation is executed. A postcondition might be that after the draw operation is executed, the figure must be updated (and that this doesn't happen later). It might also be documented if the operation changes the object state in any way (e.g., resize affects the object state). All these specifications are done as properties for an opera-

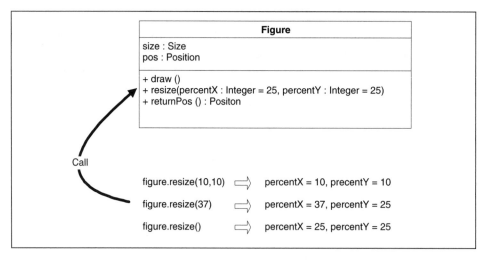

Figure 4.13 *Default values for parameters.*

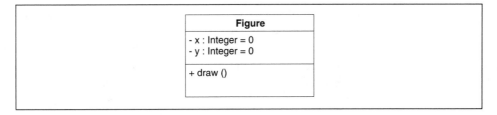

Figure 4.14 A Figure class.

tion. The properties are usually not shown directly in the class diagram, but are available from a tool (such as by clicking on an operation, all properties and their values are shown).

A persistent class is one whose objects exist after the program that created it has exited (see Figure 4.14). Persistent class objects store themselves into a database, a file, or some other permanent storage, and typically have a class–scope operation to handle the storing of the objects; for example, store (), load (...), create (). A class can be described as persistent by putting the persistent property in the name compartment (when shown in a class diagram, a property is put within curly braces, as in { persistent }).

Java Implementation

The Java code for the class in Figure 4.14 is:

```java
public class Figure
{
    private int x = 0;
    private int y = 0;

    public void draw ()
    {
        // Java code for drawing the figure
    }
};
```

The Java code for creating figure objects and calling the draw operation is:

```java
Figure fig1 = new Figure();
Figure fig2 = new Figure();
fig1.draw();
fig2.draw();
```

When objects are created, normally they should initiate attributes and links to other objects. It is possible to have an operation called create that is a class-scope operation used to create and initiate the object. It is also possible to have an operation with the same name as the class, which would correspond to a constructor in a programming language (such as in C++ or Java). A constructor is called to create and initiate an object of the class. The class in Figure 4.14 would typically have a constructor to initialize the attributes x and y to some suitable start values.

Using Primitive Types

A primitive type is a nonclass, such as integer and enumeration. There are no predefined primitive types in UML. Normally, the tool used for drawing the UML diagrams can be configured for a specific programming language, in which case, the primitive types for that language become available. If the programming language is not known (or the system being modeled shouldn't be implemented in a program), a simple subset of normal types could be used (e.g., integer, string, float). The primitive types are used for return-types, parameters, and attributes. General types such as date, integer, real, Boolean, and so on can be defined. Classes defined in any class diagram in the model can also be used to type attributes, return-types, parameters, and so on.

Relationships

Class diagrams consist of classes and the relationships between them. The relationships that can be used are *associations, generalizations, dependencies,* and *refinements.*

- An association is a connection between classes, which means that it is also a connection between objects of those classes. In UML, an association is defined as a relationship that describes a set of links, where link is defined as a semantic connection among a tuple of objects.

- A generalization is a relationship between a more general and a more specific element. The more specific element can contain only additional information. An instance (an object is an instance of a class) of the more specific element may be used wherever the more general element is allowed.

- Dependency is a relationship between elements, one independent and one dependent. A change in the independent element will affect the dependent element.

- A refinement is a relationship between two descriptions of the same thing, but at different levels of abstraction.

In the next sections, association, aggregation (which is a special case of association), generalization, dependency, and refinement relationships are presented and discussed.

Associations

An association is a connection between classes, a semantic connection (link) between objects of the classes involved in the association. An association is normally bidirectional, which means that if an object is associated with another object, both objects are aware of each other. An association represents that objects of two classes have a link between them, meaning, for example, that they "know about each other," "are connected to," "for each X there is a Y," and so on. Classes and associations are very powerful when you model complex systems, such as product structures, document structures, and all kinds of information structures.

Normal Association

The most common association is just a connection between classes. It is drawn as a solid line between two classes, as shown in Figure 4.15. The association has a name (near the line representing the association), often a verb, although nouns are also allowed. When a class diagram is modeled, it should reflect the system that is going to be built, meaning that the association names should be from the problem domain as are class names.

It is possible to use navigable associations by adding an arrow at the end of the association. The arrow indicates that the association can be used only in the direction of the arrow. However, associations may have two names, one in each direction. The direction of the name is shown by a small solid triangle either preceding or following the name, depending on the direction. It's possible to read an association from one class to the other, as in Figure 4.15: "An author uses a computer."

Figure 4.16 shows an example where a car can have one or more owners and a person can own zero or more cars. This can be expressed as part of the association in a class diagram. To express how many, we use *multiplicity*, a range that tells us

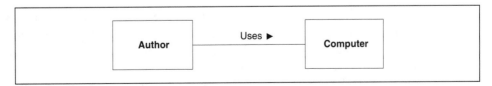

Figure 4.15 *An author uses a computer. The Author class has an association to the Computer class.*

Figure 4.16 *A person owns many (zero-to-many) cars. A car can be owned by many (one-to-many) persons.*

how many objects are linked. The range can be zero-to-one (0..1), zero-to-many (0..* or just *), one-to-many (1..*), two (2), five to eleven (5..11), and so on. It is also possible to express a series of numbers such as (1, 4, 6, 8..12). If no multiplicity is specified, then it is one (1) by default. The multiplicity is shown near the ends of the association, at the class where it is applicable (see Figure 4.17).

When we model very complex systems, especially information or business systems, it is very important to communicate the results (the model). If we can communicate our model, then it is possible at an early stage to verify, validate, and consolidate it. A class diagram is more unambigious than text. When creating the diagram, many decisions must be made that otherwise would not be. Even a small model contains a lot of information, and it is always possible to translate the model into natural language. For example, the model in Figure 4.18 can be expressed in natural language:

- An insurance company has insurance contracts, which refer to one or more customers.
- A customer has insurance contracts (zero or more), which refer to one insurance company.
- An insurance contract is between an insurance company and one or more customers. The insurance contract refers to both a customer (or customers) and an insurance company.
- The insurance contract is expressed in an (zero or one) insurance policy (a written contract of insurance).
- The insurance policy refers to the insurance contract.

The multiplicity specifies that the insurance contract is expressed in an (zero or one) insurance policy (written contract of insurance). If you call the insurance company and insure your car, there is an insurance contract, but no insurance policy. The insurance policy will be sent to you later. The point is, it is very important to model the real business, not just what it seems to be. If you model the insurance business based on the insurance policy, you might have problems. For instance, what would happen if a customer insured his car then crashed it a minute

Figure 4.17 *A navigable association says that a person can own many cars, but it does not say anything about how many people can own a car.*

later (there is no insurance policy yet, but there is an oral agreement with the insurance agent)? Alternatively, what would happen if the insurance business instituted other types of insurance policies (insurance on the Web)? If you model the "soul" of the business (the real business), you can easily handle problems that develop when the business changes because of new laws, competition, or economic shifts. In the case of insurance on the Web, you could easily add a new class called

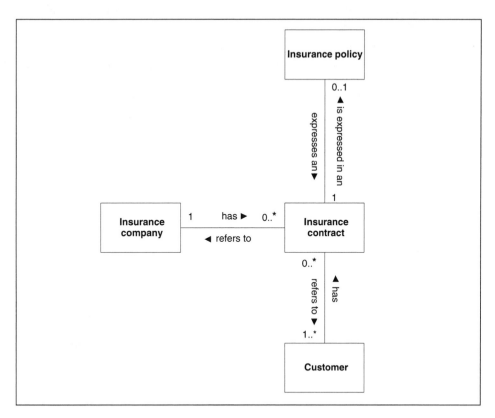

Figure 4.18 *A class diagram describing an insurance business.*

Web insurance policy. The new class could have a different behavior than normal insurance policies (e.g., that customers can change them by themselves and the changes will automatically affect the insurance contract; and the insurance policy can be sent directly to the customer by e-mail).

Object Diagram

So far, only classes have been shown in our models. Objects can be shown in an object diagram. An object diagram in UML uses the same notation and relationships as a class diagram, since the objects are just instances of the very same classes. Where a class diagram shows the class types and their relationships, the object diagram shows specific instances of those classes and specific links between those instances at some moment in time. An object diagram can thus be viewed as an example of a class diagram, and as such it is often drawn to illustrate how a complex class diagram can be instantiated into objects (see Figure 4.19). The object diagram also shows how objects from a class diagram can be combined with each other at a certain point in time.

An object is shown as a class, and the name is underscored, although an object's name can be shown optionally preceding the class name as: <u>objectname : classname</u>. The object does not have to be named, in which case only the class name is shown underscored, preceded by a colon to indicate that it is an unnamed object of the specified class. The third alternative is that only the object name is specified (underscored); the class name is not shown in the diagram.

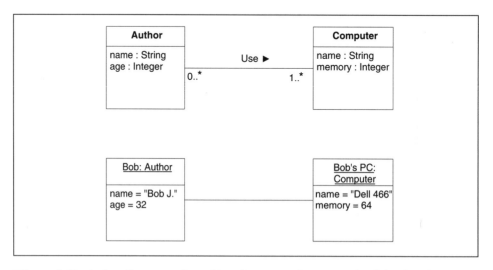

Figure 4.19 *A class diagram and an object diagram and an example of the class diagram being instantiated.*

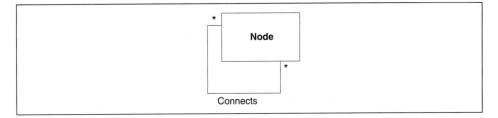

Figure 4.20 *A network consists of many nodes connected to each other.*

Recursive Association

It's possible to connect a class to itself via an association. The association still represents a semantic connection between objects, but the connected objects are of the same class. An association from a class to itself is called a *recursive association*, and is the basis for many complex models used to model things such as product structures, as shown in Figure 4.20. Figure 4.21 shows a possible object diagram for the class diagram described in Figure 4.20.

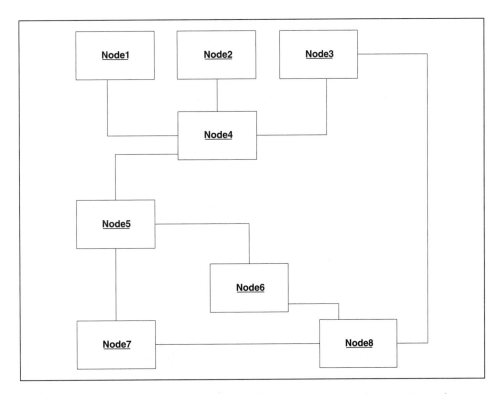

Figure 4.21 *An object diagram for Figure 4.20, in which only the object names are shown.*

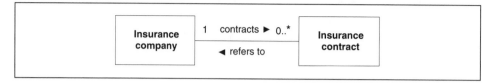

Figure 4.22 *Insurance company has associations to Insurance contract.*

Java Implementation

Figure 4.22 shows a Java implementation for the insurance company example, where the insurance company has associations to Insurance contract.

```
// Insurance_company.java file
public class Insurance_company
{
    /* Methods */

    // Insurance_contractVector is a specialization of the
    // Vector class ensuring hard typing. Vector is a standard
    // Java class for dynamic arrays.
    private Insurance_contractVector contracts;
}

// Insurance_contract.java file
public class Insurance_contract
{
    /* Methods */

    private Insurance_company refer_to;
}
```

It is easy to implement an association that is navigable or a bidirectional one-to-many association. However, in some languages, it is not that easy to implement a bidirectional many-to-many association. On the other hand, a bidirectional many-to-many association can be transformed to two one-to-many associations, as shown in Figure 4.23.

Roles in an Association

An association can have roles connected to each class involved in the association, as shown in Figures 4.24 through 4.26. The role name is a string placed near the end of the association next to the class to which it applies. The role name indicates the role played by the class in terms of the association. Roles are a useful technique for

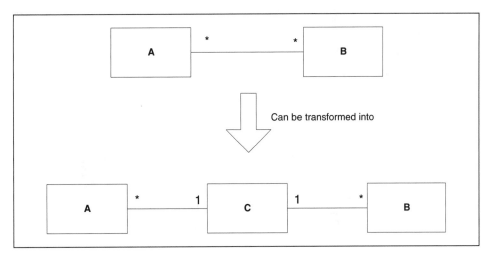

Figure 4.23 *A bidirectional many-to-many association can be transformed into two one-to-many associations.*

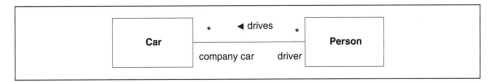

Figure 4.24 *A person plays the role of a driver and a car plays the role of a company car in terms of the drives association between Car and Person. Roles are the context in which objects act. A car can play other roles in another context, such as ambulance, police car, and so on.*

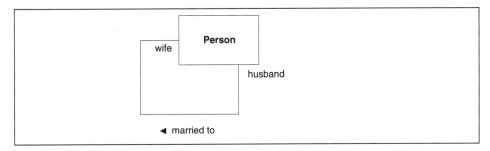

Figure 4.25 *A husband is married to a wife. Both husband and wife are people. If a person is not married, then he or she cannot play the role of husband or wife, which means that the married to association is not applicable.*

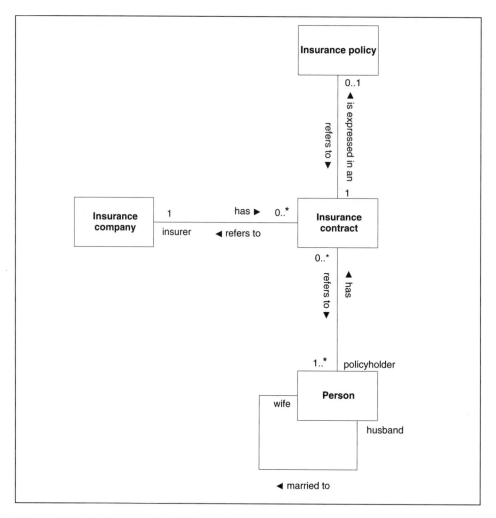

Figure 4.26 *A class can play different roles in different associations. The model from Figures 4.18 and 4.25 are combined. In this model, a person can play the role of husband, wife, or policyholder. The insurance company plays the insurer role.*

specifying the context of a class and its objects. Role names are part of the association and not part of the classes. Using role names is optional.

Qualified Association

Qualified associations are used with one-to-many or many-to-many associations. The qualifier distinguishes among the set of objects at the many end of an associa-

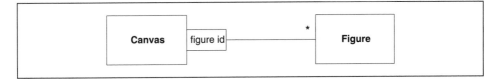

Figure 4.27 *In the Canvas class, the association is represented with a unique identification for each figure (figure id).*

tion. The qualifier specifies how a specific object at the many end of the association is identified, and may be seen as a kind of key to separating all the objects in the association. The qualifier is drawn as a small box at the end of the association near the class from which the navigation should be made. Qualified associations reduce the effective multiplicity in the model from one-to-many to one-to-one (see Figure 4.27).

Or-Association

In some models not all combinations are valid, and this can cause problems that must be handled. Figure 4.28 shows such a model. A person (policyholder) can have an insurance contract with an insurance company, and a company (policyholder) can have an insurance contract with an insurance company, but the person and the company are not permitted to have the *same* insurance contract.

A way of solving the problem is to use or-associations. An or-association is really a constraint on two or more associations. It specifies that objects of a class may

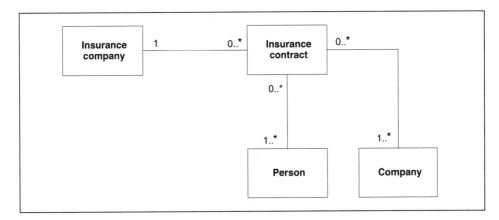

Figure 4.28 *An insurance contract cannot have associations to both company and person at the same time.*

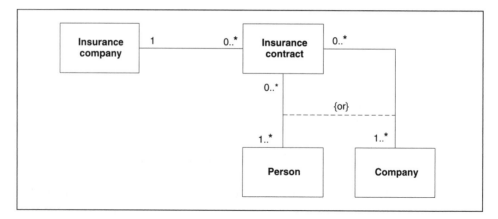

Figure 4.29 *An or-association shows that only one of the associations is valid at a time.*

participate in at most one of the associations at a time. The or-association is depicted by a dashed line between the associations that are part of the or-association, and with the specification {or} on the dashed line, as shown in Figure 4.29.

Ordered Association

The links between objects may have an implicit order; for example, windows can be ordered on a screen (one is on the top, one is at the bottom, etc.). The default value for an association is unordered. It can be shown explicitly that an association is unordered, but this is not normally the case. If there is an explicit order between the links, it is shown by putting {ordered} next to the association line near the class of the objects that are ordered, as shown in Figure 4.30. How the ordering is done (sorted) is specified either with a property of the association or inside the braces (e.g., {ordered by increasing time}).

Association Class

A class can be attached to an association, in which case it is called an association class. The association class is not connected at any of the ends of the association, but it is connected to the actual association. The association class is just like a normal class; it can have attributes, operations, and other associations. The association class is used to add extra information on a link; for example, the time the link was created. Each link of the association is related to an object of the association class. The model in Figure 4.31 shows an elevator system. The elevator control manipulates the four elevators. On each link between the elevators and the elevator con-

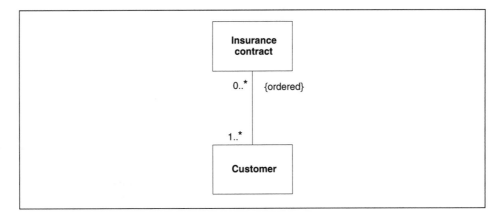

Figure 4.30 *An ordered association.*

trol, there is a queue. Each queue stores the requests from both the elevator control and the elevator itself (the buttons inside the elevator). When the elevator control chooses an elevator to perform a request from a passenger outside the elevator (a passenger on a floor), the elevator control reads each queue and chooses the eleva-

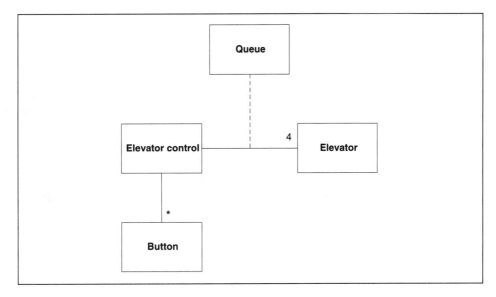

Figure 4.31 *The association class Queue could be extended with operations to add requests to the queue, to read and remove requests from the queue, and to read the length. If operations or attributes are added to the association class, they should be shown as in a class.*

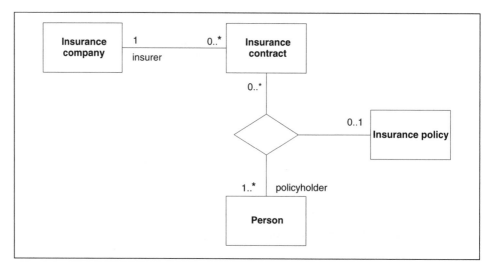

Figure 4.32 *A ternary association connects three classes.*

tor that has the shortest queue. The choice could also be made using some clever algorithm.

Ternary Association

More than two classes can be associated with each other; the ternary association associates three classes. The model in Figure 4.32 shows that a customer who plays the role of policyholder has many (zero-to-many) insurance contracts, and each insurance contract is associated with an insurance company that plays the role of insurer. On the association between customer and insurance contract, there is an (zero or one) insurance policy. The ternary association is shown as a large diamond. Roles and multiplicity may be shown, but qualifiers and aggregation (see next section) are not allowed. An association class may be connected to the ternary association by drawing a dashed line to one of the four points on the diamond.

Aggregation

Aggregation is a special case of association. The aggregate indicates that the relationship between the classes is some sort of "whole-part." One example of an aggregate is a car that consists of four wheels, an engine, a chassis, a gear box, and so on. Another example is a binary tree that consists of zero, one, or two new trees. When aggregation is used, it often describes different levels of abstraction (car consists of wheels, engine, etc.). The keywords used to identify aggregates are "consists

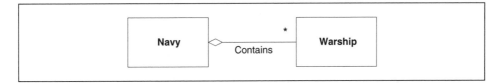

Figure 4.33 *The Navy contains many warships. Some warships can be removed and it is still a navy, and some warships can be added and it is still a navy. This is significant for a normal aggregation (but not for a composition aggregation, as described later). The parts (the warships) compose the whole (the Navy). The hollow diamond shows the aggregation.*

of," "contains," "is part of"; that is, words that indicate a whole-part relationship between the classes involved (and naturally also on their object counterparts). Special kinds of aggregation—the shared aggregate and composition aggregate—will be described shortly.

Aggregate

Figure 4.33 shows an aggregate as a line with a hollow diamond attached to one end of the line (at the wholeside, the class that contains the other class, the partside). Note, the diamond may not be attached to more than one end. Since aggregation is a special case of association multiplicity, roles (on the partside) and qualifiers may be attached to the aggregate, as in an association. An aggregate can be implemented in the same way as an association, that is, with some kind of object reference from the wholeside to the partside (and vice versa). The aggregate can also have a name (with direction) and be navigable.

Shared Aggregation

A shared aggregation is one in which the parts may be parts in any wholes, as shown in Figures 4.34 and 4.35. That an aggregation is shared is shown by its mul-

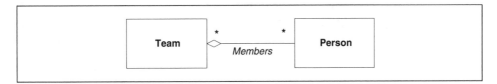

Figure 4.34 *A team is composed of team members. One person could be a member of many teams. The model shows an example of a shared aggregation, where the people are the shared parts.*

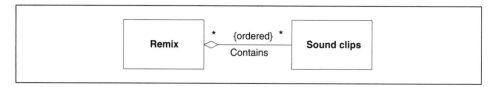

Figure 4.35 *A remix is composed of many sound clips; the same soundtrack could be a part of many remixes.*

tiplicity. The aggregation is shared if the multiplicity on the wholeside is other than one (1). Shared aggregation is a special case of a normal aggregation.

Composition Aggregation

A composition aggregation owns its parts. The composition aggregation is one with strong ownership. The parts "live" inside the whole; they will be destroyed together with its whole. The multiplicity on the wholeside must be zero or one (0..1), but the multiplicity on the partside may be any interval. A composition aggregation forms a tree of parts, whereas a shared aggregate forms a net.

There are three different ways of showing a composition aggregate. First, it can be shown with a line and a solid diamond attached to the wholeside. Second, if there is more than one part in the same aggregate (whole), they may be drawn as a tree by merging the aggregation ends into a single end. This notation is allowed for all types of aggregates. The third alternative is to put the part classes inside the whole class. These three notations are illustrated in Figures 4.36, 4.37, and 4.38.

Figure 4.39 shows an example of when an aggregate can have only one role name. The role name is at the partside. Part a is a compound aggregation with role names. Part b is an alternative compound aggregation syntax with role names. Part c shows the attribute syntax used to show compound aggregation. The roles turn into attribute names and the classes turn into attribute types.

A compound aggregate could be implemented in the same way as an association, but the whole class must control the life cycle of its parts; thus the class must destroy its parts at the same time it is destroyed. An alternative way of implementing a compound aggregate is to implement the parts as member objects of the class; that is, physically encapsulating the parts inside the whole class (see Figure 4.40).

Generalization

The definition of generalization in the UML is: "A taxonomic (taxonomy is the science of classification) relationship between a more general element and a more specific element. The more specific element is fully consistent with the more gen-

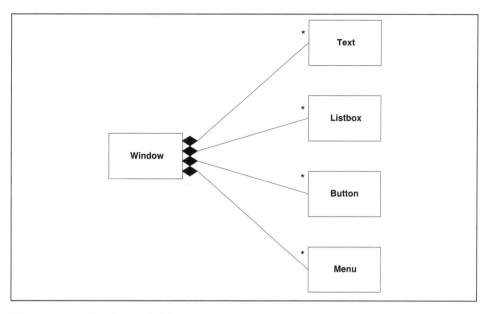

Figure 4.36 *The diamond shows the composition aggregate; the window contains (is aggregated of) many menus, buttons, listboxes, and texts. All types of aggregation can have a name.*

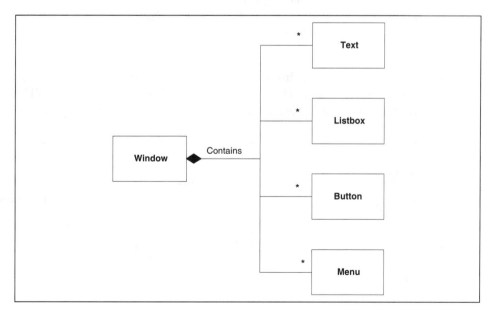

Figure 4.37 *If there is more than one part in the same aggregate (whole), they may be drawn as a tree by merging the wholeside into a single end. This is allowed for all types of aggregates. An aggregate has only one role name, and that is at the partside.*

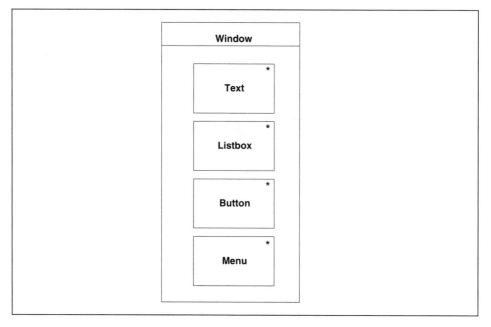

Figure 4.38 *A compound aggregate may also be shown as in the figure, where the part classes are shown inside the whole class. The multiplicity for the parts is marked in each class in the upper right-hand corner.*

eral element and contains additional information. An instance of the more specific element may be used where the more general element is allowed." Thus, generalization (sometimes called inheritance) allows elements to be specialized into new

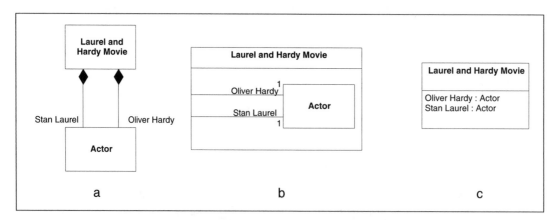

Figure 4.39 *A Laurel and Hardy movie always includes the roles Oliver Hardy and Stan Laurel.*

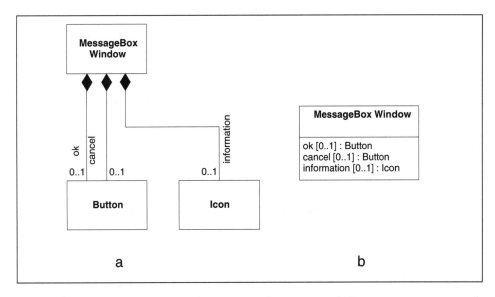

Figure 4.40 *A MessageBox Window consists of zero or one ok Button, zero or one cancel Button and zero or one information icon. A composition aggregate is shown as attributes in a class. The multiplicity is shown in Part b.*

elements, so that special cases or extensions can be easily handled as separate elements. Generalization is used for classes and use cases and for other model elements such as packages. Generalization is only used on types, never on instances (a class can inherit another class, but an object cannot inherit another object) even though the instances are indirectly affected through their type. A generalization is sometimes called an "is-a" relationship, in that one should be able to say "is-a" between the specialized element and the general element (a car *is-a* vehicle, a sales-manager *is-an* employee, etc.).

There are some variants on generalization, though they may be applicable only to certain problem domains (such as business modeling). The next section begins by describing the normal case of generalization and continues with a discussion on abstract and concrete classes. Then the variants constrained, overlapping, disjoint, and incomplete are described.

Normal Generalization

Generalization is a relationship between a general and a specific class. The specific class, called the subclass, inherits everything from the general class, called the superclass. The attributes, operations, and all associations are inherited. Attributes and operations with the public visibility in the superclass will be public in the sub-

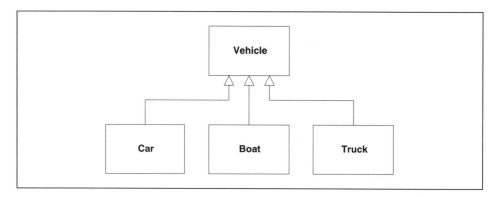

Figure 4.41 *Vehicle is a general class (superclass) derived to specific classes (subclasses) via inheritance (generalization – specialization).*

class as well. Members (attributes and operations) that have the private visibility will be inherited, but not accessible within the subclass. To protect attributes or operations from access from outside the superclass and the subclass, we can make these members protected. A protected member cannot be accessed from other classes, but is available from the class and any of its subclasses. A private member is preceded by a minus sign; a public member is preceded by a plus sign; a protected member is preceded by the pound sign (#). The visibility marker may be suppressed (not shown in the class diagram).

A class can be both a superclass and a subclass, if it is in a class hierarchy. A class hierarchy is a graph where classes are connected to each other via generalization relationships. Thus, a class can inherit from one class (in which case, it is a subclass to that class) and at the same time be inherited from another class (in which case, it is a superclass to that class). Generalization is shown as a solid line from the more specific class (the subclass) to the more general class (the superclass), with a large hollow triangle at the superclass end of the line (see Figure 4.41). As in the case with aggregation, inheritance could be shown as a tree, where the triangle is shared between all the subclasses (see Figure 4.42).

An abstract class is one that does not have any objects; or, more precisely, it is not allowed to have any objects. An abstract class is only used to inherit from, in that it describes common attributes and behavior for other classes. In the class hierarchy in Figure 4.43, it is hard to imagine objects that are vehicles that we cannot further distinguish as being a car or a boat. However, the Vehicle class is excellent to capture the commonalties between the car and boat. Vehicle is an example of an abstract class, which doesn't have any objects, but is used only to inherit from. A class can be specified explicitly as abstract by putting the tagged value { abstract } within the name compartment of the class, under the class name.

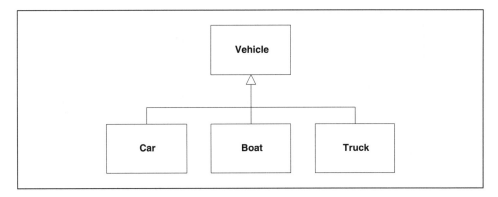

Figure 4.42 *The same model as in Figure 4.41, but the inheritance takes the form of a tree (with only one hollow triangle).*

An abstract class normally has abstract operations. An abstract operation is one that has no implementation method in the class where it is specified; only the signature is shown. A class that has at least one abstract operation must be an abstract class. A class that inherits from a class that has one or more abstract operations must implement those operations (provide methods for them) or itself become an abstract class. Abstract operations are shown with the property string { abstract } following the operation signature. They can also be shown with the operation signature in italics. Abstract operations are defined in abstract classes to specify be-

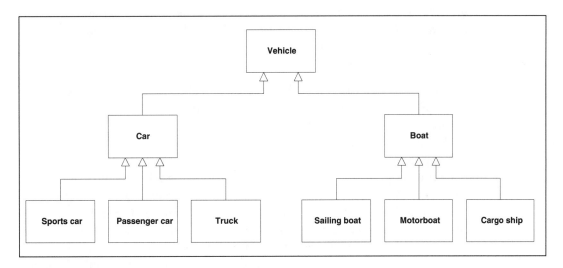

Figure 4.43 *A class hierarchy for vehicles. The Car class is subclass to Vehicle, but superclass to Sports car, Passenger car, and Truck.*

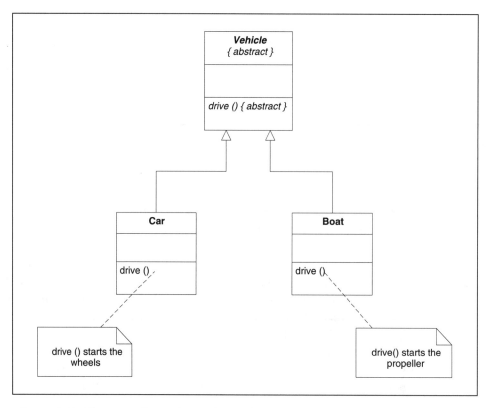

Figure 4.44 *The Car inherits the attribute color and the operation drive. The operation drive is redefined in the classes Car and Boat. The class Vehicle is abstract, which also is marked. The notes below the classes are used to comment on a class diagram.*

havior that all the subclasses must have. A Vehicle class could have abstract operations to specify that all vehicles must be able to drive, start, and stop. Thus, all classes inheriting from Vehicle must provide methods for those operations (or themselves become abstract).

The opposite of an abstract class is a concrete class, which means that it is possible to create objects from the class and that they have implementations for all operations. If the Vehicle class has specified an abstract operation drive, then both cars and boats must implement that method (or the operations themselves must be specified as abstract). The implementations are different, though. When someone tells the car to drive, the wheels move. When someone tells the boat to drive, the propeller moves (see Figure 4.44). It is easy to express that subclasses inherit an operation from a common superclass, but that they implement it in different ways.

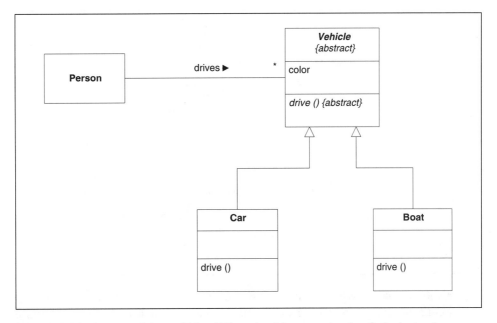

Figure 4.45 *A person drives vehicles. When the drive operation is called, the implementation used depends on whether the object used is a car or a boat. Vehicle is an abstract class showing the commonalties between cars and boats, including the association relationship to the Person class.*

As shown, the subclasses can redefine operations. A redefined operation must have the same signature (return type, name, and parameters) as the superclass. The operation being redefined can be either abstract (not have an implementation in the superclass) or concrete (have a implementation in the superclass). In both cases, the redefinition in the subclass will be used for all instances of that class. New operations, attributes, and associations can be added to the subclasses. An object of a subclass may be used in any situation where it is possible to use the superclass objects.

Figure 4.45 shows a Person class that has a drives association to the Vehicle class. The Vehicle class is abstract; that means that the actual objects that the Person drives are from the concrete subclasses Car and Boat. When the person calls (performs) the drive operation, the result depends on whether the object used in that situation is a car or a boat. If it is an object of the class Car, it will start the wheels (using the implementation as specified in the Car class). If it is an object of the class Boat, it will start the propeller (using the implementation as specified in the Boat class). This technique, where an object from a subclass acts as an object

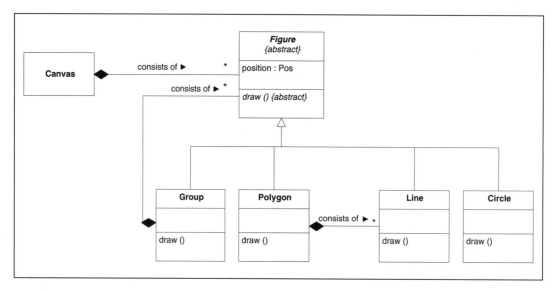

Figure 4.46 *A canvas consists of many figures. Figures could be circles, lines, polygons, or groups. A group consists of many figures. When a client asks the canvas to draw itself, the canvas asks its associated figures to draw themselves. Each figure (circles, line, polygons, or groups) is responsible for drawing itself in an appropriate way. The group draws itself through calling the draw operations in the figures that make up the group. Note that the canvas does not have to ask each figure which kind of figure it is; it just has to call the draw operation and everything else works automatically.*

from a superclass, and one or more of the operations in the superclass are redefined in the subclass, is called *polymorphism*. Polymorphism (which is Greek for many forms) means that the actual implementation used depends on the type of object to which the operation is applied. One common technique is to combine inheritance, polymorphism, and recursive associations or aggregates. Figures 4.46 and 4.47 illustrate this technique.

Discriminators can be used to specify generalization-specialization relationships. The discriminator tells on which basis we generalize and specialize. In the case with vehicles, cars, and boats, the discriminator could be propulsion. One of the main differences between cars and boats is the propulsion and that means that we can generalize and specialize with respect to the propulsion.

Java Implementation

The Java code for implementing the model in Figure 4.48 might look like:

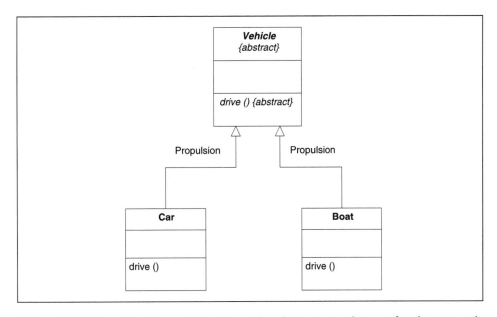

Figure 4.47 *Generalization-specialization with a discriminator that specifies that it is with respect to the propulsion that the subclasses differ.*

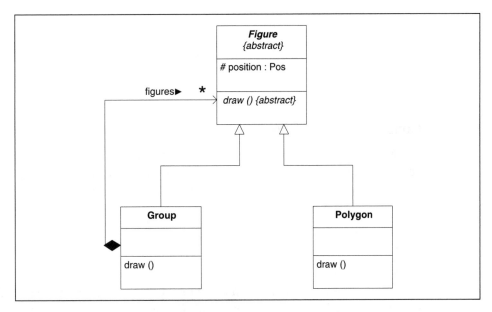

Figure 4.48 *A class hierarchy with a superclass Figure and two subclasses Group and Polygon.*

```
abstract public class Figure
{
    abstract public void draw();
    protected Pos position;
}

public class Group extends Figure
{
    public void draw ()
    {
        for (int i = 0; i < consist_of.size(), i++)
        {
            consist_of[i].draw();
        }
    }
    // FigureVector is a specialized class of the standard
    // Vector class which implements a dynamic array.
    // FigureVector adds hard type checking
    private FigureVector figures;
}

public class Polygon extends Figure
{
    public void draw ()
    {
        /* draw polygon code */
    }
}
```

Constrained Generalizations

A constraint given on a generalization specifies further information about how the generalization could be used and extended in the future. The following constraints are predefined for generalizations with more than one subclass:

Overlapping
Disjoint
Complete
Incomplete

These are semantic constraints, and may be shown in braces near the shared hollow triangle if several paths share a single hollow triangle. If the paths don't share a single hollow triangle, a dashed line should cross through all inheritance lines, and the constraints should be inserted in braces near the dashed line (see Figure 4.49).

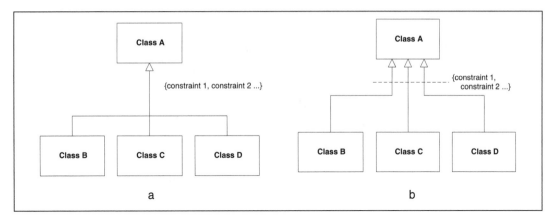

Figure 4.49 *Different ways of showing constraints on inheritance.*

Overlapping and Disjoint Generalizations

Overlapping inheritance means that any further subclasses inheriting from the subclasses in the inheritance relationship can inherit more than one of the subclasses (i.e., can use multiple inheritance with a common superclass in the inheritance tree).

Disjoint generalization is the opposite of overlapping, which means that the subclasses are not allowed to be specialized into a common subclass (as the Amphibian in Figure 4.50). Disjoint inheritance is the default; if nothing is specified, that kind of specialization using a common superclass is not allowed.

Complete and Incomplete Generalization

A constraint specifying that a generalization is complete means that all subclasses have been specified, and that no further subclassing can be done, as shown in Figure 4.51. An incomplete generalization, the default, means that subclasses may be added later on. Because one of the main goals of generalization is to allow for future extensions, incomplete generalizations are the norm.

Dependency and Refinement Relationships

In addition to association and generalization, there are two more relationships in UML. The dependency relationship is a semantic connection between two model elements, one independent and one dependent model element. A change in the independent element will affect the dependent element. As in the case with generalizations, a model element can be a class, a package, a use case, and so on. Exam-

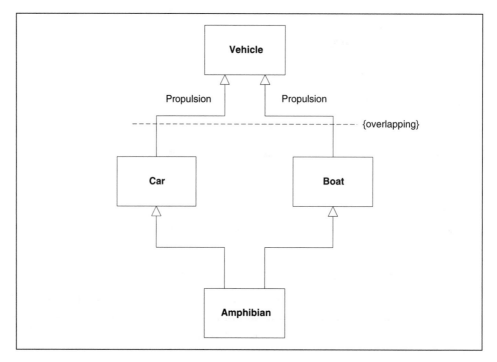

Figure 4.50 *Since the inheritance is specified as overlapping, the Amphibian class can inherit from both the Car and the Boat classes.*

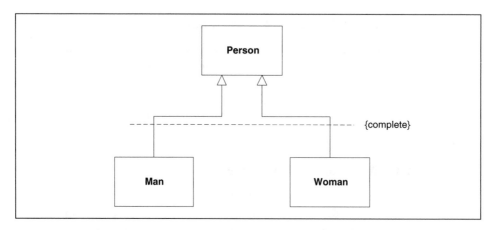

Figure 4.51 *The generalization is constrained to be complete, which means that no new subclasses may be added.*

Figure 4.52 *A dependency relationship between classes. The type of dependency is shown as stereotype; in this case, it is a "friend" dependency.*

ples of dependencies include: One class takes an object of another class as a parameter; one class accesses a global object of another class; or one class calls a class-scope operation in another class. In all these cases, there is a dependency from one class to the other, even though there is no explicit association between them. Again, a change in the independent class will affect the dependent class.

The dependency relationship is shown as a dashed line with an arrow (and possibly a label) between model elements. If a label is used, it is then a stereotype that identifies the kind of dependency. Figure 4.52 shows an example of a dependency stereotype–friend. A friend dependency means that one model element gets special access to the internal structure of the other model element (it has access even to parts with private visibility). The friend dependency is reminiscent of C++, where such a declaration can be made between classes giving special access for a "friend."

A refinement is a relationship between two descriptions of the same thing, but at different levels of abstraction. A refinement relationship can be between a type and a class that realizes it, in which case it is called a realization. Other refinements are relationships between an analysis class and a design class modeling the same thing, or between a high-level description and a low-level description (e.g., between an overview of a collaboration and a detailed diagram of the same collaboration). Refinement relationships can also be used to model different implementations of the same thing (one that is a simple implementation and another more complex, but also more efficient implementation).

The refinement relationship is shown as a dashed line with a hollow triangle between two model elements (a dashed generalization symbol; see Figure 4.53).

Figure 4.53 *Refinement relationship.*

Refinement is used in model coordination. In large projects, all models that are produced must be coordinated. Model coordination can be used to:

- Show how models on different abstraction levels are related.
- Show how models from different phases (requirement specification, analysis, design, implementation, etc.) are related.
- Support configuration management.
- Support traceability in the model.

Constraints and Derivations (Rules)

It is possible to express rules in UML; they are described as *constraints* and *derivations*. Constraints restrict a model. Examples of constraints already discussed are or–association, ordered association and inheritance constraints (overlapping, disjoint, complete, and incomplete). Derivations are rules for how things can be derived, such as the age of a person (current date minus the date of birth). The rules can be attached to any model elements, but they are especially useful for attributes, associations, inheritance, and roles and time constraints in the dynamic models that will be described later (state machines, sequence diagrams, collaboration diagrams, and activity diagrams). All rules are shown inside curly braces ({}) near the model element or in braces in a note (symbol) connected to the model element.

Associations can be derived or constrained. If a company has contracts with many customers, a derived association could be that some customers are more important VIP customers. The derived association goes directly from the class company to the class customer. A derived association has a label placed near the association, beginning with a slash followed by the name of the derivation, as shown in Figure 4.54. A constraint association can be established when one association is a subset of another association, as shown in Figure 4.55.

Attributes can also have constraints or be derived, as shown in Figure 4.56. A typical constraint for an attribute is a value range, as shown in Figure 4.57. A value range is the same as a property list for an attribute in that it specifies the possible values of the attribute. The property list is a string in any format. An example of a property string for the color attribute is {red, green, yellow}; another example of a property string for the color attribute is {0<= color <= 255}. A derived attribute is calculated in some way from other attributes. The formula for the calculation is given inside the braces under the class. A derived attribute begins with a slash, and is not stored in objects of that class (it is always calculated).

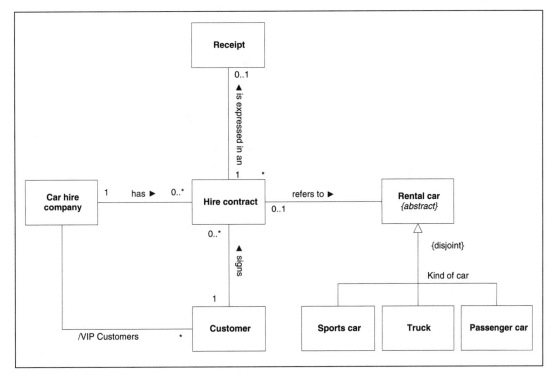

Figure 4.54 *The VIP customers are a derived association.*

Generalization has only constraints, no derivations. The constraints for generalizations are overlapping, disjoint, complete, and incomplete (as described earlier). Roles can have constraints that restrict combinations of roles played by one object. A person may normally not approve his own purchases. There are also constraints for time, but this is discussed in Chapters 5 and 6.

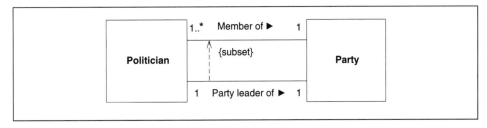

Figure 4.55 *A constraint association. The party leader of association is a subset of the member of association.*

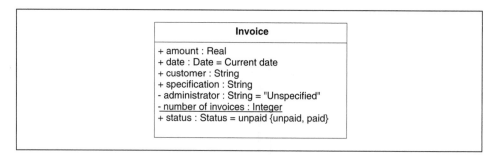

Figure 4.56 *Constraints on an attribute status.*

When rules are expressed in constraints and derivations, they refer to model elements in a model. This is done via a small syntax in UML called *navigation expression*, which comprises a basic language for specifying rules, and may sometimes have to be extended.

```
set '.' Attribute
```

The result is the value or a set of values of the attribute depending on the multiplicity of the association. The set must be an expression for an object or a set of objects.

```
set '.' role
```

The role is on the targetside of the association. The result is an object or a set of objects depending on the multiplicity of the association. The set must be an expression for an object or a set of objects.

```
set '.' '~' role
```

The role is on the sourceside of the association. The result is an object or a set of objects depending on the multiplicity of the association. This is the inverse of the association. The set must be an expression for an object or a set of objects.

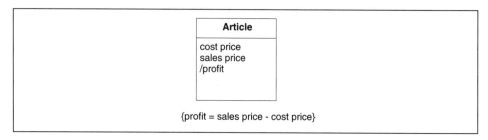

Figure 4.57 *A derived attribute profit, which is calculated from the cost and sales prices.*

```
set '[' boolean expression ']'
```

The Boolean expression is written in terms of objects within the set. The result is the subset of objects for which the Boolean expression is true. The set must be an expression for an object or a set of objects.

```
set '.' '[' qualifier value ']'
```

The qualifier value designates a qualified association that qualifies the set. It is also a value for the qualifier attribute within the qualified association. The result is the related object selected by the qualifier within the qualified association. The set must be an expression for an object or a set of objects.

Some examples are:

```
Insurance_Contract.Policyholder > 0
Person.~Policyholder.sum insured > 1000$
Car.Driver.driving license = True
Person[Supplier.Prospect] < Person[Supplier.Suspect]
```

Interfaces

A package, component, or class that has an interface connected to it is said to *implement* or *support* the specified interface in that it supports the behavior defined in the interface. The interfaces play an important role when building well-structured systems, and can be seen as contracts between collaborating clusters of model elements. The programming equivalents are OLE/COM or Java interfaces, where an interface can be specified separately from any specific class and a number of classes (or packages or components) can choose to implement that interface. An interface is described only as abstract operations, that is, a number of signatures that together specify a behavior that an element can choose to support by implementing the interface. At runtime, other objects can then be dependent on the interface alone, without knowing anything more about the class; or they may be dependent on the entire class.

The interface is shown as a small circle with a name. The interface is connected to its model element via a solid line (it is actually an association that always has the multiplicity 1–1). A class that uses the interface as implemented in a specific class is connected via a dependency relationship (a dashed arrow) to the interface circle. The dependent class is only dependent on the operations in that specific interface, not on anything else in the class (in which case, the dependency arrow should go all the way to the class symbol). The dependent class may call the operations published in the interface, which are not directly shown in the diagram.

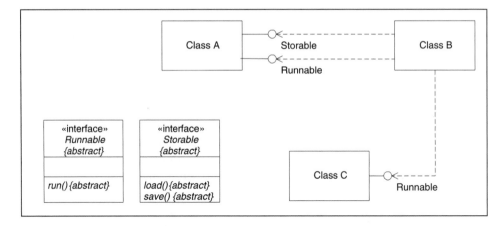

Figure 4.58 *Class A implements the interfaces Runnable and Storable. Class C implements the interface Runnable. Class B uses the interface Runnable and Storable from A, and Runnable from C. The interfaces are specified as classes with the stereotype «interface» and contain the abstract operations that the implementing classes must implement.*

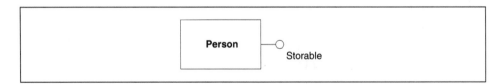

Figure 4.59 *A class Person that implements an interface Storable.*

To show the operations in an interface, the interface is specified as a class with the stereotype «interface» using the ordinary class rectangle (see Figure 4.58).

An interface can be specialized just like a class. The inheritance between interfaces is shown in a class diagram with the symbols used for classes. All interfaces have the stereotype «interface» (see Figure 4.59).

Java Implementation

The Java code for declaring both the Storable interface and the class that it implements as shown in Figure 4.59, might be:

```
interface Storable
{
    public void Save();
    public void Load();
```

```
}

public class Person implements Storable
{

    public void Save()
    {
        // Implementation of Save operation for Person
    }
    public void Load()
    {
        // Implementation of Load operation for Person
    }
}
```

Packages

A package is a grouping mechanism, whereby all kinds of model elements can be linked, as shown in Figures 4.60 through 4.63. In UML, a package is defined as: "A general-purpose mechanism for organizing elements into semantically related groups." All model elements that are owned or referenced by a package are called the package contents. As a grouping mechanism for model organization, the package instances do not have any semantics (meaning). Thus the packages only have a meaning during the model work, but is not necessarily translated into the executable system. A package owns its model elements, and that means that a model element cannot be owned by more than one package. Many methods use the term *subsystem* to describe a package.

Packages can import model elements from other packages. When a model element is imported, you refer just to the package that owns it. As in the case with most other model elements, you can have relationships between packages. However, you can have relationships only between types, not instances, because as noted, packages do not have semantics defined for their instances. The allowed relationships between packages are dependency, refinement, and generalization.

The package is shown as a large rectangle with a smaller rectangle (a tab) attached on the upper left corner of the large rectangle. If the contents (such as classes) of the package are not shown, then the name of the package is given inside the large rectangle; otherwise the name is given inside the small rectangle.

The package has similarities to aggregation. If a package owns its contents, it is *composed aggregation*; and if it refers to its contents (i.e., imports elements from other packages), it is *shared aggregation*.

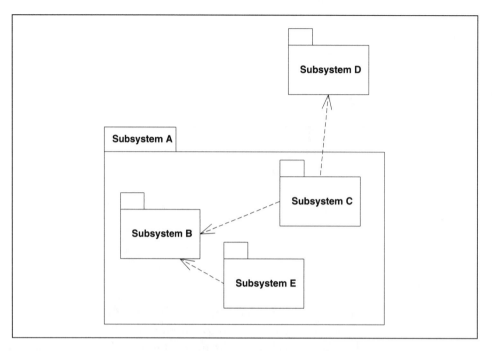

Figure 4.60 *Subsystem E is dependent on subsystem B. Subsystem C is dependent on subsystems B and D. Subsystems B, C, and E are inside subsystem A. All subsystems are represented as packages.*

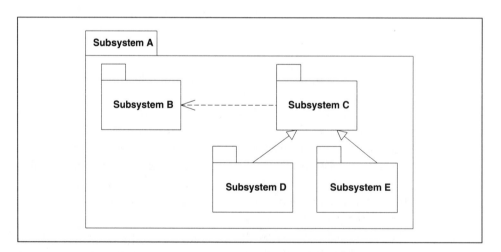

Figure 4.61 *Subsystems D and E are specialized from the generalization subsystem C. Subsystems B, C, D, and E are in subsystem A. Subsystem C depends on B (it typically has imported elements from it).*

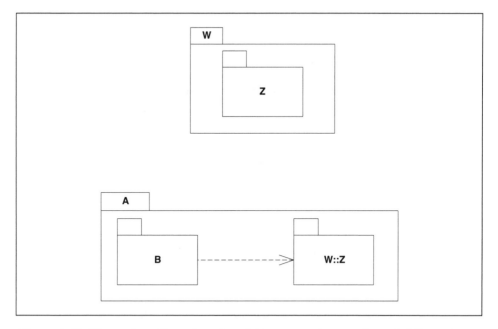

Figure 4.62 *The package Z inside package W is imported into package A. The package B is dependent on the imported package Z.*

A package may have visibility just like classes, showing how other packages can access its contents. UML defines four degrees of visibility: private, protected, public, and implementation. The default visibility for a package is public. Public visibility means that other elements can see and use the contents in the package. Private means that only the package that owns an element or a package that imports the model element can use it. If the visibility is protected, only the package that owns or imports the model element can use it; but it is also possible for specialized packages to access the model elements inside the generalized packages. The difference between private and protected visibility for packages is the inheritance: Only packages with the protected visibility can use model elements from the generalization package. The last visibility is implementation; it is also allowed for attributes, but there is no special symbol for it. Implementation is similar to private, but model elements that have a dependency to a package cannot use the elements inside that package if it has implementation visibility. Importing from a package is described as a dependency (with the stereotype «imports»), which means that if a package has the visibility implementation, no other package can import from that package.

A package may have an interface that publishes its behavior. The interface is shown with a small circle connected via a solid line to the package, as is the case

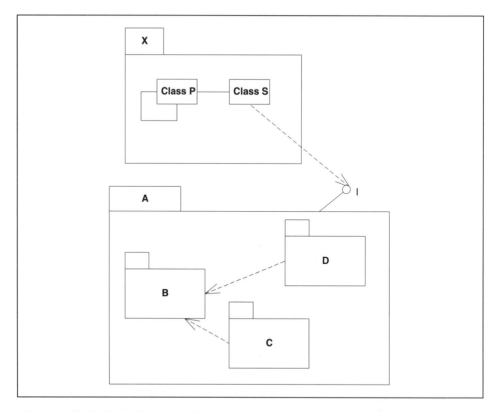

Figure 4.63 *Package X contains classes P and S. Package A has an interface I. Class S inside package X is dependent on interface I in package A.*

with classes. Typically one or more classes within the package then implement that interface.

Templates

Templates are fully supported in some languages such as C++, while others such as Java have no equivalent. Figure 4.64 shows a template as a parameterized class. The parameters to the template are used to create a real class that can be used. Thus, a template is a class that has not been fully specified, but where the final specification is done through the parameters to the template. The parameters can be classes or primitive types, for example, integers or Booleans. The parameterized class is used to specify groups of classes. A parameterized class can be an array, where the in-stantiated classes of the template then could be an array of cars, an array of colors,

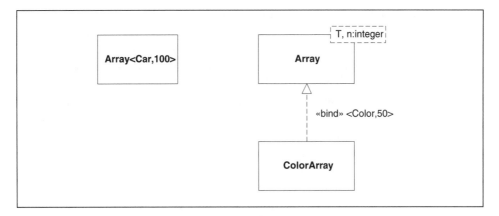

Figure 4.64 *A parameterized class Array with the parameters T (a class) and n (an integer). Two instantiations are shown, one just by specifying the name of the template and the parameters within a class symbol, and the other by specifying a refinement relationship from the instantiated class to the template.*

and so on. The parameterized class has a parameter list containing the name and type of each parameter, separated by commas. If one of the parameters is a class, it is optional to show the type in the parameter list. This means that the parameter list [T:class, A:integer] is the same as [T, A:integer]. The parameter list is shown in a dashed rectangle in the upper right-hand corner of the rectangle for the parameterized class. An instantiation of the template (the specification of a class) is shown with an ordinary class rectangle, but there the class name describes from which template it is instantiated and with which parameters, for example, Array<Car, 100>. It is also possible to show the relationship of an instantiated class and its template with a refinement relationship, using the stereotype «bind» followed by the actual parameters used in the class.

Model Quality

How do we know if a model is good or not? A modeling language can give us a syntax and semantics to work with, but it cannot tell us whether a good model has been produced. This opens the very important subject of model quality. What is important when we design models is what we are saying about reality. Models give expression to whatever it is we are studying (reality, a vision, etc.).

In a model, it is very important that the essence of the problem domain is captured. In financial systems, we are often modeling invoices but not the debt. In most businesses, the invoices as such are of no real importance, but the debts are.

An invoice is just a representation of a debt, so it should be modeled to reflect that. Another example is bank accounts. During the '70s and '80s, many banks modeled bank accounts. The customers (bank account owners) were just a part of the bank accounts (a bank account was modeled as a class or an entity and the customer as an attribute). The first problem was that the banks could not handle a bank account with many owners. The second problem was that the banks could not conduct marketing work involving customers without a bank account because they did not have the addresses.

Thus, one dimension of model quality must be the relevance of the model. A relevant model captures the important aspect of whatever is being studied. Other dimensions of model quality are that the model should be easy to communicate, have an explicit goal, be easy to maintain, be consistent, and have integrity. Different models of the same thing but with different purposes (or perspectives) should be able to be integrated (model integration).

No matter which method and modeling language have been used, there are other problems. When we make the models, we become a part of the business, which means that we must consider the effects of our intervention on the business. It is very important to handle all aspects of our intervention such as politics, culture, social structure, and power. If we fail to do this, it might not be possible to discover and capture all the real needs of the customer (note, the stated requirements are not always the same as the customers' needs). In particular, problems with internal politics, social patterns, informal structure, and power surrounding the customers must be taken into consideration.

What Is a Good Model?

A model is good when it is possible to communicate it, when it fits its purpose, and when we have captured the essentials. A good model takes time to create; it is normally done by a team, one composed to fit a certain purpose. One purpose might be to mobilize the forces to discover the needs of an organization. Other purposes might be to model a requirement specification, perform an analysis, or draw a technical design for an information system. When people are allocated to teams, it must be done with the team purpose in mind. Teams for modeling a business or an information system may be composed of customers, modeling experts, and problem domain experts.

Can We Communicate the Model?

Why must models be easy to communicate? All projects, large and small, are about communication. People are talking to each other. They are reading each other's documents and discussing their contents. Thus the primary idea behind models is to be able to communicate them. If we are creating models that no one reads or understands, then it doesn't make sense to do them at all. Models are not done because a method or a project leader stipulates it. Models are done to communicate with and unite our forces to achieve the highest productivity, efficiency, and quality as possible.

Does the Model Fit Its Purpose?

A model should have an explicit purpose that everybody using it recognizes. All models have a purpose, but often that purpose is implicit, and that makes it harder to use and understand them. Analysis and design models might be models of the same systems, but they are still different models and focus on different topics (or details). It is also necessary to have an explicit purpose for the model in order to verify and validate it. Without an explicit purpose, we might, for instance, verify an analysis model as if it were a design model.

Capturing the Essentials

Many models just involve documents in the business—for example, invoices, receipts, insurance policies. If the models just involve documents, what happens when the business changes? In practice, this is a huge problem. It is necessary to capture the essence of the business (the core) and model around those core concepts, to be able to handle changes properly. Model the core business and then model the representation of that core business. If the core (e.g., debt) is modeled, small changes in the business can be handled by alterations in the classes that represent the core classes (e.g., invoice as a representation of debt).

Name Conventions

Names on the model elements should be derived from the problem domain; they should not have a prefix or suffix. It is important that elements be assigned relevant names, especially classes, associations, roles, attributes, and operations. When elements are named from the domain, it is easier to communicate the model.

Model Coordination

Different models of the same thing must be able to be integrated and related to each other. One aspect of model coordination is integration. Integration means that if a set of models have the same purpose (although they may have different perspectives, e.g., dynamic, functional, static) and represent the same thing, it should be possible to put them together without introducing inconsistencies.

Relationships between models on different levels of abstraction is another important aspect. It is one of the keys to succeeding with traceability in software engineering. Relationships between different levels of abstraction can be visualized with the refinement relationship in UML. This means that models are coordinated on each level of abstraction and between the different levels of abstractions.

Model Complexity

Even if the models we design can be communicated, have an explicit purpose, capture the essentials in the business, and are coordinated, we can still run into problems if the models are too complex. Extremely complex models can be difficult to survey, verify, validate, and maintain. Often it is a good idea to start with a simplification, and then go into greater detail using model coordination. When the problem domain is very complex, divide the models into more models (using sub-models—e.g., packages) and through that process control the situation.

Summary

When we model, we are expressing the details of what it is we are studying, thus it is very important that the model capture the essence of the object of study. An object is something we can say things about and manipulate (in some way). An object exists in the real world (or more precisely, our understanding of the real world). An object could be a part of any system in the world—a machine, an organization, or a business. A class is a description of zero, one, or many objects with the same behavior. Classes and objects are used to discuss systems.

When we model, we use a modeling language such as UML that provides the syntax and semantics to create a model. The modeling language, however, cannot tell us whether we have done a good job. So the model quality must be explicitly focused, which means that all models must have an explicit and clear purpose and that they capture the essence of what is being studied and modeled. All models should also be easy to communicate, verify, validate, and maintain.

UML supports static, dynamic, and functional modeling. Static modeling is supported by class diagrams, which consist of classes and relationships between them. The relationships could be associations, generalizations, dependencies, or refinements. An association is a connection between classes, which means that it is also a connection between the objects of those classes. A generalization is a relationship between a more general element and a more specific element. The more specific element can contain only additional information. An instance (an object is an instance of a class) of the more specific element may be used where an instance of the more general element is allowed. Dependency is a relationship between elements, one independent and one dependent. A change in the independent element will affect the dependent element. A refinement is a relationship between two descriptions of the same thing, but at different levels of abstraction.

5 *Dynamic Modeling*

A ll systems have a static structure and dynamic behavior, and the UML provides diagrams to capture and describe both these aspects. Class diagrams are best used to document and express the static structure of a system—the classes, objects, and their relationships. State, sequence, collaboration, and activity diagrams are best used to express the behavior (the dynamics) of a system, to demonstrate how the objects interact dynamically at different times during the execution of the system.

Class diagrams model intellectual and physical things and the relationships between those things. Describing the static structure of a system can reveal what the system contains and how those things are related, but it does not explain how these things cooperate to manage their tasks and provide the functionality of the system.

Objects within systems communicate with each other; they send messages to each other. For example, the customer object Joe sends a message buy to the salesman object Bill to do something. A message is typically just an operation call that one object invokes on another object. How objects communicate and the effects of such communication are referred to as the dynamics of a system; that is, how the objects collaborate through communication and how the objects within the system change state during the system's lifetime. Communication among a set of objects in order to generate some function is called an *interaction*, which may be described by three kinds of diagrams: sequence, collaboration, or activity.

The dynamic diagrams described in this chapter are:

- *State diagrams* that describe which states an object can have during its life cycle, and the behavior in those states, along with what events cause the state to change; for example, an invoice can be paid (state paid) or unpaid (state unpaid).

119

- *Sequence diagrams* describe how objects interact and communicate with each other. The primary focus in sequence diagrams is time. The sequence diagram shows how a sequence of messages are sent and received between a set of objects in order to perform some function.
- *Collaboration diagrams* also describe how objects interact, but the focus in a collaboration diagram is space. To focus on space means that the relationships (the links) between the objects (in space) are of particular interest, and therefore explicitly shown in the diagram.
- *Activity diagrams* are yet another way of showing interactions, but they focus on work. When objects are interacting with each other, the objects also perform work in terms of activities. These activities and their order are described in activity diagrams.

Since the sequence, collaboration, and activity diagrams all show interactions, often you must make a choice as to which diagram to use when documenting an interaction. Your decision depends on which aspect is considered the most important.

In addition to the static structure and dynamic behavior, functional views can be used to describe systems. Functional views illustrate the functionality a system provides. Use cases are functional system descriptions; they describe how actors can use a system. As we've discussed, use cases are normally modeled at an early stage (e.g., requirement analysis) to describe and capture how an actor might use a system. Use-case models should capture only how an actor might use a system, not how the system is built. Classes and interactions implement use cases in the system. The interactions are expressed in sequence, collaboration, and/or activity diagrams, thus there is also a link between a functional view and a dynamic view of the system. The classes used in the implementation of the use cases are modeled and described in class diagrams and state diagrams (a state diagram is attached to a class, subsystem, or system). Use cases and their relationship to interactions are described in Chapter 3.

Interaction between Objects (Messages)

In object-oriented programming, an interaction between two objects is performed as a message sent from one object to another. In this context, it is important that the word "message" not be taken too literally, in that a message is "sent" as in a communication protocol. A message is most often implemented by a simple operation call, when one object calls an operation in another; when the operation has been executed, the control is returned to the caller along with a return value. A

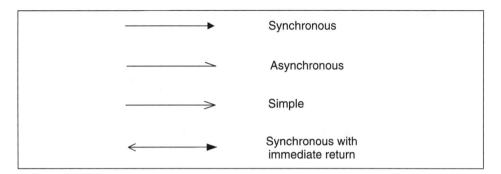

Figure 5.1 *Message types notation.*

message can also be an actual message sent through some communication mechanism, either over the network or internally on a computer, though this is most common in real-time systems. Messages are shown in all the dynamic diagrams (sequence, collaboration, state, and activity) as a means of communicating between objects. A message is drawn as a line with an arrow between the sender and the recipient of the message. The arrow type indicates the message type.

Figure 5.1 shows the message types used in the UML. They are:

- *Simple*: Represents a flat flow of control. It shows how the control is passed from one object to another without describing any details about the communication. This message type is used when details about the communication are not known or not considered relevant in the diagram. It is also used to show the return of a synchronous message; that is, it is drawn from the object that handles the message back to the caller to show that the control is passed back.

- *Synchronous*: A nested flow of control, typically implemented as an operation call. The operation that handles the message is completed (including any other nested messages being sent as part of the handling) before the caller resumes execution. The return can be shown as a simple message, or the return can be implicit when the message has been handled.

- *Asynchronous*: Asynchronous flow-of-control, where there is no explicit return to the caller and where the sender continues to execute after sending the message without waiting for it to be handled. This is typically used in real-time systems where objects execute concurrently.

The simple and synchronous messages can be combined into one message line with the synchronous message arrow at one end and the simple return arrow at the other. This indicates that the return is almost immediate after the operation call.

State Diagram

State diagrams capture the life cycles of objects, subsystems, and systems. They tell the states an object can have and how events (received messages, time elapsed, errors, and conditions becoming true) affect those states over time. A state diagram should be attached to all classes that have clearly identifiable states and complex behavior; the diagram specifies the behavior and how it differs depending on the current state. It also illustrates which events will change the state of the objects of the class.

States and Transitions

All objects have a state; the state is a result of previous activities performed by the object, and is typically determined by the values of its attributes and links to other objects. A class can have a specific attribute that specifies the state, or the state can be determined by the values of the "normal" attributes in the object. Examples of object states are:

- The invoice (object) is paid (state).
- The car (object) is standing still (state).
- The engine (object) is running (state).
- Jim (object) is playing the role of a salesman (state).
- Kate (object) is married (state).

An object changes state when something happens, which is called an event; for example, someone pays an invoice, starts driving the car, or gets married. There are two dimensions of dynamics: the interaction and the internal state changes. Interactions describe the object's external behavior and how it interacts with other objects (by sending messages or linking and unlinking to each other). Internal state changes describe how objects are altering states—for example, the values of its internal attributes. State diagrams are used to show how objects react to events and how they change their internal state; for instance, an invoice changes state from unpaid to paid when someone pays it. When an invoice is created, it enters the state of unpaid (see Figure 5.2).

State diagrams may have a starting point and several end points. A starting point (initial state) is shown as a solid filled circle, and an end point (final state) is shown as a circle surrounding a smaller solid circle (a bull's-eye). A state in a state diagram is shown as a rectangle with rounded corners. Between the states are state transitions, shown as a line with an arrow from one state to another. The state transitions may be labeled with the event causing the state transition, as shown in Figure 5.3. When

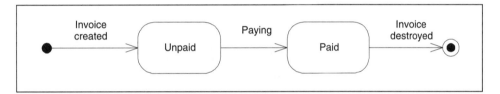

Figure 5.2 *A state diagram for invoices. The solid filled circle indicates the starting point of invoices (object created). The circle surrounding the solid filled circle indicates the end point (object destroyed). The arrows between the states show state transitions and the events that cause them.*

the event happens, the transition from one state to another is performed (it is sometimes said that the transition "fires" or that the transition "is triggered").

A state may contain three kinds of compartments, as shown in Figure 5.4. The first compartment shows the name of the state, for example, idle, paid, and moving. The second compartment is the optional state variable compartment, where attributes (variables) might be listed and assigned. The attributes are those

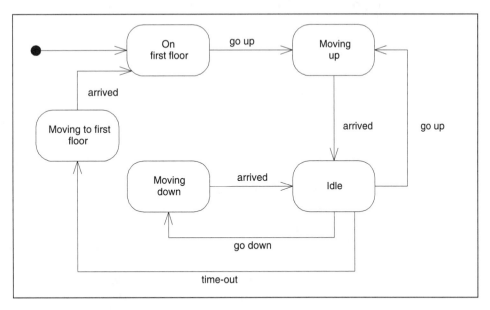

Figure 5.3 *A state diagram for an elevator. The elevator starts at the first floor. It can be moving up or down. If the elevator is idle on one floor, a time-out event occurs after a period of time and moves the elevator back to the first floor. This state diagram does not have an end point (final state).*

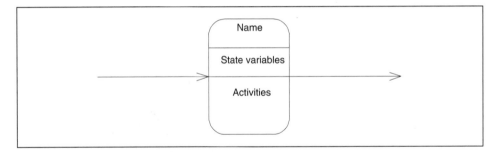

Figure 5.4 *Name, state variable, and activity compartments.*

of the class displayed by the state diagram; sometimes, temporary variables are useful in states, for example, counters. The third compartment is the optional activity compartment, where events and actions might be listed. Three standard events may be used in the activity compartment: *entry*, *exit*, and *do*. The entry event can be used to specify actions on the entry of a state; for instance, assigning an attribute or sending a message. The exit event can be used to specify actions on exit from a state. The do event can be used to specify an action performed while in the state; for example, sending a message, waiting, or calculating. These standard events may not be used for other purposes. The formal syntax for the activity compartment is:

```
event-name argument-list '/' action-expression
```

The event-name can be any event, including the standard events entry, exit, and do. The action-expression tells which action should be performed (e.g., operation calls, incrementing attribute values, etc.). It is also possible to specify arguments to the events (entry, exit, and do events do not have any arguments; see Figure 5.5).

A state transition normally has an event attached to it, but it is not necessary. If an event is attached to a state transition, the state transition will be performed when the event occurs. A do–action within a state can be an ongoing process (e.g., waiting, polling, operation control, etc.) performed while the object is in the given state. A do–action can be interrupted by outside events, meaning that an event on a state transition may interrupt an ongoing internal do–action.

If a state transition does not have an event specified, the attached state will change when the internal actions in the source state are executed (if there are any internal actions such as entry, exit, do, or user–defined actions). Thus, when all the actions in a state are performed, a transition without an event will automatically be triggered (see Figure 5.6).

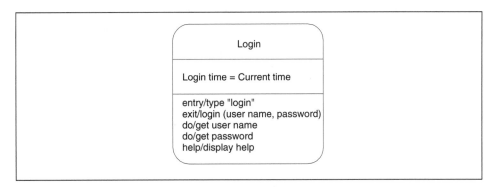

Figure 5.5 *A state called login, where the login time is assigned to the current time, and where a number of actions are performed on entry, exit, and while in the state. The help/ display help is a user-defined event and action within the action compartment.*

The formal syntax for specifying a state transition is:

```
event-signature '[' guard-condition ']' '/' action-expression
'^' send-clause
```

where the event-signature syntax is defined as:

```
event-name '(' parameter ',', ...')'
```

and the send-clause syntax is:

```
destination-expression '.'destination-event-name '(' argument
',' ...')'
```

where the destination-expression is an expression that evaluates an object or a set of objects. Examples of event-signatures, guard-conditions, action-expressions, and send-clauses are given next.

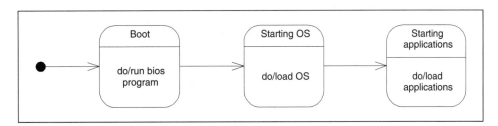

Figure 5.6 *State transitions without explicit events. The transitions occur when the activities in each state have been performed.*

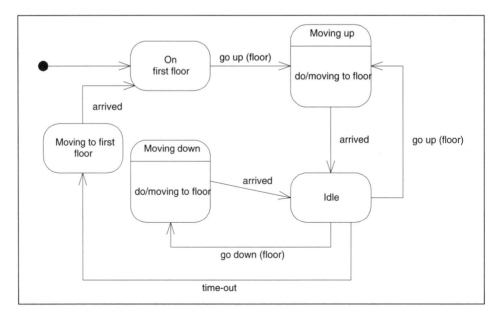

Figure 5.7 *The event of the transitions between the On first floor and Moving up states has a parameter, floor (the type of the parameter is suppressed); as has the transition between Idle and Moving up and between Idle and Moving down.*

Event-Signature

Figure 5.7 shows an event-signature, which consists of an event-name and parameters, specifying the event that triggers a transition, along with additional data connected to the event. The parameters are a comma-separated list of parameters with the syntax:

```
Parameter-name ':' type-expression, Parameter-name ':' type-
expression ...
```

where the parameter-name is the name of the parameter and the type-expression is the type of the parameter, for example, integer, Boolean, and string. The type-expression may be suppressed, that is, not shown.

Examples of state transitions with event-signature are:

```
draw (f : Figure, c : Color)
redraw ()
redraw
print (invoice)
```

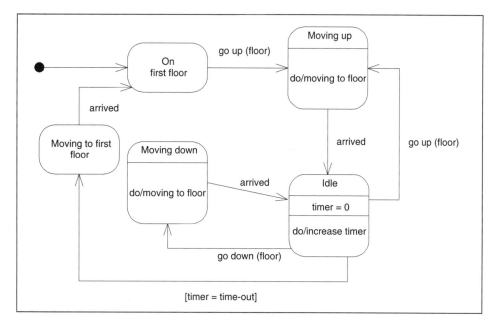

Figure 5.8 *The Idle state assigns zero to the attribute timer, then it increases the timer continuously until the event go down or go up occurs or until the guard-condition timer = time-out becomes true.*

Guard-Condition

Guard-condition is a Boolean expression placed on a state transition. If the guard-condition is combined with an event-signature, the event must occur *and* the guard-condition must be true for the transition to fire. If only a guard-condition is attached to a state transition, the transition will fire when the condition becomes true (see Figure 5.8). Examples of state transitions with a guard-condition are:

```
[t = 15sec]
[number of invoices > n]
withdrawal (amount) [balance >= amount]
```

Action-Expression

Action-expression is a procedural expression executed when the transition fires, as shown in Figure 5.9. It may be written in terms of operations and attributes within the owning object (the object that owns all of the states) or with parameters within the event-signature. It is possible to have more than one action-expression on a

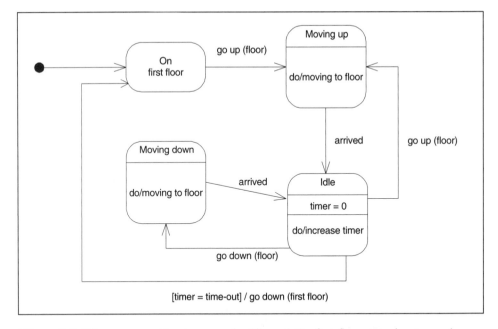

Figure 5.9 *The state transition between the Idle and On first floor states has a guard-condition and an action-expression. When the timer attribute is equivalent to the Time-out constant, the action* go down *(first floor) is performed; then the state is changed from Idle to On first floor.*

state transition, but they must be delimited with the backward slash (/) character. The action-expressions are executed one by one in the order specified (from left to right). Nested action-expressions or recursive action-expressions are not allowed. It is, however, possible to have a state-transition that contains only an action-expression. Examples of state transitions with an action-expression are (:= is used for assignment):

```
increase () / n := n + 1 / m := m + 1
add (n) / sum := sum + n
/flash
```

Send-Clause

The send-clause is a special case of an action. It is an explicit syntax for sending a message during the transition between two states. The syntax consists of a destination-expression and an event-name. The destination-expression should be one that evaluates an object or a set of objects. The event-name is the name of an event meaningful to the destination object (or set of objects). The destination object can also be the object itself.

```
[timer = Time-out] / go down (first floor)
```

can be translated to a send-clause as:

```
[timer = Time-out] ^ self.go down (first floor)
```

Other examples on state transitions with a send-clause are:

```
out_of_paper()^indicator.light()
left_mouse_btn_down(location) / color:=pick_color(location) ^
pen.set(color)
```

State diagrams should be easy to communicate and understand (as all models should), but sometimes it is tricky to express complex internal dynamics (the object's internal states and all the state transitions) and at the same time create a model that is easy to communicate. In each situation, the modeler must decide whether to model all internal dynamics as they appear, in detail, or to simplify them to make it easier to understand the model (a simplification could be temporary).

Events

An event is something that happens and that may cause some action (see Figure 5.10). For example, when you press the Play button on your CD player, it starts playing (provided that the CD player is turned on, a CD is loaded, and the CD player is otherwise in order). The event is that you press the Play button, and the action is that it starts playing. When there are well-defined connections between events and actions, it is called *causality*. In software engineering, we normally model causal systems in which events and actions are connected to each other. It is not causal for example, if you drive too fast on the highway and the police stop you, because the action of the police stopping you is not sure to happen; thus there is no well-defined connection between the event (driving too fast) and the action (the police stopping you).

The definition of an event can be found in the *Cambridge Dictionary of Philosophy* [Cambridge 96], by looking at the definition of entity (under metaphysics):

Every entity must be either an individual thing (e.g., Socrates and this book), or a property (e.g., Socrates' color and the shape of this book), or a relation (e.g., marriage and the distance between two cities), or an event (e.g., Socrates' death), or a state of affairs (e.g., Socrates' having died), or a set (e.g., the set of Greek philosophers).

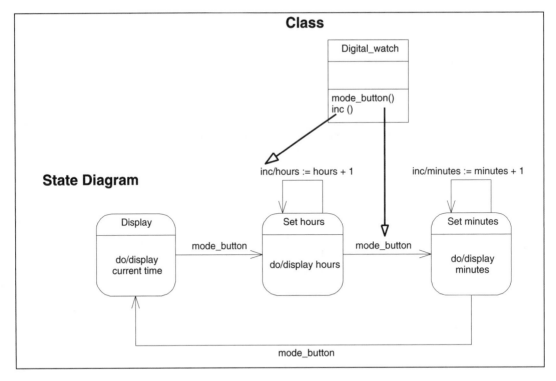

Figure 5.10 *The Digital_watch class with its corresponding state diagram. The figure shows how events in the state diagram are related to operations within the class. The watch has three states: its normal display state showing the time, and two states for setting the clock (hours and minutes, respectively).*

There are four kinds of events within the UML:

- *A condition becoming true*: This is shown as a guard-condition on a state transition.

- *Receipt of an explicit signal from another object*: The signal is itself an object. This is shown as an event-signature on state transitions. This type of event is called a message.

- *Receipt of a call on an operation by another object (or by the object itself)*: This is shown as an event-signature on state transitions. This type of event is also called a message.

- *Passage of a designated period of time*: The time is normally calculated after another designated event (often the entry of the current state) or the passage of a given amount of time. This is shown as a time-expression on state transitions.

Note that errors are also events and may be useful to model. The UML does not give any explicit support for error events, but it can be modeled as a stereotyped event; for example:

«error» out_of_memory

It is important to know some basic semantics about events. First, events are triggers that activate state transitions; these events are processed one at time. If an event potentially can activate more than one state transition, only one of the state transitions will be triggered (which one is undefined). If an event occurs, and the state transition's guard-condition is false, the event will be ignored (the event will not be stored, triggering the transition when the guard-condition later becomes true).

A class can receive or send messages; that is, operation calls or signals. The event-signature for state transitions is used for both. When an operation is called, it executes and produces a result. When a signal object is sent, the receiver catches the object and uses it. Signals are ordinary classes, but used only for sending signals; they represent the unit sent between objects in the system. The signal classes may be stereotyped with the «signal» stereotype, which constrains the semantics of the objects, meaning that only they can be used as signals. It is possible to build signal hierarchies supporting polymorphism, so that if a state transition has an event-signature specifying a specific signal, all the subsignals will also be receivable by the same specification (see Figure 5.11).

Java Implementation

State diagrams are in some cases redundant information, depending on whether the operations within the classes have specified algorithms. In other words, a class behavior may be specified within operations as algorithms or explicitly by state diagrams (or both). When state diagrams are implemented in an object-oriented programming language, they are implemented either directly in the algorithms (with case statements, etc.) or they are implemented with separate mechanisms, such as finite state machines or function tables. It is outside the scope of this book to describe this in detail; however, Figure 5.12 illustrates the principles for implementing a state diagram directly into the operations of the class.

The UML does not give any advice on how to implement signal events in a programming language. Nevertheless, implementing the signals is rather straightforward: They are implemented as classes with both attributes and common operations. The classes that are to receive the signals must have a corresponding operation that receives the signal object as an argument.

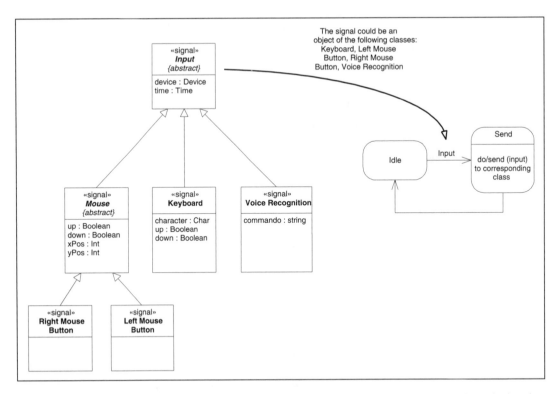

Figure 5.11 *A signal class hierarchy with an abstract superclass. The state diagram on the right-hand side receives input signals (including subsignals to the Input class). Only concrete signals may be sent (because the abstract signal class does not have any instances).*

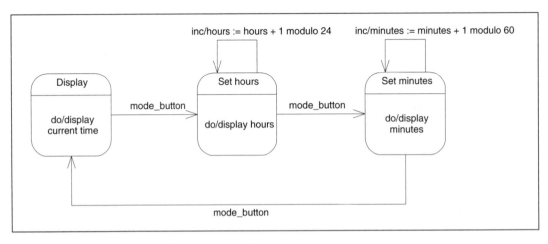

Figure 5.12 *A state diagram for a digital watch.*

The Java code for a class with the state diagram shown in Figure 5.12 would look something like this:

```java
public class State
{
    public final int Display = 1;
    public final int Set_hours = 2;
    public final int Set_minutes = 3;
    public int value;
}

public class Watch
{
private State state = new State();
private DigitalDisplay LCD = new DigitalDisplay();

public Watch ()
    {
        state.value = State.Display;
        LCD.display_time();
    }

public void mode_button ()
    {
        switch (state.value)
        {
        case State.Display :
           LCD.display_time();
           state.value = State.Set_hours;
           break;
        case State.Set_Hours :
           LCD.display_hours();
           state.value = State.Set_minutes;
           break;
        case State.Set_minutes) :
           LCD.display_time();
           state.value = State.Display;
           break;
    }
public void inc()
    {
        case (state.value)
        {
```

```
            case State.Display :
                ;
                break;
            case State.Set_hours:
                LCD.inc_hours();
                break;
            case State.Set_minutes:
                LCD.inc_minutes();
                Break;

        }

    }
```

Sending Messages between State Diagrams

State diagrams may send messages to other state diagrams. This is shown either by actions (i.e., specifying the receiver in the send-clause) or with dashed arrows between the state diagrams. If dashed arrows are used, the state diagrams must be grouped inside their objects (the class rectangle symbol is then used). The rectangle symbol may also be used for modeling subsystems or systems (a sort of macro class). Two different techniques can be used to draw dashed arrows between state diagrams that represent messages.

The first way is to draw the dashed arrow from a transition within the source object to the border of the target object (this is the alternative to the text syntax in the send-clause). Then a transition should be drawn within the target object, which corresponds to and catches the specified message.

The second way is to draw a dashed line from the source object to the target object, indicating that the source object is sending the message some time during its execution. However, the target object must also have a corresponding transition signature to catch the message (see Figure 5.13).

Substates

A state may have nested substates, whereby internally the state has its own substates that can be shown in other state diagrams. The substates may be and-substates or or-substates. An or-substate indicates that a state has substates, but only one at a time, as shown in Figure 5.14. For instance, a car may be in the running state, which has two different substates: forward and backward. These are or-substates because they may not be true at the same time. The nested substates can be displayed in another state diagram by expanding the running state in the initial state diagram.

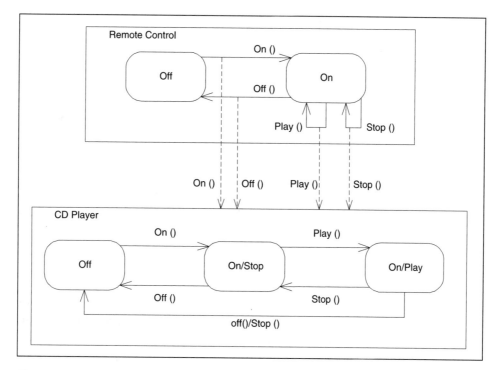

Figure 5.13 *The remote control sends messages to the CD player.*

On the other hand, the running state can also have many concurrent substates (and–substates): forward and low speed, forward and high speed, backward and low speed, backward and high speed. When a state has and–substates, several of them can be true in parallel, indicating that a state can have substates that are both or–

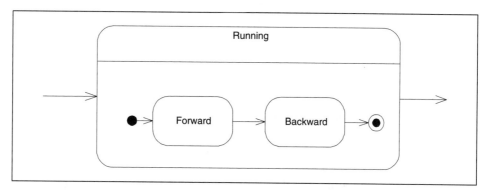

Figure 5.14 *An or-substate.*

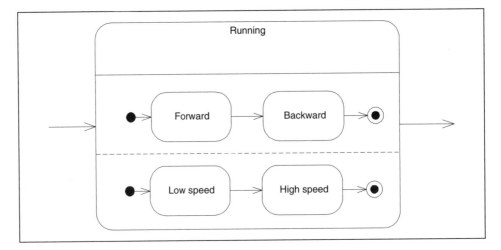

Figure 5.15 *An and-substates (combined with or-substates).*

substates and and-substates, as shown in Figure 5.15. And-substates are also called concurrent substates, and can be used when modeling the states of concurrent threads. This is discussed in more detail in Chapter 6.

History Indicator

A history indicator is used to memorize internal states; for example, it remembers a state so that it's possible to go back to that state at a later time, in case an activity has to be interrupted or reversed. A history indicator applies to a state region, in which it is placed. If a transition to the indicator fires, the object resumes the state it had last within that region. A history indicator is shown as a circle with an H inside. It may have several incoming transitions, but no outgoing transitions (see Figure 5.16).

Sequence Diagram

Sequence diagrams illustrate how objects interact with each other. They focus on message sequences, that is, how messages are sent and received between a number of objects. Sequence diagrams have two axes: the vertical axis shows time and the horizontal axis shows a set of objects. A sequence diagram also reveals the interaction for a specific scenario—a specific interaction between the objects that happens at some point in time during the system's execution (e.g., when a specific function is used).

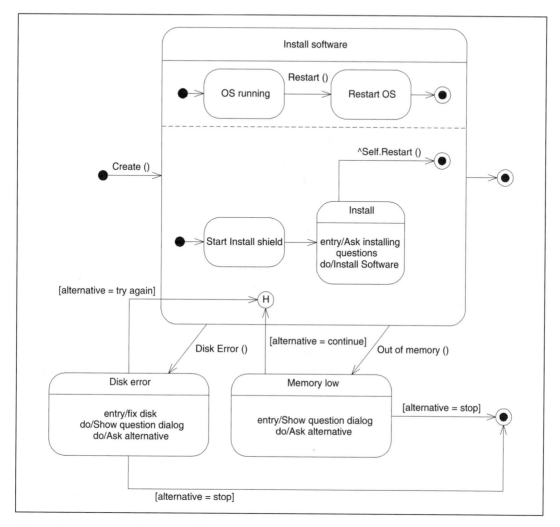

Figure 5.16 *An install program. The history indicator is used to handle errors such as "out of memory" and "disk error," when some specific error states handle these errors. After the error states have been performed, the history indicator is used to go back to the state that applied before the error.*

On the horizontal axis are the objects involved in the sequence. Each is represented by an object rectangle with the object and/or class name underlined. And a vertical dashed line, called the object's lifeline, indicates the object's execution during the sequence (i.e., messages sent or received and the activation of the object). Communication between the objects is represented as horizontal message lines between the objects' lifelines. The arrow specifies whether the message is synchronous, asynchronous, or simple (previously defined in this chapter). To read the sequence diagram, start at the top of the diagram and read down to view the exchange of messages taking place as time passes.

Generic and Instance Form

Sequence diagrams can be used in two forms: the generic form and the instance form. The instance form describes a specific scenario in detail; it documents one possible interaction. The instance form does not have any conditions, branches, or loops; it shows the interaction for just the chosen scenario. The generic form describes all possible alternatives in a scenario, therefore branches, conditions, and loops may be included. For example, the scenario "opening an account" in a sequence diagram using the generic form would be described with all possible alternatives: where everything is successful, where the customer isn't allowed to open an account, where money is immediately deposited in the account, and so on. The same scenario documented with the instance form of a sequence diagram would have to choose one specific execution and stick to that case; for example, one diagram could show the successful opening of an account. If all cases must be shown using instance form diagrams, a number of them would have to be drawn.

A message is a communication between objects that conveys information with the expectation that action will be taken. The receipt of a message is normally considered an event. Messages can be signals, operation calls or something similar (e.g., RPC (Remote Procedure Calls) in C++ or RMI (Remote Method Invocation) in Java). When a message is received, an activity starts in the receiving object; this is called *activation*. Activation shows the focus of control, which object(s) executes at some point in time. An activated object is either executing its own code or is waiting for the return of another object to which it has sent a message. Activation is drawn as a thin rectangle on the object's lifeline. The lifeline represents the existence of an object at a particular time; it is drawn as a dashed line extending from the top to the bottom of the diagram. The messages are shown as arrows (synchronous, asynchronous, or simple) between the object lifelines. Each message may have a signature with a name and parameters, for example:

```
print (file : File)
```

The messages may also have sequence numbers, though they are seldom used because the sequence is given explicitly in the diagram. Returns (from synchronous messages such as operation calls) are also shown as arrows (using the simple arrow); but note, returns are not always shown (see Figure 5.17).

Messages can also have conditions. A condition must be true for the message to be sent and received. Conditions are used to model branches or to decide

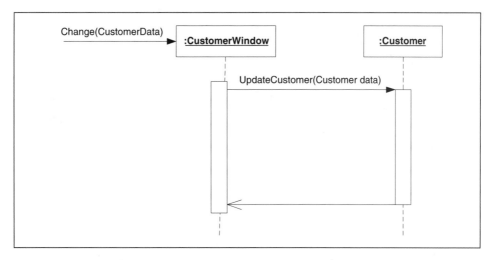

Figure 5.17 *A sequence diagram with one scenario starting with the Change message. The return of the UpdateCustomer message is shown.*

whether or not to send a message. If conditions are used to describe branches, several message arrows are drawn with conditions that exclude each other; in other words, only one message is sent at a time, as shown in Figure 5.18. If branches are

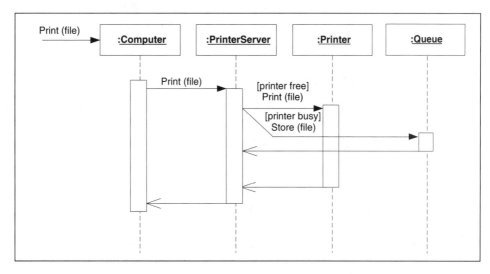

Figure 5.18 *The messages from the PrinterServer to the Printer has conditions that show how alternatives are described in a sequence diagram. Either the Print message to the Printer or the Store message to the Queue is sent.*

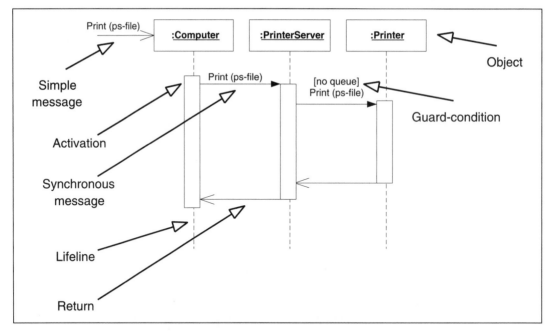

Figure 5.19 *The concepts used in a sequence diagram.*

modeled with conditions that do not exclude each other, the messages are sent concurrently. A message can also be sent from an object to itself, in which case, the message symbol is drawn from the object symbol to itself, as shown in Figure 5.19.

Concurrent Objects

In some systems, objects run concurrently, each with its own thread of control. If the system uses concurrent objects, it is shown by activation, by asynchronous messages, and by active objects. This topic is discussed further in Chapter 6.

Labels that Define Iteration and Constraints

Sequence diagrams can have labels and comments in the left or right margin. The labels can be of any kind such as timing marks, descriptions of actions taken during activation, constraints, and so on, as shown in Figure 5.20. Iteration is typically documented using a margin comment, as shown in Figure 5.21. It is also possible to express timing constraints with labels. For instance, it might be useful to constrain the time between two messages and the time it takes for a message to arrive (the transition time).

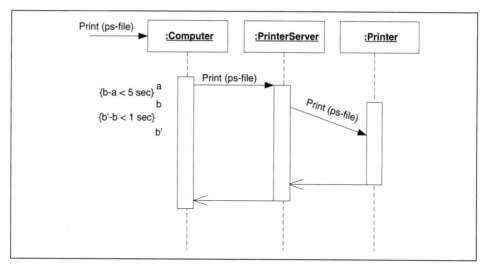

Figure 5.20 *Labels used to specify time constraints. The time between a and b must not be longer than five seconds. The message Print from the PrinterServer must be received within one second. A slanted arrow shows that the time between sending and receiving the message is substantial. As usual, constraints are shown inside braces.*

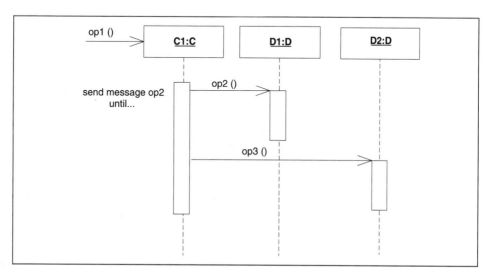

Figure 5.21 *Iteration expressed in the margin.*

Creating and Destroying Objects

Sequence diagrams may show how objects are created and destroyed as part of the scenario documented. An object may create another object via a message. The object created is drawn with its object symbol placed where it is created (on the vertical time axis). The message that creates or destroys an object is normally a synchronous message (a solid arrow). When an object is destroyed, it is marked with a large X; it is further indicated by drawing the lifeline of that object only to the point at which it was destroyed (see Figure 5.22).

Recursion

Recursion is a technique used in many algorithms. Recursion occurs when an operation calls itself, as shown in Figure 5.23, where it is depicted as an activation added onto itself. The message (when an operation calls itself) is always synchronous, and is marked as such in the sequence diagram. The return is shown as a simple message.

Collaboration Diagram

Collaboration diagrams focus both on the interactions and the links between a set of collaborating objects (a link is an instance of an association). The sequence and collaboration diagram both show interactions, but the sequence diagram focuses on time and the collaboration diagram focuses on space. The links show the actual objects and how they are related to each other; and an object can be shown with its internal structure (the objects it consists of are drawn inside the object). As with sequence diagrams, collaboration diagrams may be used to illustrate the execution of an operation, a use-case execution, or simply an interaction scenario in the system.

As noted previously, concurrency and asynchronous messages will not be described here. They are described in Chapter 6. A technique by which collaboration diagrams are parameterized is described in Chapter 9.

Collaboration diagrams show objects and their links to each other, as well as how messages are sent between the linked objects. The objects are drawn in the same way as classes, but their names are underlined (the object symbol). The links are drawn with lines (which look like associations, but without multiplicity). On a link, a message can be attached with a message label that defines, among other things, a sequence number for the message. The label requires a special syntax, given shortly. A collaboration diagram starts with a message that initiates the entire interaction or collaboration, for example, an operation call (see Figure 5.24).

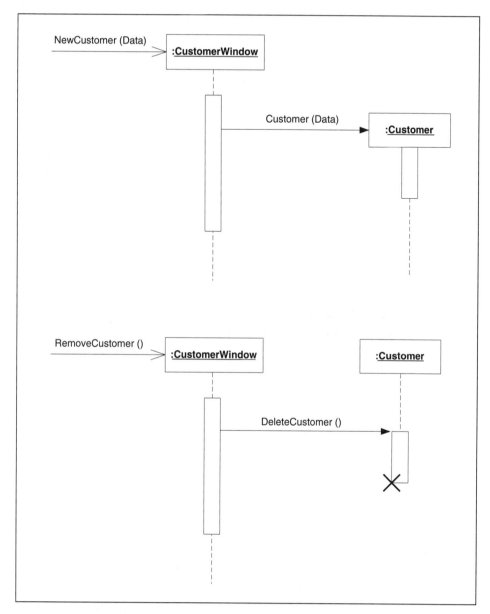

Figure 5.22 *The Customer message creates a new object of the Customer class (this is typically handled by the constructor of the Customer class, having the same name as the class). The DeleteCustomer operation destroys a customer object. The return from a creation or destruction may be shown explicitly, but it is not in these diagrams.*

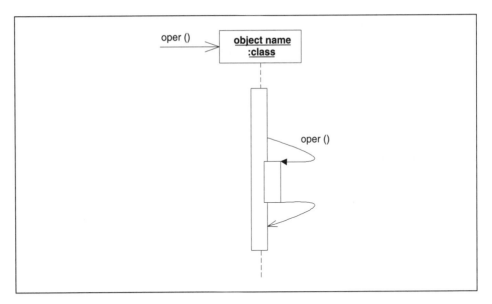

Figure 5.23 *The oper () operation calls itself. There must be a condition in the operation that stops the recursion. The return is explicitly shown.*

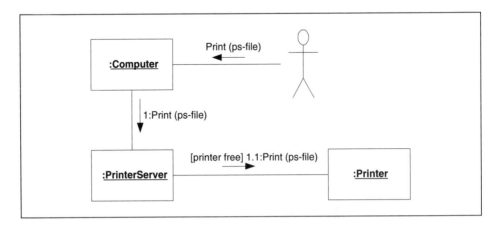

Figure 5.24 *An actor sends a Print message to the Computer. The Computer sends a Print message to the PrinterServer. The PrinterServer sends a Print message to the Printer if the printer is free.*

Message Flow

A message label (the label placed on a message) in a collaboration diagram is specified with the syntax:

```
predecessor guard-condition sequence-expression return-value :=
signature
```

where the predecessor is specified with the syntax:

```
sequence-number ',' ... '/'
```

The predecessor is an expression for synchronization of threads or paths, meaning that the messages connected to specified sequence-numbers must be performed and handled before the current message is sent (i.e., execution is continued). The list of sequence-numbers is comma-separated.

The guard-condition is specified with the syntax:

```
'[' condition-clause ']'
```

The condition-clause is normally expressed in pseudo-code or an actual programming language. The UML does not prescribe a specific syntax.

The sequence-expression has the syntax:

```
[integer | name][recurrence] ':'
```

The integer is a sequence-number specifying the message order. Message 1 always starts a sequence of messages; message 1.1 is the first nested message within the handling of message 1; message 1.2 is the second nested message within the handling of message 1. An example sequence could be: message 1, message 1.1, 1.2, 1.2.1, 1.2.2, 1.3, and so on. Thus the numbering can delineate both the sequence and nesting of messages (when the messages are synchronous, nested operation calls and their returns). The name represents a concurrent thread of control; this is discussed further in Chapter 6. For instance, 1.2a and 1.2b are concurrent messages sent in parallel. The sequence-expression should be terminated with a colon (:).

Recurrence represents a conditional or iterative execution. There are two choices:

```
'*' '[' iteration-clause ']'
'[' condition-clause ']'
```

The iteration-clause is used to specify iteration (repeated execution), where the iteration-clause is a condition for the iteration, such as [i := 1...n]. For example, a message label containing an iteration could be shown as:

```
1.1 *[x = 1..10]: doSomething()
```

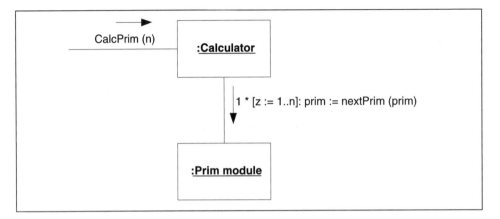

Figure 5.25 *Iteration and return-value shown in a collaboration diagram.*

The condition-clause is normally used for specifying branches, not for guard-conditions. [x<0] and [x=>0] are two condition-clauses that may be used for branching, in which only one of the conditions is true; thus, only one of the branches will be executed (sending the message connected to that branch). Both condition-clauses and iteration-clauses are meant to be expressed in pseudo-code or in the syntax of an actual programming language.

The return value should be assigned to a message-signature. A signature is composed of a message-name and an argument list. The return value shows the value retrieved as the result of an operation call (a message). An example of this would be the message label 1.4.5: x := calc (n) (see Figure 5.25). Examples of message labels are:

```
1: display ()
[mode = display] 1.2.3.7: redraw()
2 * [n := 1..z]: prim := nextPrim (prim)
3.1 [x<0]: foo()
3.2 [x=>0]: bar()
1.1a,1.1b/1.2: continue()
```

Links

A link is a connection between two objects. Any role names of the objects in the link can be shown at the link's ends, along with qualifiers in the links. Both qualifiers and roles are also specified in the class diagram that contains the objects' classes. There are also some stereotypes that may be attached to the role of the objects in the link (the link role): global, local, parameter, self, vote, and broadcast.

- *Global* is a constraint applied to a link role, specifying that the corresponding instance is visible because it is in a global scope (the instance is available through a global name known throughout the system).

- *Local* is a constraint applied to a link role, specifying that the corresponding instance is visible because it is a local variable in an operation.

- *Parameter* is a constraint applied to a link role, specifying that the corresponding instance is visible because it is a parameter in an operation.

- *Self* is a constraint applied to a link role, specifying that an object can send messages to itself.

- *Vote* is a constraint applied to a message, constraining a collection of return messages. The vote constraint specifies that the return value is selected through a majority vote of all the return values in the collection.

- *Broadcast* is a constraint applied to a set of messages, specifying that the set of messages are not invoked in a certain order.

Lifetime of an Object

Objects that are created during a collaboration are designated with {new}, as shown in Figure 5.26. Objects that are destroyed during the collaboration are signified by the constraint {destroyed}. Objects that are both created and destroyed during the same collaboration are designated as {transient}, which is equivalent to { new } { destroyed } (see Figure 5.27).

Using Collaboration Diagrams

Collaboration diagrams can be used to show quite complex interactions between objects. However, learning the numbering scheme of messages can take some time, but once learned, is rather easy to use. The main difference between collaboration diagrams and sequence diagrams is that collaboration diagrams show the actual objects and their links (the "network of objects" that are collaborating), which in many situations can ease the understanding of the interaction. The time sequence is easier to see in the sequence diagram, where it can be read from top to bottom. When deciding which diagram to use to show an interaction, the general guideline is to choose a collaboration diagram when the objects and their links facilitate understanding the interaction, and to choose a sequence diagram when only the sequence needs to be shown.

Figure 5.28 shows a more complex collaboration diagram. A Sales Statistics window (message 1), creates a Statistics Summary object (1.1), which will collect

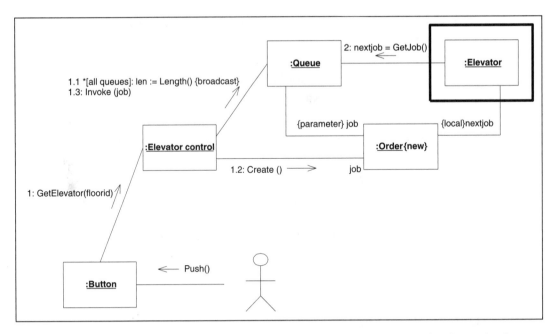

Figure 5.26 *A collaboration where an actor pushes a button to get an elevator to his floor. The elevator control object checks how long the job queues of all the elevators are and chooses the shortest. It then creates a job order object and invokes it by putting in a queue. The elevator object runs concurrently and picks up jobs from the queues. The elevator is an active object, meaning that it executes concurrently with its own thread of control. Active objects will be further discussed in Chapter 6.*

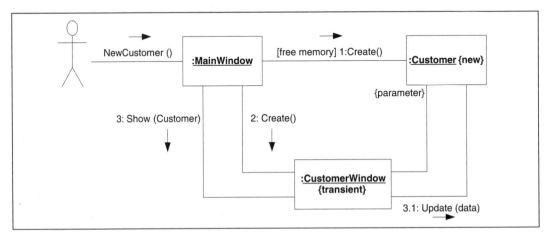

Figure 5.27 *The object MainWindow receives the message NewCustomer, and creates a Customer object. A CustomerWindow is created, and the customer object is then passed to the CustomerWindow which allows for update of the customer data.*

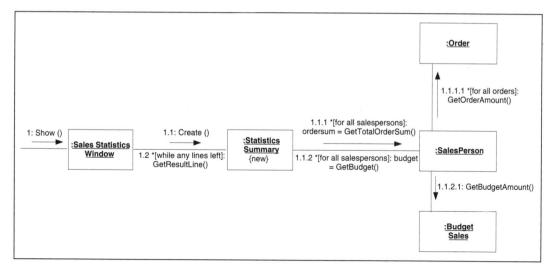

Figure 5.28 *A collaboration diagram that summarizes sales results.*

the statistics to display in the window. When the Statistics Summary object is created, it will iterate all salespersons to get the total order sum (1.1.1) and the budget (1.1.2) for each salesperson. Each salesperson object gets its order sum by iterating all its orders, getting the amount for each (1.1.1.1), and adding them together; and its budget by getting the amount from a budget sales object (1.1.2.1). When the Statistics Summary object has iterated all salespersons, it has been created (the return of message 1.1). The Sales Statistics window then gets the result lines from the Statistics Summary object (the result line is a formatted string describing the result of one salesperson) and shows each line in its window. When all the result lines have been read, the show operation on the Sales Statistics window returns and the collaboration is finished.

Activity Diagram

Activity diagrams capture actions and their results. They focus on work performed in the implementation of an operation (a method), and the activities in a use-case instance or in an object. The activity diagram is a variant of a state diagram and has a slightly different purpose, which is to capture actions (work and activities that will be performed) and their results in terms of object-state changes. The states in the activity diagram (called action-states) transition to the next stage directly when the action in the state is performed (without specifying any events as in the normal state diagram). Another difference between activity diagrams and state diagrams is that their actions may be placed in *swimlanes*. A swimlane groups activities, with respect to who is responsible for them or where they reside in an organization. An activity diagram is an alternative way of describing interactions, with the possibility of expressing how actions are taken, what they do (change of object states), when they take place (action sequence), and where they take place (swimlanes).

Activity diagrams may be used for different purposes, including:

- To capture the work (actions) that will be performed when an operation is executing (the instance of the operation implementation). This is the most common usage of activity diagrams.

- To capture the internal work in an object.

- To show how a set of related actions may be performed, and how they will affect objects around them.

- To show how an instance of a use-case may be performed in terms of actions and object state changes.

- To show how a business works in terms of workers (actors), workflows, organization, and objects (physical and intellectual factors used in the business).

Actions and Transitions

An action is performed to produce a result. The implementation of an operation may be described as a set of related actions, which is later translated to code lines. As defined earlier an activity diagram shows the actions and their relationships and can have a start and an end point. A start point is shown as a solid filled circle; the end point is shown as a circle surrounding a smaller solid circle (a bull's-eye). The actions (action states) in an activity diagram are drawn as rectangles with rounded corners (the same notation used in state diagrams; see Figure 5.29).

Within the action, a text string is attached to specify the action or actions taken. The transitions between the actions have the same syntax as in state diagrams, except for events. Events may be attached only to the transition from the start point to the first action. Transitions between actions are shown with an arrow, to which guard-conditions, a send-clause, and an action-expression may be attached. Often nothing is specified, indicating that the transition will be triggered as soon as all the activities in the action-state have been performed (see Figure 5.30).

Transitions are protected by guard-conditions, which as noted previously must be true for the transition to trigger, using the same syntax as guard-conditions in state diagrams. Decisions are made using guard-conditions; for example, [yes] and [no]. A diamond-shaped symbol is used to show a decision point, as shown in Figure 5.31. The decision symbol can have one or more incoming transitions and two

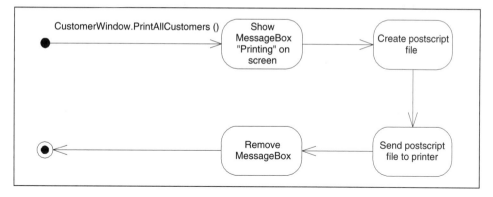

Figure 5.29 *When someone calls the PrintAllCustomer operation (in the CustomerWindow class), the actions start. The first action is to show a message box on the screen; the second action is to create a postscript file; the third action is to send the postscript to the printer; and the fourth action is to remove the message box from the screen. The transitions are automatic; they occur as soon as the action in the source state is performed.*

or more outgoing transitions labeled with guard-conditions. Normally, one of the outgoing transitions is always true.

A transition is divided into two or more transitions that result in parallel actions. The actions are executed concurrently, although they can also be executed one by one. The important thing is that all the parallel transitions be performed before they unite (if they ever unite). A bold line is drawn to show that a transition is divided into several branches, and shows the actual split into parallel actions. The bold line is also used to show the unification of the branches (see Figure 5.32).

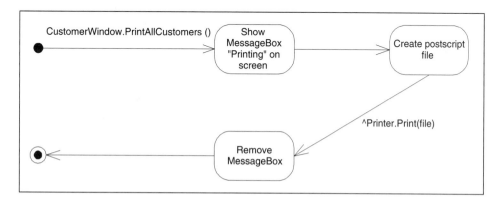

Figure 5.30 *The transition between the second and the third actions has a send-clause that sends a Print(file) message to the Printer object.*

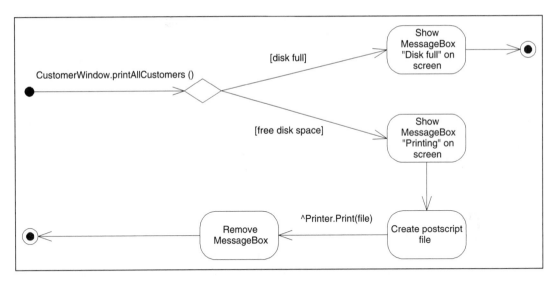

Figure 5.31 *If the disk is full, MessageBox "Disk full" is shown. Otherwise MessageBox "Printing" is shown.*

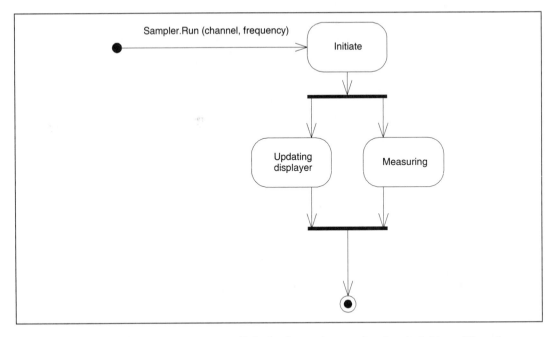

Figure 5.32 *When the Run operation is called, the first action to take place is Initiate. Then the actions Updating display and Measuring are performed simultaneously (concurrently or by alternating).*

Swimlanes

As already stated, a swimlane groups activities, normally with respect to their responsibility. Swimlanes are used for several different purposes; for example, to show explicitly where actions are performed (in which object), or to show in which part of an organization work (an action) is performed. Swimlanes are drawn as vertical rectangles. The activities belonging to a swimlane are placed within its rectangle. The swimlane is given a name that is placed at the top of the rectangle (see Figure 5.33).

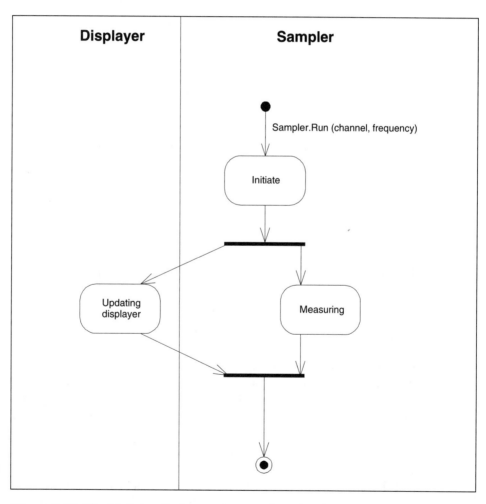

Figure 5.33 *The Updating displayer action is performed within the Displayer. The Initiate and Measuring actions are performed within the Sampler.*

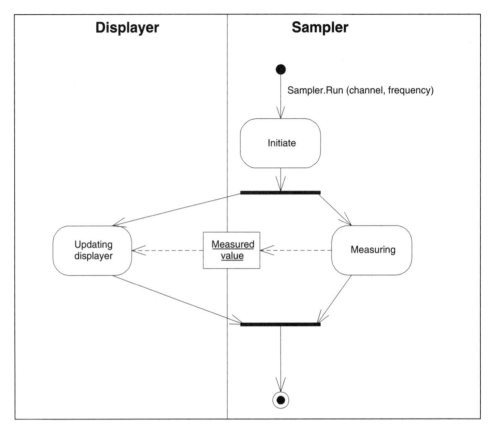

Figure 5.34 *The Measuring action supplies the Updating displayer action with measured values (measured value is an object).*

Objects

Objects can be shown in activity diagrams. They are either input to or output from the actions, or they can simply show that an object is affected by a specific action. Objects are shown as object rectangles with the object and/or class name inside them. When an object is input to an action, it is shown as a dashed arrow extending from the object to the action; when the object is output from an action, it's shown as a dashed arrow extending from the action to the object. When the object is affected by the action, it's shown as a dashed line between the action and the object. Optionally, the state of the object can be shown below the class name and inside the brackets, such as [planned], [bought], [filled], and so on (see Figure 5.34).

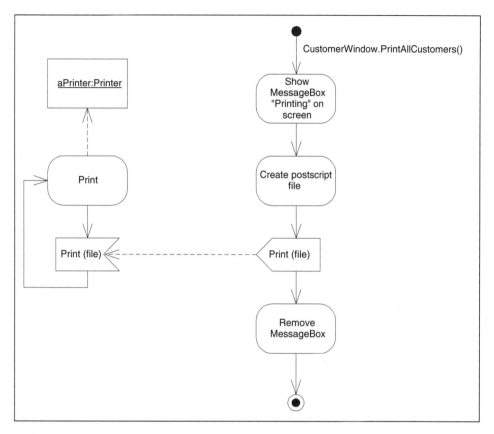

Figure 5.35 *Between Create postscript file and Remove MessageBox, a Print signal is sent. The signal contains a file that is received and printed in the Printer object.*

Signals

Signals may be sent or received in activity diagrams (signals were described earlier in this chapter). There are two symbols, one for sending and one for receiving a signal. The send symbol corresponds to the send-clause attached to a transition. As with the send-clause, both the send and receipt symbols are attached to a transition; however, graphically the transition is divided into two transitions with a send or a receipt symbol in between.

The send and receipt symbols may be attached to the objects that are the receivers or the senders of the messages. This is done by drawing a dashed line with an arrow from the send or receipt symbol to the object. If it is a send symbol, the arrow points to the object; if it is a receipt symbol, the arrow points to the receipt symbol. It is optional to show the objects. The send symbol is a convex pentagon; the receipt symbol is a concave pentagon, as shown in Figure 5.35.

Business Modeling with Activity Diagrams

According to Nilsson (1991), when modeling businesses, these important aspects should be studied and described in the models: resources, rules, goals, and actions (workflow). There are two kinds of resources: physical and information. Workers (actors within the business) are examples of resources; they are physical objects. Other physical objects might be items that are produced, consumed, or handled. Information objects are often objects that are handled within an information system. Information objects carry information about the business. The business rules restrict the use of the resources, both physical items and information. For instance, one rule might be that a physical item must not be damaged during delivery. Another rule might be that some information is strategic and must be kept confidential. The use of these resources is the actual work, called the workflow.

The goals of the business motivate the workflow, where the resources are used in accordance with specified rules. In business modeling, it is often important to separate physical objects from information objects. Physical objects are those that exist in the real world (or our understanding of the world), for example, cars, customers, and contracts. Information objects carry information about the business, whether about work or physical things (objects). Thus customer objects in an information system are not the actual customers; they contain information about the actual customers. Stereotypes may be used to separate physical objects from information objects within activity diagrams. The stereotype «Information» might, for instance, be used to indicate that an object is an information object; similarly, the stereotype «Physical» might be used to indicate that an object represents the actual physical object. When objects are handled, produced, or consumed, they are changing their states, which can be described in activity diagrams (see Figure 5.36).

All businesses have an organization, and might sometimes be of interest in the models. In activity diagrams, swimlanes are used to represent organizations. Workers are considered resources, and might be treated as physical objects although usually they are treated as actors. An actor is a system (a human being is also considered a system) acting in the business. Normally, workers are human beings employed in the business and performing the work. The actors are driving the workflow, and are supported by information and other systems. Actors can be modeled with the stickman icon in UML or using the stereotype «actor» (see Figure 5.36).

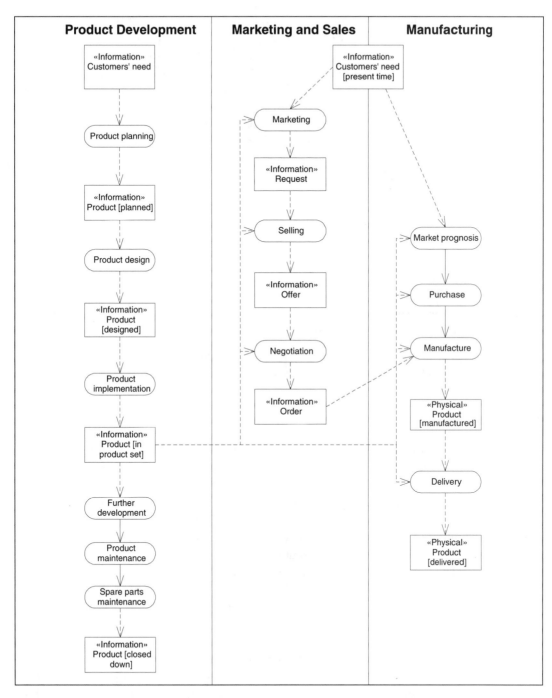

Figure 5.36 *A business pattern for manufacturing described with an activity diagram.*

The approach to modeling business with activity diagrams may be complemented with use cases or other techniques to capture the requirements of the system (the business system). Note that with this approach, objects are identified and classified into information or physical items. The identified information objects may become a proper foundation for analyzing and building a system to support the modeled business. Using activity diagrams has similarities to implementing workflow techniques such as IDEF0 (a standard visual process modelling language). Therefore, the actions might be described as in those techniques.

Actions may be described in many ways. One practical approach is to describe them with the following headings:

- *Definition*: A formal or informal description of the action.

- *Purpose*: A description of the purpose of the action.

- *Characteristic*: Typically repetitive or one-time shot.

- *Method of measurement*: When it is possible and desirable to measure the actions, the method of measurement should be described.

- *Actors/Roles*: Which actors and roles are required to perform the action.

- *Information technology*: What kind of information system support is required.

- *Rules, policies, and strategies*: Any documents, strategies, or policies that restrict the performance of the actions should be mentioned.

Summary

All systems have a static structure and dynamic behavior. The structure may be described with static model elements such as classes, relationships, nodes, and components. The behavior describes how the elements within the structure interact over time. These interactions normally are deterministic and may be modeled. Modeling the dynamic behavior of the system is called dynamic modeling, which is supported by the UML. There are four different diagrams, each with a different purpose: state, sequence, collaboration, and activity.

The state diagram is used to describe the behavior of and the internal states within a class (it can also be used for subsystems and entire systems). It focuses on how objects over time change their states, depending on events that occur, the behavior and the actions performed in the states, and when transitions occur. An event can be a condition becoming true, the receipt of a signal or an operation call, or just passage of a designated period of time.

The sequence diagram is used to describe how a set of objects interact with each other in a specific scenario. It focuses on message sequences, that is, how messages are sent and received between a set of objects. Sequence diagrams have two axes; the vertical axis shows time and the horizontal axis shows the objects involved. The primary aspect of the sequence diagram is time.

The collaboration diagram is used to describe how objects interact in space, meaning that besides the dynamic interaction, it also explicitly shows how the objects are linked to each other. There is no axis for time; instead, the messages are numbered for sequence.

The activity diagram is used to describe how things are done, the work that is performed. Activity diagrams can be used for operations, classes, or use cases, but they may also be used just to show workflow. Activity diagrams can be used to model businesses where work and workers, organizations, and objects are shown.

6   *Advanced Dynamic Modeling: Real-Time Systems*

Some of the broad range of systems that can be modeled with UML are real-time systems. There is no established definition of what really constitutes a real-time system, but intuitively it is a system in which timing is very important. The system must handle external events within constrained time limits, execution is concurrent, and the performance of the system often needs to be optimized (the system has to be "fast"). Under this rather broad definition, most systems can be considered in some way real-time systems, and thus need to have timing specifications and constraints identified in their modeling.

Figure 6.1 shows a real-time system:

- *Where timeliness is important*: The system performs its functions within specified time limits ("response time"). All specified time deadlines must be met.

- *That is reactive*: The system is continuously responding to events from the external environment that "drives" the execution of the system.

- *With concurrently executing threads of control, where different parts of the software run in parallel*: The concurrent execution can be performed in a "real" parallel system with several processors; each thread executes on its own processor. Alternatively, it can be performed in a simulated environment with only one processor, but the real-time operating system schedules threads to share the processor (passes the control to them one at a time). Concurrency enables an efficient utilization of the hardware and is used in creating good models of systems where external events occur asynchronously.

- *With very high requirements on most of the nonfunctional requirements such as reliability, fault tolerance, and performance.*

161

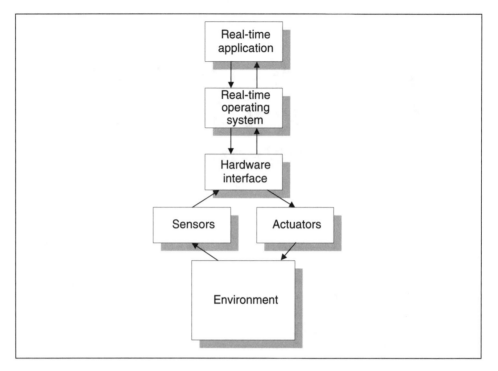

Figure 6.1 *A real-time system.*

- *Not deterministic:* It is impossible to formally prove that the system will work in all situations under all conditions, due to the complexity of concurrency, external asynchronous events that may occur in any order, and the hardware involved.

Real-time system models need specifications for time requirements, asynchronous event handling, communication, concurrency, and synchronization. And because real-time systems are often distributed, the models also have to show the distribution of the system. The diagrams most affected by real-time aspects are the dynamic model diagrams such as sequence and collaboration diagrams, where concurrency and time specifications can be added. It is, however, important to understand that even the most specialized real-time system also have static structures, which have to be modeled using those diagrams as well (such as class and deployment diagrams).

A real-time system is often highly integrated with its physical environment, in that it receives events and information through sensors and controls devices through actuators. Thus a real-time system often works closely with specialized hardware and has to handle low-level interrupts and hardware interfaces. A system that involves tightly integrated specialized hardware and software is called an *embedded system*. Embedded systems can be found in cars, consumer electronics, manufacturing machines, and many others. An embedded real-time system often uses a small real-time operating system that can be fitted easily into a system with limited memory capacity. An embedded system must be fast enough to communicate and control its hardware and to handle and react to all the events that occur, even in a worst-case situation (where everything happens at once).

Real-time systems are often divided into *hard* and *soft* categories. In a hard real-time system, a late (or incorrect) response is considered an unacceptable error that can result in loss of life. Examples of hard real-time systems are airplane control software, life surveillance systems, and automatic train control systems. Soft real-time systems can accept a late response occasionally; for instance, in a digital telephone system, it may take a long time to connect a call, or the connection may fail; neither scenario is considered a serious or dangerous error.

Obviously, then, the demands are greater when designing real-time systems, especially hard real-time systems. The system must be fault-tolerant, meaning that exceptional errors in software and hardware must be handled by the system and that under no circumstances may the system become inoperable. Nevertheless, exceptions and errors that do occur must be handled ("expect the unexpected"). To be able to handle even the worst-case situations of many events happening at the same time, performance must be optimized and tuned so that there is a big reserve that can be utilized when necessary.

Object Orientation and Real-Time Systems

A common question about object-oriented modeling is whether object orientation really can be used to model real-time systems. Given the high demands on performance of real-time systems and the common misconception that objects are just data stored in relational databases, many would give a skeptical answer to this question. Clearly, given the complexity of real-time systems, the need to design precise and descriptive models is more important than in normal systems. But as long as the modeling language supports both traditional object-oriented concepts and real-time concepts, object orientation and real time mix very well.

There are implementation issues, such as that the underlying environment must have adequate support for real-time constructs (processes or threads, and communication and synchronization mechanisms). There are also times when the implementation of a model has to be optimized, to allow for maximum performance. This is typically the case when there are too many layers of abstraction, resulting in a performance cost with too much communication between a number of objects to handle a specific event. In such a situation, implementation shortcuts have to be taken in conflict with the ideal model (usually at the cost of getting a more complex and harder-to-maintain system).

As mentioned, an object-oriented real-time system requires an operating system that supports real-time constructs. The operating system could be either a standard operating system such as Windows, OS/2, or UNIX, or a specialized real-time operating system optimized for embedded real-time systems. The quality of the real-time services (performance, reliability, ease of programming) depends on the operating system used, and is not really a property of the object-oriented language or method. Object orientation is used to model the system being built, and to map those models onto the services provided by the operating system. Naturally, the quality of the object-oriented design affects the quality of the finished system.

The primary concept introduced when modeling systems with concurrent execution is that of active classes. An object of an *active class* (an active object) can execute its own thread of control, and thus take the initiative to perform actions without being sent a message. In a system with several active objects, several threads of control will be executing concurrently. This introduces new problems to handle, such as communication between active objects and their synchronization when they share resources. The opposite of an active class is a *passive class*, which is the "normal" class discussed so far. An object of a passive class will execute only when it is sent a message (e.g., an operation is called); and when the operation returns, it will hand back the control to its caller. A real-time system is a mix of active and passive objects.

Concurrency in object-oriented systems can be viewed either through the explicit or the implicit concurrency model (as described in M. Awad et al., 1996). The explicit concurrency model describes concurrency separately from the objects by defining processes at an early stage of analysis, and then treating processes and objects as separate modeling entities. The system is decomposed into a number of processes, and each process is internally modeled as an object-oriented system to design the internal structure (naturally, classes can be reused in several processes). The process and object concepts are separated, and the system is divided into processes whereby each process is modeled internally as an object-oriented system of its own.

The implicit concurrency model delays the design of concurrency. The system is modeled as objects, where in an early analysis, all objects are considered to have their own execution threads; that is, be active objects (or, as a variant, only those objects explicitly marked as active have their own execution thread). Gradually, through architecture and detailed design, the ideal analysis models are mapped onto an implementation with the support of services from the underlying real-time operating system. In the final implementation, only those objects that really need to be are implemented as active. Although UML can support both the implicit and explicit concurrency models, it has better support for the implicit concurrency model. Active classes, asynchronous communication, and synchronization can be modeled in early phases and gradually be translated into the services and capabilities of the implementation environment.

Hardware handling is typically done through hardware wrapper classes, which are designed to present interfaces to the hardware and to model the capabilities of the hardware. These hardware wrappers handle the communication protocol to the device and the interrupts that the device can generate. Using such hardware classes enables the low-level protocol to be hidden, and a low-level interrupt to be quickly translated into a higher-level event in the rest of the system. Depending on the nature of the hardware, a wrapper class can be either an active or a passive class.

Real-Time Concepts

This section presents the basic mechanisms for modeling real-time systems in UML. The subsections show how these mechanisms are used in the dynamic model diagrams presented in Chapter 5. The mechanisms presented are the definitions of active classes and objects (concurrency), communication between active objects, and the synchronization of active objects, as shown in Figure 6.2.

Active Classes and Objects

Active classes are used to model the concurrent behavior of the real world, and to create a model that uses the system resources as efficiently as possible. An active

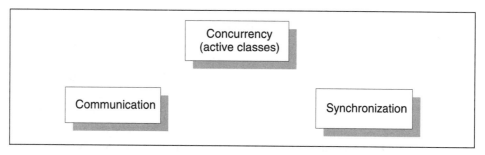

Figure 6.2 *The different mechanisms for modeling real-time systems.*

class is a one that owns an execution thread and can initiate control activity. An active class (or actually an instance of an active class, an active object) executes in parallel with other active objects and initiates actions by itself (in its own code or by sending messages to others). An active class is thus the "unit" that executes concurrently. In contrast to active classes are the passive classes, which are all "normal" classes in the system. A passive object (of a passive class) is able to execute only when some other object (passive or active) performs some operation on it (sends a message to it).

An active class is implemented as a process or a thread. A process is a "heavyweight" thread of control; a thread is a "lightweight" thread of control. The important difference between process and thread is that a process normally encapsulates and protects all its internal structure by executing in its own memory space, while a thread executes in a memory space shared with other threads; this memory space can contain shared information (such as other objects). A process is initiated by an executable program, and can be viewed as a system of its own. Note, in some operating systems, a process is equivalent to a thread, so these definitions of process and thread concepts should be taken as a guideline rather than literally. The concepts can also be combined so that, inside a process, a number of threads execute and share the memory space.

Active classes are typically implemented through a class library that has a superclass, ActiveClass. This superclass is inherited by all classes that should be active, and contains the mapping of process or thread operations such as start, stop, suspend, resume, priority handling, and so on to the corresponding operating system calls that implement these functions in the underlying operating system. Normally, an abstract operation called run in the superclass must be implemented in the concrete active subclass. The implementation of this operation specifies the execution thread code of the active class; that is, the code that executes in parallel with other execution threads. Typically the run operation executes in an eternal loop, reading input signals or interacting with synchronization mechanisms and performing the work of the active class.

Active objects interact through communication and synchronization mechanisms. The communication mechanism can be an ordinary operation call between objects (synchronous messages in the object-oriented world; or the communication mechanism may be one supported by the operating system, such as mailboxes or queues where messages or signals can be sent and received asynchronously. Synchronization mechanisms are techniques used to control the execution of concurrent threads, to prevent conflicting or ineffective resource usage (e.g., multiple threads using the same resource concurrently, or a consumer trying to read and work on some information before the producer is finished supplying the information).

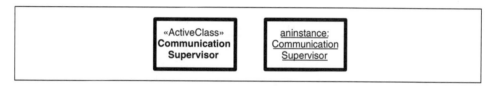

Figure 6.3 *An active class and an object of that active class.*

Active objects are usually larger than passive objects, because they own or reference a number of other objects. Sometimes a package (the UML equivalent of a subsystem) is controlled through an active object that makes the package run concurrently with other packages. However, it is important to realize that even in a hard real-time system, there are a lot more passive objects than active objects. A cost is connected with creating a thread or process, and the system will become overly complex and slow if too many active objects are defined.

An active class (or object) is shown in UML as a class or object rectangle drawn with a thick line. If the name inside the rectangle contains a class name, the symbol represents an active class; if the name is an underlined object, the symbol represents an active object. The class is of the stereotype «ActiveClass», which should be visible when the class is shown in a class diagram (see Figure 6.3).

An active class or object is often depicted with its internal structure embedded, as shown in Figure 6.4, and typically uses several other classes to define its internal structure. These internal classes are normally passive, but they may be other active classes.

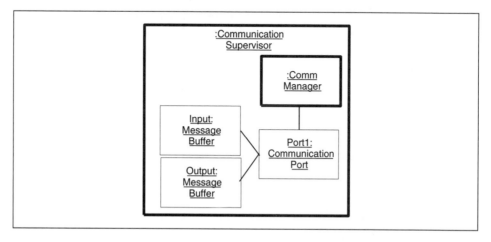

Figure 6.4 *An active object with its internal structure in terms of other active or passive objects.*

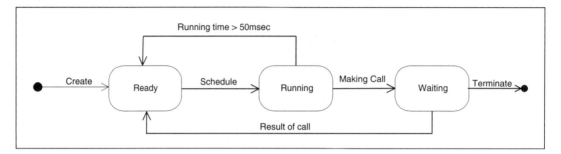

Figure 6.5 *States of an active object with the events that cause transitions.*

States of an Active Class

An active class often changes its behavior depending on some internal state (or in some cases, on the overall state of the system). The states of an active class and its behavior are modeled in a state diagram, as described in Chapter 5. The state diagram shows the possible states of the active class—which events are accepted in each state and the transition and actions performed when a specific event occurs (see Figure 6.5). Timing constraints are not shown in the state diagram, except perhaps as notes.

Communication

When passive objects communicate with each other, it is normally done through operations (synchronous message sending). One object calls in an operation (sends a message to) another object, and the calling object waits for the operation to execute and then to have control returned when the operation is done (possibly along with a return value from the operation). As part of the operation call, data can be passed between the objects as parameters.

A number of mechanisms can be used to enable active objects to communicate with each other. Active objects must be able to execute concurrently and to send messages to other active objects without having to wait for the operation to be finished. Some of the most common mechanisms used when communicating between active objects are:

- *Operation calls*: An ordinary call on an operation in an object. This is the equivalent of sending a synchronous message to an object, whereby the caller waits for the operation to finish and return.

- *Mailboxes/Message queues*: A technique that defines mailboxes or message queues. A message is placed in the mailbox by the sender, and at some point read and handled by the receiver. This technique allows for asynchronous messages; a sender can place a message in the mailbox and immediately continue to execute.

- *Shared memory*: A block of memory is reserved for communication, so that two or more active objects can write and read information. The block has to be guarded by some kind of synchronization mechanism so that concurrently executing objects don't try to write and/or read the information at the same time. The shared memory technique is normally used when some large data structure has to be worked upon by several objects.

- *Rendezvous*: A technique by which specific rendezvous points in the execution of two threads are defined. The first thread to reach its rendezvous point stops and waits for the other thread to reach its corresponding rendezvous point. When both threads are at the rendezvous point, they exchange information and then start to execute concurrently again.

- *Remote procedure calls* (*RPCs*): RPCs handle distribution of the concurrent threads to separate computers in a network and allow the threads to be written in different languages. The calling thread identifies an operation in an object that it wants to call, then furthers this request to the RPC library. The RPC finds the object in the network, packages the request into a universal format and sends the request over the network. On the receiving side, the request is translated from the universal format to the format that the receiving object wants, and the call is made. When the call is finished, the result is returned in a similar manner. Thus, the RPC is both a communication and a synchronization mechanism.

The mechanisms described here are implementation techniques that are mapped onto the properties of the operating system. In modeling, the communication between active objects is described using events, signals, and messages; it is not until the design phase that the actual implementation techniques are chosen.

Communication can be asynchronous or synchronous. Asynchronous communication is unpredictable; that is, an event can occur at any time in the execution of the system, and it is not possible to know when a specific event will be sent. Synchronous communication is predictable in that it can occur only at specified times in the execution of the system (which can be identified by reading the control flow in the code). A real-time system uses both asynchronous and synchronous communication. Typically, external events in the environment happen asynchronously while parts of the internal communication in the system are synchronous. When discussing message sending between objects, asynchronous and synchronous communications have also come to indicate whether the sending object waits for the message to be handled (synchronous message sending) or not (asynchronous message sending).

Events

In a real-time system, events are drivers of system activity. An event is something that occurs in the system or in the environment, and something to which the system must react to and handle. All events that can occur must be defined; furthermore, the system's behavior when the event happens must be defined. The behavior is often connected to the state of an object in that the same event can cause different behaviors depending on the state of the object when the event occurs. An event can also cause a transition from one state to another.

In UML, there are four different categories of events:

- *A condition becoming true*: A guard-condition that becomes true is considered an event. This is typically implemented through an active object that monitors this condition and notes when it has become true.

- *The receipt of an explicit signal object*: A signal object is sent from one object to another. The signal object, which is considered a message, is of a signal class and may contain attributes and operations. Signal objects are typically sent through some operating system mechanisms, such as a mailbox or queue. Signal objects can be sent asynchronously.

- *The receipt of an operation call*: One object calls an operation in another object. This operation call, which is considered a synchronous message, passes information through parameters and the return value.

- *A passage of time*: A specified amount of time passing is also an event, sometimes called a periodic event. Such an event is used to describe an intended delay in processing or time-outs if some other event hasn't occurred within a specified time. A passage-of-time event is implemented either through a sleep call, which suspends the execution of the thread for a specified amount of time, or a request to the operating system of a time-out message, which is then sent to the requesting object when the specified time has elapsed.

Events can be divided into logical and physical categories. A physical event is low-level, at the hardware level; a logical event is a higher-level representation of that occurrence. The physical event "interrupt on port 4H" could be translated into the logical event "alarm from the infrared sensor device." Since logical events are at a higher level of abstraction, the models preferably should be defined with logical events rather than low-level physical events. Physical events should be translated into logical events as close to their detection as possible (this is typically done through an active object with a state diagram, which, depending on the current state, can make an interpretation and translation of the physical event into a logical event).

Properties such as a categorization of the event, priority, time-handling requirements, or administrative information can be defined for events. To do so, it is often suitable to define the event as a class and define those properties as tagged values of the class; or, if the information is connected to the actual instances, as attributes of the class.

Signals

Signals are defined in UML as "a named event that can be raised." A signal is described as a class with the stereotype «signal» that represents an event that occurs in the system. Since the signal is described as a class, it can have attributes and operations to carry both information and behavior about the event. Signals are passed between objects in the system, either synchronously or asynchronously, and are messages (only the message passed between communicating objects also contains a signal object, and is not only an operation call).

Signals are described in class diagrams, and all the signals in a real-time system are modeled in a hierarchy, as shown in Figure 6.6. This makes it possible to group

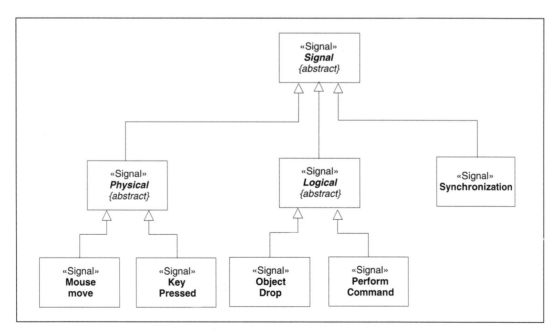

Figure 6.6 *A hierarchy of signal classes.*

a number of signals by having a common superclass. A receiver of a signal can then specify that it accepts objects of a specified superclass, which then means that it accepts signal objects of the superclass or any of its specialized subclasses. A superclass in such a hierarchy can also contain general information about the signal, such as a priority, time sent, and so on.

As signals are a special case of events, they can be divided into logical or physical signals carrying either low-level hardware information or higher-level interpretation of what the event means in terms of the execution of the system.

Messages

Objects communicate through messages; specifically, messages are used to communicate between passive objects, between active and passive objects, or between active objects. A message is implemented by a simple operation call, or as a signal object that is put in a mailbox or queue. The receipt of a message is normally considered an event in a real-time system. Messages are shown in a number of UML diagrams—sequence, collaboration, state, and activity—to illustrate communication between objects.

Figure 6.7 shows the message types in UML. They are defined as follows:

- *Simple*: Represents a flat flow of control. A simple message shows how the control is passed from one object to another without describing any details about the communication. This message type is used when details about the communication are not known or not considered relevant in the diagram. It is also used to show the return of a synchronous message; it is drawn from the object that handles the message back to the caller to show that the control is passed back (possibly along with some result).

- *Synchronous*: A nested flow of control, typically implemented as an operation call. The operation that handles the message is completed (including any further messages being sent as part of the handling) before the caller resumes execution. The return can be shown in a sequence diagram as a simple message, or the return can be implicit when the message has been handled. A

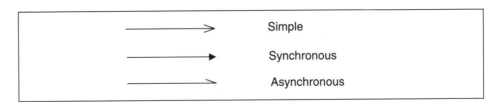

Figure 6.7 *Message types in UML.*

synchronous message between active objects indicates wait semantics; the sender waits for the message to be handled before it continues to execute (i.e., the sender waits for the receiver to be ready to handle it *and* it waits for the receiver to acknowledge that it actually has been handled).

- *Asynchronous*: Asynchronous flow-of-control where there is no explicit return to the caller. An asynchronous message between objects indicates no-wait semantics; the sender does not wait for the message to be handled before it continues to execute.

Simple and synchronous messages can be combined into one line, with the synchronous message arrow at one end and the simple return arrow at the other. This indicates that the return of control is virtually immediate.

Other message types are extensions to the basic UML, such as a *balking* message (a message that is sent only if the receiver is ready to accept it) and a *time-out* message (that will be canceled if it is not handled within a specified amount of time). These message types and other similar variants are described as *stereotypes of messages*.

Synchronization

Synchronization is the process of coordinating concurrently executing threads with each other, so that they do not improperly interfere with each other (e.g., that they are not concurrently trying to modify or access a shared resource at the same time) and that they interact in an efficient order. Synchronization is necessary in any system that has concurrency. Not only are the active objects concerned with this, but also all passive objects that are shared between active objects.

The problems that can occur if synchronization is not properly handled are:

- *Incorrect shared access*: Resources or passive objects that are shared between active objects can cause problems if they are accessed concurrently. If one thread calls an operation in a passive object, the operation can execute some code lines that set attributes in the object. Anytime during the execution of the operation, the thread can be suspended by the operating system, which then schedules another thread for execution. This other thread calls the same or another operation in the same object, now on an object that is not in a safe state (since the last call to that operation hasn't finished yet). Let's say that the operation executes to the end and that the first thread then is scheduled, resuming execution at the point where it was suspended. The attributes of the object have changed, and the final result of the operation is undetermined. What is needed is *mutual exclusion* between the threads, so that only one thread at a time executes the operation and no other thread can access that operation until the first thread has finished it. The problem with shared access concerns both the objects that are shared as well as other shared resources (devices such as printers, communication ports, etc.).

- *Inefficient resource usage*: Often there are dependencies between the execution of different threads. One thread might depend on another thread to make some preparation of the data it is using. The first thread could be continuously executing in a busy-wait loop, checking over and over again to determine whether the other thread is finished. This is a big waste of machine resources. A better solution is to have a synchronization mechanism to coordinate the thread with the preparing thread, to ensure it is not scheduled to execute until it has been notified that the first thread has finished its work.

- *Deadlocks*: A deadlock occurs when a number of threads all are waiting for each other. As an example, a system could have two communication ports, A and B, guarded by some synchronization mechanism. Two threads (possibly two instances of the same active class) at some point need both of these communication ports. One thread manages to reserve port A, and the other manages to reserve port B. The first thread now waits for port B to be released, and the second thread waits for port A, while neither of them is releasing the port it has reserved. This is a deadlock, which totally stops the system from continuing to run correctly.

- *Starvation*: A starvation problem is when one thread never gets to run. It occurs when the priorities of the threads are defined in such a way that it is impossible or very difficult for one thread to ever get control. Consequently, the task of the thread is never performed, which in turn leads to other difficulties.

The mechanisms used to synchronize threads are concepts such as *semaphores*, *monitors*, or *critical regions*. They all share the common characteristics that they guard a specific code block so that only one thread at a time gets access to it. The code block then contains the code to reserve or use a resource such as a device or a shared object. The mechanisms also have operations to wait for a resource (or actually, the code block guarding the resource) to be released without continuous "busy waiting," which is waste of processor resources. The mechanisms need to be supported by the operating system because they have to be implemented using indivisible low-level instructions, and several programs executing concurrently are involved.

Resolving the synchronization problems described earlier also calls for the scheduling of the threads, which is done through setting priorities. Obviously a thread with higher priority has precedence and is scheduled to run before a thread of lower priority. In some operating systems, it is also possible to parameterize the scheduling algorithm or even to choose the scheduling algorithm. The simplest way to control the scheduling is in the code of the active objects, where they can voluntarily give up the control by calling functions such as sleep (which makes the thread idle for a specified amount of time) or by waiting for a communication or synchronization mechanism such as a mailbox or semaphore to be signaled or released.

The built-in support for synchronization in UML is limited, but it can be defined through extensions using stereotypes or properties. A class or an operation can have its concurrency requirements defined through a Concurrency property with the possible values Sequential, Guarded, and Synchronous. If a property is set for a class, it affects all operations in the class, otherwise only the operation for which the property is set is affected. The meanings of the values are:

- *Sequential*: The class/operation is intended only for use in a single thread of control (not concurrently by several threads).

- *Guarded*: The class/operation will work in the presence of multiple threads of control, but it needs an active collaboration of the threads to achieve mutual exclusion. The threads normally have to lock the object/operation before using it, and unlock it afterward.

- *Synchronized*: The class/operation will work in the presence of multiple threads of control; the class itself handles this. This feature is being built in more modern programming languages, such as Java, where an operation can be declared as synchronized; then the handling of synchronization of that operation is automatic so that only one thread at a time can access it.

If synchronization must be modified more explicitly, a semaphore class can be defined and instantiated to semaphores whenever the synchronization between active objects has to be shown. Another possibility is to define a stereotype semaphore that is used for all classes whose instances are shared and should be guarded by a semaphore (in that case, the semaphore is implicitly connected to the class that is stereotyped). Synchronization mechanisms other than semaphores can of course be modeled as classes or stereotypes as well.

Scheduling

As briefly introduced previously, another technique used to synchronize active objects is to schedule them. Scheduling is the process of deciding which thread should run next in a situation where several threads are conceivable. Scheduling is done by the operating system, which allocates the processor to a thread using some predefined algorithm (e.g., a round-robin algorithm, by which every thread gets a specified time slot, or a dynamic priority algorithm, which is based on giving priority to the threads that are in the foreground interacting with the user).

The programmer can control parts of the scheduling, normally by setting priorities of the threads or by setting parameters of the scheduling algorithm. In a complex situation where detailed control is needed of the scheduling, a *supervisor thread* can be designed. The supervisor thread, given maximum priority, gives the control to the application threads according to how it has been programmed (the algorithm defined in the supervisor code).

In UML, the priority of an active object is most suitably noted as a tagged value of the active class. There is no predefined tagged value for such a value, but it can easily be defined. The value range depends on the resolution of the operating systems; for example, it can be just low, medium, or high priority, or a value range between 1 and 32. Normally the priority set during modeling needs to be tuned when testing prototypes or early releases of the system.

Implementation of Concurrency and Synchronization in Java

The Java programming language has built-in support for threads. As usual, the quality and performance of the real-time constructs depend on the underlying operating system on which the Java program executes. The upcoming code shows an active class that inherits from a predefined Thread class (part of the Java API). As part of that inheritance, the abstract run operation must be implemented in the class and must define the actual code to be run in the thread. An eternal loop is defined in the code; and inside the loop, some synchronous and asynchronous message sending is done (to send the asynchronous message, signal and mailbox classes must be defined; they are not predefined in Java). The loop also sleeps for 10 milliseconds.

The thread objects are instantiated in the static main function, which is where all Java programs begin execution. In this main function, two objects of the DemoThread class are created and started; they will run in parallel execution, sharing the processor and being scheduled by the operating system. Using Java, the different real-time constructs that have been shown are relatively easy to map to code.

```
class DemoThread extends Thread
{
    public void run()
    {
        try
        {
            // Do forever
            for (;;)
            {
                // Synchronous message to System.out object
```

```
                    System.out.println("Hello");

                    // Asynchronous message placed in Global_mailbox
                    // Needs definition of class Signal and Mailbox
                    // elsewhere.
                    Signal s = new Signal("Asynch Hello");
                    Global_mailbox.Put(s);

                    // Waits for 10 milliSeconds.
                    sleep(10);
                }
            }
        catch (InterruptedException e)
        {
        }
    }
    public static void main(String[] arg)
    {
        // Create an instance of the active class (thread)
        DemoThread t1 = new DemoThread();
        // Start execution
        t1.start();
        // Create another instance of the active class
        DemoThread t2 = new DemoThread();
        // Start execution
        t2.start();
    }
}
```

Real-Time Modeling in UML

This section describes all the real-time modeling constructs in the UML. There are
no special diagrams for expressing real time; instead, real-time modeling information is added to the normal UML, especially the dynamic diagrams. UML has definitions for specifying the following types of information:

- *Time*: Time specifications and constraints are best defined in sequence diagrams, where time is the primary aspect. However, time specifications can be
added to other diagrams as notes.

- *Concurrency*: Concurrency is described as active classes (using the stereotype
«ActiveClass» and drawn with a thick line around the class or object rectangle). Properties of the active class (e.g., priority) can be defined as tagged val-

ues of the class. A mapping to the implementation environment can be made through the component stereotypes «Process» and «Thread».

- *Asynchronous events*: UML supports asynchronous messages sent between threads or initiated from asynchronous events in the environment.

- *Synchronization*: Synchronization can be described either as properties of classes or operations (the Concurrency property) or as classes/stereotypes that define mechanisms such as a semaphore, monitor, or critical region.

- *Distribution*: Threads deployed in a distributed system are described in a deployment diagram (which in turn uses components from a component diagram to represent processes and threads).

Figures 6.8 through 6.11 show selected examples of a house alarm system. The system consists of a main unit to which a number of sensors and alarms are connected. The sensors detect movements in the guarded area, and the alarms generate sounds and/or lights to scare off an intruder. The total area that can be guarded is divided into cells, where a cell contains some sensors and some alarms that guard a specific area. When a cell is activated, the alarm functionality is on; when it is deactivated, it is not guarding the area.

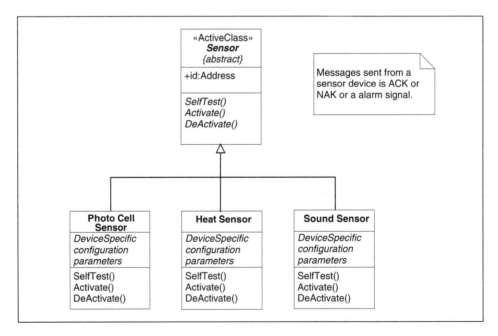

Figure 6.8 *The alarm system has sensors.*

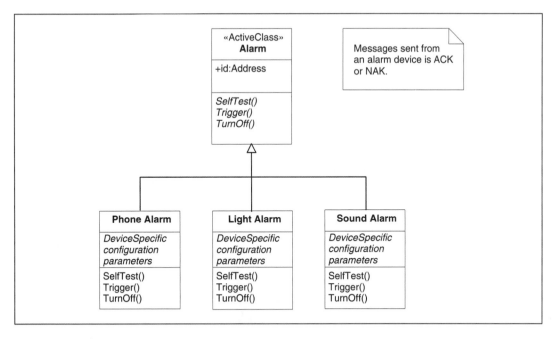

Figure 6.9 *Alarms.*

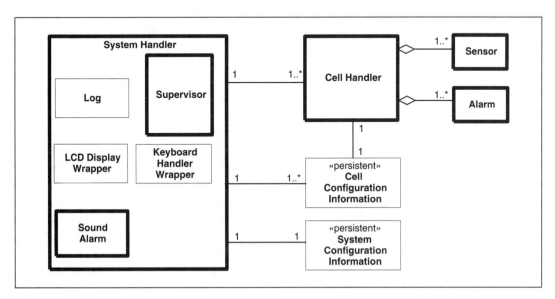

Figure 6.10 *Active and passive objects in the house alarm system.*

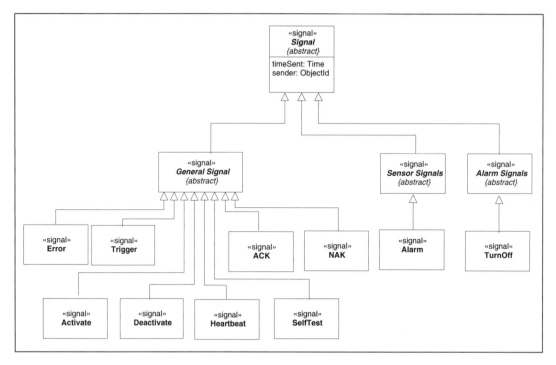

Figure 6.11 *A signal hierarchy for the house alarm system.*

The sensors are devices that will detect activity in a specific area. They are modeled as a number of classes specializing an abstract Sensor class that defines the interface to sensors. The Sensor class is active; it has its own thread of control that handles the low-level interrupts from the actual device. A sensor can be activated or deactivated, it can be tested, and it can generate ACK, NAK, and an alarm signal.

The alarms are devices to scare off an intruder by means of sound and light effects, or by calling and sending information to an alarm phone number. An alarm can be triggered or turned off and it can be tested; the signals it can generate are either ACK or NAK. Like the sensors, the alarms are modeled as an active class that handles the low-level communication with the device.

A class diagram of the system illustrates how the sensors and alarms are integrated into a system solution. Sensors and alarms are connected to a Cell Handler, an active class that handles a specific cell. A Cell Handler object reads its configuration from a persistent object holding the current configuration of the cell (the sensors and alarms it is connected to and other configuration parameters). The Cell Handler is connected to the System Handler, which is an active class that handles the user communication through a user panel that has an LCD display and a small keyboard. Through this user interface, the system can be configured, activated, and deactivated. All such changes are stored in cell and system configuration information classes. The System Handler also contains a supervisor thread, which continuously communicates with all the Cell Handlers. The supervisor performs self-tests on the devices, and receives "heartbeat" signals from the Cell Handler (signals sent from the Cell Handler to indicate that it is running correctly). It will also receive an alarm signal from a cell, in which case it normally will broadcast a trigger signal to other cells, causing all alarms in the entire system to start. The System Handler has a log in which it stores all events; it also has an internal sound alarm that can be used under all circumstances, even if the connections to the other alarms have been cut (the main unit would have a battery unit in case of power failure).

The signals in the system comprise part of the static structure of the house alarm system. They are collected into a hierarchy, whose organization is open to discussion. In the solution in the house alarm example, there are three types of signals: general, sensor, and alarm. The general signals can be used both between the System Handler and the Cell Handler, as well as to the devices. All asynchronous communication in the system is done using signals.

State Diagram

A state diagram identifies the states and behavior of an active object. The behavior changes in different states during the object's life cycle. (Normal (nonconcurrent) state diagrams were described in Chapter 5, along with the other dynamic modeling diagrams.) An active object's state can be refined into concurrent substates, where a number of actions are often performed concurrently. The result of the nested substates determines the overall state of the active object. The substates are state machines with start and stop states, and they can maintain their states for longer periods of time (e.g., for the total execution of the system). The substates don't have to be executing in their own threads, though that is often the case.

Concurrent substates are shown by dividing the graphic region of the state into subregions using dashed lines. Each subregion is a concurrent substate, may have an optional name, and contains a nested state diagram with disjoint states (see Figure 6.12).

The activation phase can be modeled using concurrent substates, where the substates show the actions and states of current interest for the alarms, the sensors, and the Cell Handler, respectively. Only if and when all these substates have reached their stop state has the overall state of the system been activated; otherwise, the system has been placed in an activation failure state. The concurrent substates are in this case also performed concurrently.

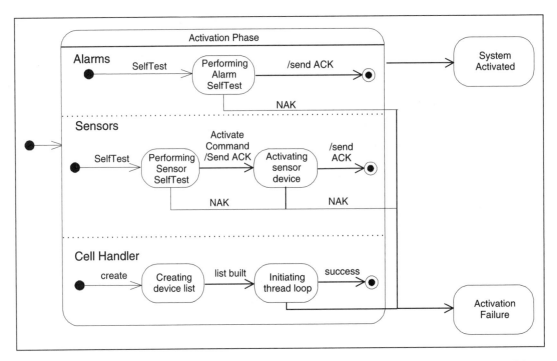

Figure 6.12 *Concurrent substates in a state diagram. The state diagram describes the activation of the entire system.*

Complex transitions can be used as an alternative to concurrent substates. A complex transition may have multiple source or target states, and either splits control into concurrent threads that run in parallel or unifies concurrent threads into a single thread. In this way, parts of a state diagram are performed in parallel, but the difference from using concurrent substates is that the concurrent states in a complex transition are not state machines of their own; they are states on the same level performed in parallel.

A complex transition is either a state transition whereby the control is divided into two or more new states being performed concurrently, or a state transition whereby two or more states are synchronized in one new state. A complex transition is shown as a short vertical bar, which may have one or more solid arrows extending from states to the bar (called the source states). It may also have one or more solid arrows from the bar to states (destination states). A transition string may be shown near the bar. Only when the object is in all of the source states and the transition guard string is true does the transition fire, which means that concurrent execution either begins or ends.

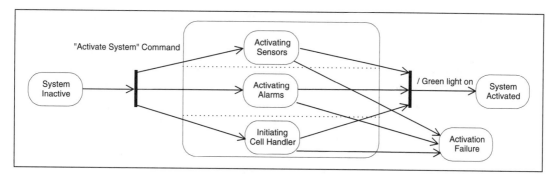

Figure 6.13 *A complex transition where the control flows are divided into concurrent threads that run in parallel and later become synchronized again.*

A simpler model of the activation phase is to show it with complex transitions as in Figure 6.13. By definition, the activities in each of the regions are done concurrently, and only when they all are performed is the transition to the system activated state complete.

Sequence Diagram

A sequence diagram shows how a number of objects interact in a specific situation. The primary aspect is time, which is determined by reading the diagram from top to bottom. Naturally then, a sequence diagram is appropriate for specifying time and timing constraints in real-time systems. These time specifications are usually written in any of the margin comment areas of the diagram (the script); for example, a specification of the maximum time between two messages, or a comment on how long an object should wait before it sends another message to another object. As an aid, time marks (indicating a specific point in the sequence, e.g., A or B) can be defined in the script and then later referred to in the specifications (e.g., A − B < 10 sec).

In the sequence diagram, different messages can be used to show different types of communication between the objects. A simple message can show that the message type is not yet known or is irrelevant; or it may give a return value from a synchronous message. A synchronous message in a concurrent system provides wait semantics; that is, that the sending object waits for the receiving object to handle the message. An asynchronous message reveals that the sending object does not wait, but continues to execute immediately after having sent the message (any result is typically sent back as an asynchronous message as well). Transmission delays can be depicted by a slanted message arrow indicating that the message will be received at a later time than when it is sent (the maximum transmission time can be specified in the margin).

Active objects are drawn as object rectangles with a thick line. The activation (when an object has execution control) is depicted as a thin rectangle on the lifeline from the activation point until the object is no longer activated. A passive object is activated only while it is handling a message; it loses the activation when the result is returned, whereas an active object typically maintains control and performs activities while both sending and receiving other events.

Branching, iteration, recursion, creation, and destruction of objects have the same notation as for nonconcurrent systems and are described in Chapter 5.

Figure 6.14 shows again the activation sequence of the system where the System Handler gives an order to the Cell Handler to activate itself. The Cell Handler then sends a synchronous message (makes an operation call) to the Cell Configuration object asking for information; it returns the configuration data. The Cell

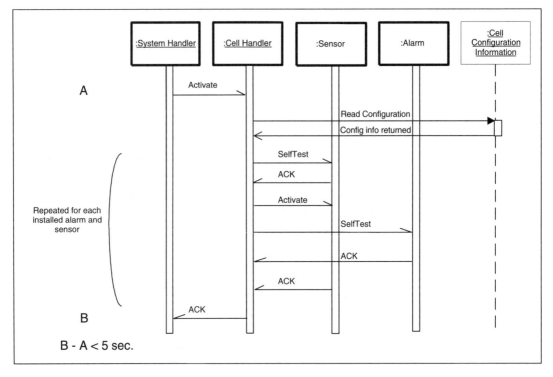

Figure 6.14 *The alarm activation sequence documented in a sequence diagram. Most messages are sent asynchronously except for the reading of the Cell Configuration Information, which is done synchronously with a normal operation call.*

Handler then sends self-test signals to all devices, to acknowledge that they are working correctly. The sensor devices also need an activate signal to become activated. Note that the Sensor and Alarm rectangles' names are not underlined, indicating that they actually represent the classes. Instead of drawing a number of sensors and alarm objects in this sequence diagram, the alternative of using classes to show a number of objects has been used. The communication with sensors and alarms, which is done through asynchronous messages, is repeated for each installed device (described in the left margin). When all devices have been correctly tested and activated, an acknowledgment signal is sent to the System Handler.

This sequence diagram describes the exact scenario of a successful activation. It is also possible to describe a more general case, in which error alternatives would also have been documented. Note that time specifications can be added in the script in the left margin of the diagram. In this case, the time from activation to the point at which the system actually is activated should not take longer than five seconds.

Collaboration Diagram

A collaboration diagram shows both a context (a set of objects and their relationships) and an interaction (how the objects cooperate to perform a specific task). It is very useful for showing interactions in a real-time system, because it can illustrate a structure of both active and passive objects interacting. More than one thread of execution can be shown in the same diagram, as well as parallel sending of messages. The message sequence is identified by numbering the messages with labels.

Active objects are drawn as an object rectangle with a thick line, often with its internal structure. As just noted, a collaboration diagram is excellent for showing the interaction between a set of active objects, along with the internal structure of those active objects (often composed of passive objects).

The message types are the same as in the sequence diagram (simple, synchronous, and asynchronous) and have the same meanings and symbols. The label containing the message sequence replaces the vertical time sequence in the sequence diagram. Messages sent in parallel can be described using letters in the sequence number expression. For instance, the sequence numbers 2.1a and 2.1b of two messages in the collaboration diagram indicate that those messages are sent in parallel. The message label can also implicitly contain synchronization information through the predecessor specification. A predecessor specifies other messages that must be performed before the message flow is enabled (i.e., the message is sent). That means that the predecessor can be used to synchronize active objects so that the work is performed in the right order even if several active objects execute concur-

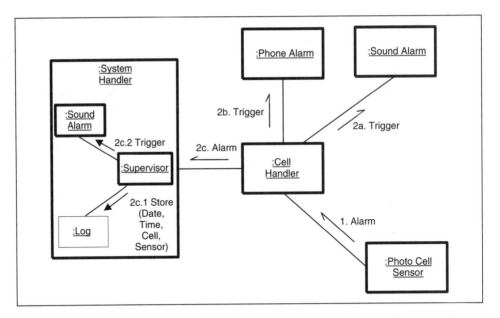

Figure 6.15 *A sensor has detected a movement and initiates an alarm in the system that is documented in a collaboration diagram.*

rently. A message label can also have a guard-condition that must be fulfilled for the message to be sent. The guard-condition can thus contain synchronization conditions requiring that a resource be available before it is used.

Timing annotations can be added to a collaboration diagram, though not as clearly as in a sequence diagram. They are normally added as notes or constraints of the elements in the diagrams.

The collaboration diagram in Figure 6.15 shows the interaction when a sensor detects something. It then sends an asynchronous alarm signal to the Cell Handler. Next the Cell Handler sends in parallel asynchronous trigger signals to all alarms (in this case, a phone and a sound alarm) and an asynchronous alarm signal to the System Handler. Inside the System Handler, the alarm signal is handled synchronously—the supervisor thread first calls the internal sound alarm and then writes the event to the log. A collaboration diagram provides a good picture of both the structure of the involved objects and their interaction.

Activity Diagram

The activity diagram is used primarily for sequential flow control. An activity diagram is typically connected to an operation in a class, and thus is not as important as the other dynamic diagrams in terms of real-time specification, though it is still usable in such a system.

The activity diagram contains action states, whose actions need to be performed before a transition to a new state can be made (an external event is thus not necessary). Conditions and decisions can be added to the diagram; a decision diamond indicates which way the execution should go (which action state should be performed next). Action states can be performed in parallel, which is shown by dividing the execution flow line into several lines, each one going into a separate action state. The actions in the states are then performed in parallel. The objects affected by the activities in the action states can be shown by drawing object rectangles and connecting them either as input to or output from an action state with dashed arrow lines.

The activity diagram can also demonstrate the sending and receiving of messages, which is interesting when modeling real-time systems. The action state symbols can be complemented by symbols indicating that a message is being sent (a convex pentagon resembling a rectangle with a triangular point on one side) or received (a concave pentagon resembling a rectangle with a triangular notch in one side). Dependency arrows can be drawn from the message symbols to the objects that are the senders or receivers of the messages.

One possible use of the activity diagram in real-time systems is to specify the run operation of an active class, since this operation shows the concurrent behavior of the objects of that class. Figure 6.16 shows the run operation in the Cell Handler, in which the eternal thread loop can be seen. The operation waits for signals and, depending on the signal received, performs some activities to handle it. It then sends a heartbeat signal to the System Handler, requests a time-out signal from the operating system so that it is guaranteed to receive a signal in that time, and returns to waiting for a new signal. In Figure 6.16, the activities for handling the activate, deactivate, and time-out signals have been collapsed into superactivities to prevent the diagram from becoming too complex.

Component and Deployment Diagram

The component and deployment diagrams describe the physical architecture of the system, which includes how the classes are implemented in different code components and how the resulting executable components are allocated to nodes (computers and other devices) in which they execute. These diagrams are described in more detail in Chapter 7.

The real-time aspects of these diagrams are that active classes are allocated to components, in which they are implemented and executed (a component can be both a source code component and an executable code component). A component

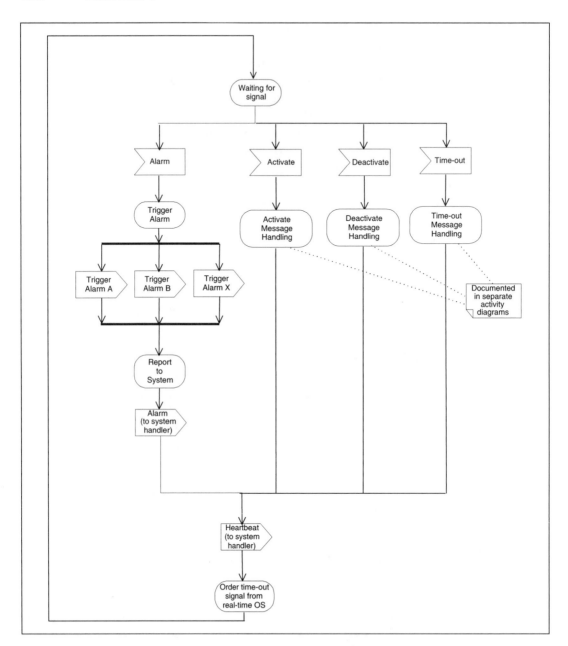

Figure 6.16 *The run operation defined for the active Cell Handler class. Parallel activities can be shown in the activity diagram along with the synchronization of those activities (the triggering of alarms). The handling of the activate, deactivate, and time-out messages have been collapsed here into a superactivity, but they can be expanded into a separate activity diagram to show the details.*

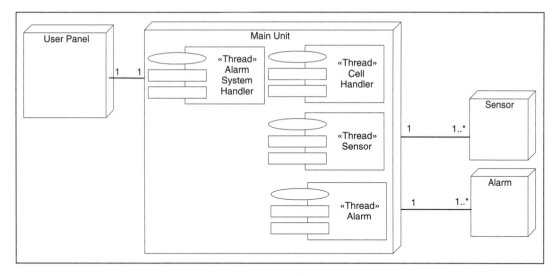

Figure 6.17 *The deployment diagram for the house alarm system.*

can have either the «Process» or «Thread» stereotype, specifying whether the active class is implemented as a process or a thread. The active classes are physically deployed and distributed among the actual computers in the system via the components in which they are implemented. Thus, there is a trace between the logical classes and where they are executing in the computers, and vice versa, from the programs in the computers back to their descriptions in the logical view of the system.

In the house alarm system, the physical architecture shows a main unit with a user panel that has connections to a number of sensors and alarms. The components have all been allocated to the main unit, which has all the software in the system, including all the threads (see Figure 6.17).

Adapting to Real-Time Systems

Although UML has a number of mechanisms for modeling real-time systems, it is often necessary to use the extension mechanisms to adapt UML in a real-time project. The extension mechanisms can be used to adapt UML to a specific method, organization, or application domain. The mechanisms are described in detail in Chapter 8.

A standard stereotype, «ActiveClass», defines a class (and its objects) as active. The stereotype is drawn with a thick line. There are also standard stereotypes, «Process» and «Thread», used with components to describe whether a component is implemented as a thread or a process. More stereotypes can be defined to identify the mapping of the logical model to the implementation environment: «Semaphore», «Mailbox», «Exception», «Interrupt», and others. Stereotypes can also be used to clarify the models, for example, with stereotypes such as «HardwareWrapper» or «Scheduler», to explain the role of a specific class or component. Stereotypes can also define different types of messages.

Properties (tagged values) are used to define the concurrency of a class or an operation (with the values Sequential, Guarded, or Synchronized). User-defined tagged values can be assigned to active classes to specify a priority tag or other scheduling information.

Timing constraints are often used in a real-time system, and most often are noted in the sequence diagram script, although they can be added freely to any diagram as a constraint within braces close to the affected element.

Special Real-Time Modeling Concerns

There are some special concerns when modeling real-time systems. Naturally, concurrency, communication, and synchronization are the most important factors, but fault tolerance, performance optimization, and distribution must also be dealt with when modeling real-time systems.

Fault Tolerance

Fault tolerance is the capability of a system to function in the presence of hardware and software failures. In many real-time systems, a system failure is simply not accepted under any circumstances. As mentioned earlier, if the real-time software controls an airplane, a car, or a medical control unit, a system failure could mean the difference between life and death. Such systems must be capable of handling the most abnormal situations, where either the hardware or software fails to work as expected. A system with a high degree of reliability is one in which the results are predictable and the system is robust. The system must gracefully handle errors, and under all circumstances stay in operation (the system can be depended on). There are a number of techniques for achieving this status:

- *Error and exception handling*: Certain aspects of fault tolerance can be handled through "normal" error and exception handling. Errors must be anticipated in all situations, and extra safety-catch exceptions must be defined, then generated whenever an exceptional event occurs. Exception handlers are defined at appropriate places in the code to handle the exceptions and to make sure that the system continues to function.

- *Multiple systems*: A technique involving multiple systems is used in applications such as that implemented in the space shuttle, where both the hardware and software is doubled or even tripled. In multiple systems, malfunctioning hardware or software is directly replaced with its back-up unit. The software may have been written by different teams; and only when all software systems give the same order, is it implemented (except in a situation where a decision must be made, in which case a majority rules). On a smaller scale, a system can have a supervisor process that monitors the execution of the system; in case of a serious situation, the supervisor can take charge, causing an alarm or a possible restart of the system.

- *Formal proofs*: Mathematical methods used to analyze concurrent execution and message exchange can detect common problems such as deadlocks, starvation, concurrent use, and so on. Even such formal mathematical methods require a lot of work, and they can be used to detect possible error situations in a hard real-time system.

In UML, a few mechanisms can be used to try to achieve fault tolerance, even if there is no specific mechanism for that purpose. If communication is not guaranteed, all sequence diagrams must contain specifications delineating what happens if a message is lost. This typically requires time-outs that will occur in case a message (such as an acknowledgment) is lost. State diagrams can be modeled with fault states at the outmost level, so that whenever an unexpected event occurs, the object is transferred to a fault state that contains suitable handling.

Performance Optimization

The use of abstraction, which is a keystone in object-oriented development, can unfortunately lead to degradation of real-time performance. When performance optimization is important, a conflict might arise between the "ideal" object-oriented model on one hand and performance on the other, so that the actual implementation has to be optimized. That includes taking shortcuts in the communication between objects (so that an object gains direct access to an object to which it normally does not have access) and merging classes to decrease the number of layers between different parts of the software. This can improve the performance, though at the cost of decreasing the modularity of the software.

As part of the optimization, it is necessary to also look at the active objects. If possible, active objects should be implemented as threads rather than as processes. Threads can execute together in the same memory space and have less overhead than processes; furthermore, the handling of threads is definitely "cheaper" for the operating system in terms of performance. It is also necessary to check if active objects can be merged, thereby avoiding the sharing of passive objects, with all the synchronization handling that would then be required.

Other guidelines for achieving higher performance are:

- Use synchronous communication (e.g., operation calls) instead of asynchronous communication.
- Reuse message objects or other frequently used objects instead of continuously re-creating them.
- Avoid copying objects between different memory spaces.

Such detailed optimization work may be necessary when trying to achieve maximum performance from a real-time system. However, the first place to look for optimization possibilities is the overall design level. Often an improved overall design can mean huge gains in performance, gains that are almost impossible to achieve by optimizing the lowest level. To guide you to the "right" places, consider a tool such as a profiler (a profiler shows where the processor spends its execution of a program; that is, which parts of the program are most often used).

Distribution

A real-time system is often distributed, which is modeled in UML in the deployment diagram where components are distributed across nodes. Sending messages and objects between the different nodes can be easy if a system such as OLE or CORBA is present; otherwise the distribution mechanisms must be designed and implemented manually.

A distribution mechanism includes packing and unpacking complex objects to and from streams of bytes (sometimes called *serializing*) that can be sent on a communication line. It also includes the task of instituting a global object identification system, so that objects can address each other without knowing the exact location of the objects. There must also be server processes or threads to enable the object to register and then resolve requests to that object into actual operations on the object.

Process Issues

There has been a lack of methods for building real-time systems in general, and object-oriented real-time modeling has been no exception. Building real-time systems, especially hard real-time systems, has often been treated as craftsmanship whereby highly experienced developers build the systems "in their head." Considering that hard real-time systems often govern life-and-death situations, you may wonder whether this is a disciplined engineering solution.

As a basis for building object-oriented real-time systems, all the knowledge from building ordinary object-oriented systems can be used. Like all other systems, real-time systems have a static structure in terms of classes and objects, which are related to each other using association, generalization, and dependencies. And a real-time system has a behavior that can be described using dynamic models, and a development and a deployment view that can be modeled in component and deployment diagrams. The special areas that need to be handled when defining a process/method for real-time systems are:

- Determination of the model for separating processes/threads and objects.
- Identification and definition of active classes.
- Communication and synchronization of active classes.
- Mapping of the real-time aspects to the implementation environment.

Since processes and threads are similar to objects (they encapsulate information and behavior, and communicate using some sort of messages), a model must be determined for how to use these concepts when building systems that will need them. Traditionally, the most common solution was to first define a model of large-sized processes that communicated using operating system primitives, and then to design an object-oriented model of passive objects inside each process (the explicit concurrency model). Thus every process was seen as a system in itself, and the process and object concepts were handled separately. More modern methods follow the implicit concurrency model, where concurrency is integrated into the object-oriented world using active classes. The system is then totally described in object-oriented models, where active objects can execute concurrently.

The reasons for identifying a class as active typically are:

- *Asynchronous events in the environment*: When the environment undertakes events asynchronously, and there are hard-time requirements for reacting to these events, active objects must be introduced to handle them. These active classes are mapped to the asynchronous events in the real world and can be itemized to give higher priority to some events.
- *Periodic handling*: Work that must be performed periodically is normally modeled as active classes that sleep for a prescribed amount of time, wake up, perform their work, and then go back to sleep again.
- *Time-critical functions*: Functions dictated by time constraints can be modeled as an active class that is given higher priority than others. In a preemptive system, a thread with higher priority will always suspend all other threads with lower priority, thereby gaining full access to the machine resources.
- *Computational tasks in background*: Tasks can be considered background work, which can be performed in isolation and usually at lower priority. Such tasks

are printing, collecting statistics, or doing other computational work that isn't time critical. This kind of work can be placed in an active object with lower priority, which executes only when there's time "left over" from the system's normal execution.

When the active classes have been identified, the issues of communication and synchronization immediately arise. Real-time systems can have asynchronous messages that must be handled both in the modeling language and the method. Typically, the communication between active objects is asynchronous, while the internal communication in an active object is synchronous. All objects that share two or more active objects must have built-in protection against concurrent use, and this must be identified when modeling (it is nearly impossible to "find" the correct synchronization mechanisms just by conducting tests).

Finally, an object-oriented real-time method must take into consideration the implementation environment. The models must be mapped easily to primitives in the environment; and sometimes, the performance requirements dictate that more ideal models be easily translated into more optimized implementation solutions.

Attempts have been made to define object-oriented methods specifically targeted at real-time systems. ROOM (Real-Time Object-Oriented Modeling language) is a modeling language (B. Selic et al., 1994) complemented with heuristics and work organization guidelines for creating models of real-time systems. The language is based on an actor concept (not to be confused with actors in use cases) that is an active class. Actors are described as a state machine, which can have nested substates. The active class is defined with interface components called ports. Each port defines a protocol: input and output messages and their legal ordering. An actor can have several ports and thus reflect different roles of the actor. Passive data objects can also be modeled, and actors can be placed in layers. ROOM also incorporates a programming language, which can be used to express low-level details such as message passing and data manipulation. ROOM models are executable so that they can be executed in a tool to observe the behavior of the model.

OCTOPUS (M. Awad et al., 1996) is an adaptation of OMT (J. Rumbaugh et al., 1991) to real-time systems. Requirements of the system are modeled by use cases, and a context diagram describes an overview of the system. The system architecture phase divides the system into subsystems, which are described in an analysis using structural, functional, and dynamic models from the OMT method. The dynamic models have special real-time support in terms of activities and models for event lists, event groups, event sheets, state charts, action tables, and significance tables. A subsequent design phase details the interaction between objects in object interaction threads (which are very similar to collaboration diagrams in UML). From these object interaction threads, decisions are made about suitable processes and interprocess messages, and translated into a program in an implementation» phase.

Summary

A real-time system is one in which timeliness is important; it is reactive, has concurrently executing threads, and is not deterministic. To specify a model for a real-time system, time requirements, concurrency, asynchronous communication, and synchronization must be considered. A real-time system is often embedded, meaning that the software is tightly integrated with specialized hardware. Real-time systems can be categorized as hard or soft. A hard real-time system is one in which a failure could mean loss of life; thus fault tolerance is of the utmost importance.

Real time and object orientation are integrated through the definition of active classes and objects. An active class has its own thread of control and thus can initiate actions by itself. That is in contrast to "normal" passive objects, which execute only when some other object performs some operation on it and passes back the control when the operation returns. Active classes and objects are implemented through processes or threads supported by the operating system.

Active objects communicate either through ordinary operation calls (called synchronous messages in the object-oriented world) or through specialized mechanisms such as mailboxes or message queues in which messages can be delivered asynchronously. An asynchronous message means that the sender doesn't wait for the receiver to be ready to accept the message, nor does it automatically wait for any return result. The behavior of active objects is modeled using events; an asynchronous message signal is one type of event. Other events are that a guard-condition becomes true, a passage of time elapses, or a synchronous message is received from another object (e.g., an operation call).

Synchronization mechanisms are things such as semaphores or critical regions that protect a specific code area, which in turn protects some shared resource such as a passive object or a device. Synchronization mechanisms are used to prevent problems such as conflicts in parallel usage of shared objects, deadlocks, or just inefficient resource usage of the processor caused by having threads executing in endless "busy wait" loops.

UML has support for defining active classes, as classes of the stereotype «ActiveClass»; the class rectangle is drawn with a thick line. The concurrent behavior of an active class can be shown with concurrent substates or complex transitions in a state diagram. Active classes and objects can then be used in all types of diagrams, such as class, sequence, and collaboration diagrams. Collaboration diagrams are particularly suited to documenting concurrent behavior because they can show both the context of a collaboration, including both active and passive objects, and the concurrent communication using asynchronous messages. Activity diagrams can be used to show the detailed specification of certain handling; for example, the handling of received signals in a thread.

To define a method/process for object-oriented real-time systems, these aspects must be addressed: determine a basic model for separating processes/threads from objects; identify and define active classes, communication, and synchronization of the active classes; and, finally, design a suitable mapping to an implementation environment. Although there are methods on the market today (such as ROOM or OCTOPUS) for modeling real-time systems, there is still a lack of methodology for combining real-time systems and object orientation.

7 *Physical Architecture*

A system architecture is a blueprint of all the parts that together define the system: their structure, interfaces, and the mechanisms that they use to communicate. By defining an appropriate architecture, it makes it easier to navigate the system, to find the location of a specific function or concept, or to identify a location to which to add a new function or concept to fit into the overall architecture. The architecture must be detailed enough so that it can be mapped to the actual code. An architecture that is both easy to navigate and sufficiently detailed must also be scaleable, meaning it can be viewed on different levels. The architecture, for example, should provide a top-level view that includes only a few parts; from there, the developer should be able to select one part and examine its internal architecture, which consists of more parts. Using a tool, it should be possible to "zoom into" different parts of the system to study them in greater detail.

A well-defined architecture allows the insertion of new functions and concepts without imposing problems on the rest of the system (such as in an old monolithic system where one small change in one part of the system could cause something seemingly unrelated to stop working because of complex relationships between different parts of the system).

The architecture should serve as a map for the developers, revealing how the system is constructed and where specific functions or concepts are located. Over time, this map may have to be changed during development because of important discoveries and experiences along the way. The architecture must "live" with the system as the system is being developed, and should constantly reflect the system's construction in all phases and generations. Naturally, the base architecture is defined in the first version of the system, and the quality of this initial architecture is vital for enabling developers to change, extend, and update the functionality of the system.

The UML definition of architecture is:

Architecture is the organizational structure of a system. An architecture can be recursively decomposed into parts that interact through interfaces, relationships that connect parts, and constraints for assembling parts.

Buschmann et al. (1996) offers another definition of software architecture:

A software architecture is a description of the subsystems and components of a software system and the relationships between them. Subsystems and components are typically specified in different views to show the relevant functional and nonfunctional properties of a software system. The software architecture of a system is an artifact. It is the result of the software design activity.

The architecture is described in a number of views, and each view concentrates on a specific aspect of the system. The complete picture of the system can be made only by defining all views. In UML, these views are usually defined as use-case view, logical view, concurrency view, component view, and deployment view. A broader separation usually divides the architecture into logical and physical architectures. The logical architecture mainly specifies the functional properties of the system and is driven by the functional requirements of the system; the physical architecture deals primarily with nonfunctional aspects such as reliability, compatibility, resource usage, and deployment of the system. These architectures are described further in this chapter.

Experienced developers sometimes seem to have a "magic" ability to define good architectures. But this skill comes from having designed a lot of systems, which gives them a knowledge for which solutions work and which don't. They typically reuse solutions that have worked well in the past. In fact, recently, a lot of work has been directed toward trying to identify architectural patterns or frameworks ("solutions") that are repeatedly used by experienced developers when designing software architectures. Buschmann et al. (1996) has defined the following architectural patterns:

- *Layers pattern:* A system decomposed into groups of subtasks in which each group of subtasks is at a particular level of abstraction.
- *Pipes and filters pattern*: A system that processes a stream of data, where a number of processing steps are encapsulated in filter components. Data is passed through pipes between adjacent filters, and the filters can be recombined to build related systems or system behavior.
- *Blackboard pattern*: A system where several specialized subsystems assemble their knowledge to build a partial or approximate solution to a problem for which no deterministic solution strategy is known.

- *Broker pattern*: A system where decoupled components interact by remote service invocations. A broker component is responsible for coordinating communication and for transmitting results and exceptions.

- *Model-view-controller pattern*: A system that divides an interactive system into three components: A model containing the core functionality and data, one or more views displaying information to the user, and one or more controllers that handle user input. A change-propagation mechanism ensures consistency between user interface and model.

- *Microkernel pattern*: A system that separates a minimal functional core from extended functionality and customer-specific parts. The microkernel also serves as a socket for plugging in these extensions and coordinating their collaboration.

Rumbaugh et al. (1991) also defined a number of architectural frameworks:

- *Batch transformation*: Data transformation of the entire input set.

- *Continuous transformation*: Data transformation performed continuously as inputs arrive.

- *Interactive interface*: System driven by external interactions.

- *Dynamic simulation*: System that simulates evolving real-world objects.

- *Transaction manager*: System concerned with storing and updating data, often including concurrent access from different physical locations.

Further descriptions of these patterns and frameworks can be found in Rumbaugh et al. (1991) and Buschmann et al. (1996). Naturally no system uses just one of these frameworks or patterns. Various patterns are used in different parts of the system and at different scales. A layers pattern can be used to define the architecture of a specific subsystem, while in one of the layers in the subsystem another pattern can be used to organize it internally. To become a good software architect, you must have the ability to know the design of the architectural patterns, when they should be used, and how to combine them.

With all these definitions in mind, what comprises a good architecture? Here are some guidelines for answering that question.

- A correct description of the parts that define the system, both in terms of the logical architecture and the physical architecture.

- A map of the system on which a developer can easily locate where a specific functionality or concept is implemented. The functionality or concept may be either application-oriented (a model of something in the application domain) or design-oriented (some technical implementation solution). This also implies that requirements of the system should be traceable to the code that handles it.

- Changes and extensions should be easy to make in a specific location in the system, without the rest of the system being negatively affected.

- Simple, well-defined interfaces and clear dependencies between different parts, so that an architect can develop a specific part without having a complete understanding of all the details in the overall system.

- Support for reuse by both incorporating reusable parts into the design and allowing the design of generic parts that can be used in other systems.

An architecture that comprises all these qualities is not easy to design, and sometimes compromises have to be made. But defining a good base architecture is one of the most important steps in the development of a successful system. If it is not done conscientiously, the architecture will come to be defined bottom-up by the code, resulting in a system that is difficult to change, extend, maintain, and understand.

Logical Architecture

As noted, the logical architecture deals with the functionality of the system, allocating functionality to different parts of the system and specifying in detail how the solutions work. The logical architecture contains the application logic, but not the physical distribution of that logic into different processes, programs, or computers. The logical architecture gives a clearer understanding of the construction of the system to make it easier to administrate and coordinate the work (to use the human developer resources as efficiently as possible). Not all parts of the logical architecture have to be developed within the project; class libraries, binary components, and patterns can often be bought.

The logical architecture answers questions such as:

- What functionality does the system deliver?

- Which classes exist, and how are those classes related to each other?

- How do the classes and their objects collaborate to deliver the functionality?

- What are the timing constraints on functions in the system?

- What would be a suitable plan for a number of developers to follow to develop this architecture?

In UML, the diagrams used to describe the logical architecture are use-case, class, state, activity, collaboration, and sequence. These diagrams have all been described in previous chapters. A common architecture is the three-layered structure where the system is divided into an interface layer, a business object layer, and a database layer. A diagram showing such a logical architecture, including a possible internal architecture of each layer, is shown in Figure 7.1. From the packages, other diagrams can be reached which describe the classes in each package and their internal collaboration.

Physical Architecture

The physical architecture deals with a detailed description of the system, in terms of the hardware and software that the system contains. It reveals the structure of the hardware, including different nodes and how these nodes are connected to each other. It also illustrates the physical structure and dependencies of the code modules that implement the concepts defined in the logical architecture; and the distribution of the run-time software in terms of processes, programs, and other components. The physical architecture attempts to achieve an efficient resource usage of the hardware and the software.

The physical architecture answers questions such as:

- In which programs or processes are classes and objects physically located?
- On which computers do the programs and processes execute?
- Which computers and other hardware devices are in the system, and how are they connected to each other?
- What are the dependencies between different code files? If a specific file is changed, which other files have to be recompiled?

The physical architecture describes the decomposition of the software and hardware. A mapping is drawn from the logical architecture to the physical architecture, whereby the classes and mechanisms in the logical architecture are mapped onto components, processes, and computers in the physical architecture. This mapping allows the developer to "follow" a class in the logical architecture to its physical implementation; or vice versa, to trace the description of a program or a component back to its design in the logical architecture.

As previously described, the physical architecture is concerned with the implementation, and thus is also modeled in implementation diagrams. The implementation diagrams in UML are the component and the deployment diagrams. The component diagram contains the software components: the code units and the structure of the actual files (source code and binary). The deployment diagram shows the run-time architecture of the system, covering both the physical devices and the software allocated to them.

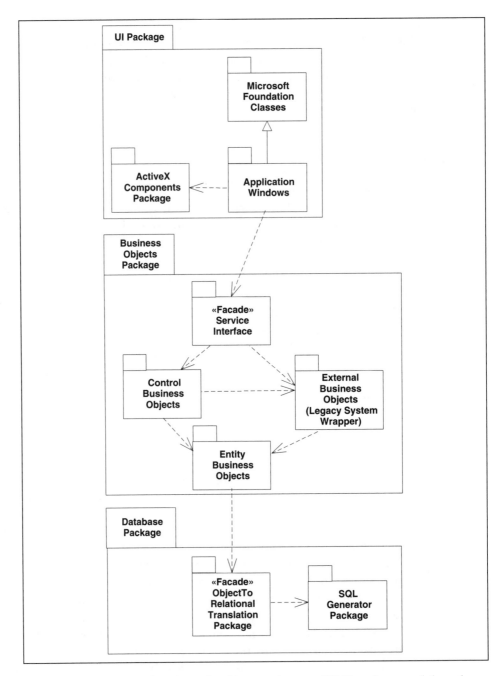

***Figure* 7.1** *A common three-layered architecture shown as UML packages and dependencies between the packages.*

Hardware

The hardware concepts in the physical architecture can be divided into:

- *Processors*: These are the computers that execute the programs in the system. A processor can be of any size, from a microprocessor in an embedded system to a supercomputer.

- *Devices*: These are the support devices such as printers, routers, card readers, and so on in the system. They are typically connected to a processor that controls them. There may be a fine line between what is a processor and what is a device (most devices have their own CPUs), but generally a processor runs parts of the software created specifically for the system.

- *Connections*: Processors have connections to other processors. They also have connections to devices. The connections represent a communication mechanism between two nodes, and can be described as both the physical medium (for example, optical cable) and the software protocol (for example, TCP/IP).

Software

Traditionally the software in a system architecture was rather loosely defined as consisting of "parts." Other words for "part" could be package, module, component, namespace, or subsystem. A common name for the modular unit handled in the architecture is subsystem, a miniature system within a larger system. It has an interface and is internally decomposed either into more detailed subsystems or into classes and objects. Subsystems can be allocated to processes in which they execute (and the processes can be allocated to computers on which they execute).

In UML, a subsystem is modeled as a package of classes. A package organizes a number of classes into a logical group, but defines no semantics for the group. In the design, it is often common to define one or more components as the façade to a subsystem. The façade component provides the interface to the subsystem (package) and is the only component visible to the rest of the system. By using a façade, the package becomes a very modular unit, in which the internal design can be hidden and only the façade component has dependencies to other modules in the system. When viewing the package, it is the façade component that is interesting for those who want to use the services of the package, and sometimes only the façade needs to be shown in diagrams. Packages are used both in the logical design, where a number of classes can be packaged into a unit, and in the physical architecture, where a package encapsulates a number of components (typically implementing the classes in the logical design).

The façade construction has a representation in UML, but is then applied to a package. A package contains a façade package that references other elements, but owns no elements of its own. The façade package represents the package in which it is enclosed, and it is annotated as a façade by the stereotype «facade» to that package. Although this is a possible model of the façade concept, the model solution with a façade component (representing a façade class) should also be considered and used.

The main concepts in describing the software are components, processes, threads, and objects.

- *Component*: A component in UML is defined as "a reusable part that provides the physical packaging of a collection of model element instances." This means that a component is a physical implementation (for instance, a source code file) that implements logical model elements as defined in class diagrams or interaction diagrams. A component can be viewed at different stages of the development, such as at compile time, link time, and run time. In a project, the definition of a component is often mapped to the implementation environment (i.e., the programming language and tools used).

- *Processes and threads*: A process represents a heavyweight flow of control, while a thread represents a lightweight flow of control (a discussion of these issues can be found in Chapter 6). They are both described as stereotyped active classes, and active objects are allocated to an executable component in which they run.

- *Objects*: Objects (passive) are those without an execution thread of their own. They run only when someone sends a message to them (calls one of their operations). They can be allocated to a process or thread (an active object) or directly to an executable component.

Component Diagram

The component diagram describes software components and their dependencies to each other, representing the structure of the code. The components are the implementation in the physical architecture of the concepts and the functionality defined in the logical architecture (classes, objects, their relationships, and collaborations). The components are typically the implementation files in the development environment (see Figure 7.2).

A software component can be any of these:

- *Source component*: A source component is meaningful at compile time. It is typically a source code file implementing one or more classes.

- *Binary component*: A binary component is typically object code that is the result of compiling a source component. It could be an object code file, a static

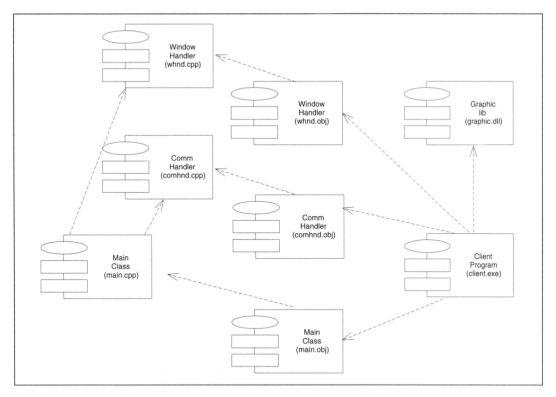

Figure 7.2 *Component diagrams that show a number of components—source, binary, and executable—and their dependencies.*

library file, or a dynamic library file. A binary component is meaningful at link time or, in the case of a dynamic library, at run time (a dynamic library is loaded by the executable component at run time).

- *Executable component*: An executable component is an executable program file that is the result of linking all binary components (either static at link time or dynamic at run time). An executable component represents the executable unit that is run by a processor (computer).

A component is shown in UML as a rectangle with an ellipse and two smaller rectangles to the left (this is the symbol used in the Booch method to represent a module). The name of the component is written below the symbol or inside the large rectangle.

Components are types, but only executable components may have instances (which they have when the program they represent is executing in a processor). A component diagram shows only components as types. To show instances of com-

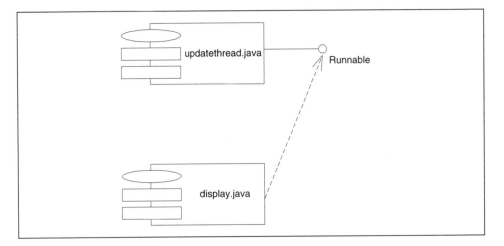

Figure 7.3 *Interfaces and dependencies.*

ponents, a deployment diagram must be used, where instances of executable components are allocated to node instances in which they execute.

A dependency connection between components, shown as a dashed line with an open arrow, means that one component needs another to be able to have a complete definition. A dependency from one source code component A to another component B means that there is a language-specific dependency from A to B. In a compiled language, it could mean that a change in B will require a recompilation of A, because definitions from component B are used when compiling A. If the components are executable, dependency connections can be used to identify which dynamic libraries an executable program needs to be able to run.

A component can define interfaces that are visible to other components. The interfaces can be both interfaces defined at the source-code level (as in Java) or binary interfaces used at run time (as in OLE). An interface is shown with a line from the component with a circle at the end. The name of the interface is placed next to the circle. Dependencies between components can then point to the interface of the component being used (see Figure 7.3).

Compile-Time Components

Compile-time components are the source components that contain the code produced in the projects, as shown in Figure 7.4. Other components such as link-time and run-time components are generated from the compile-time components. Some stereotypes that can be used for compile-time components are:

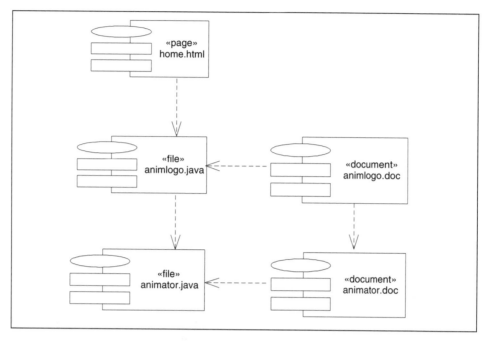

Figure 7.4 *Dependencies between source-code components.*

- *«file»*: A representation of a file containing source code.
- *«page»*: A representation of a Web page.
- *«document»*: A representation of a document (containing documentation rather than compilable code).

A dependency from one compile-time component to other compile-time components reveal which other components are needed to make its definition complete; for instance, which other compile-time components does it include in its definition (see Figure 7.4)?

Link-Time Components

A link-time component is used when linking the system. It is typically the object code representing the result of compiling a compile-time component or a library that is the result of compiling one or more compile-time components. A special case is the dynamic link library (DLL), which is linked to a run-time component at run time rather than at link time. The stereotype «library» can be used to show that a component is a static or dynamic library.

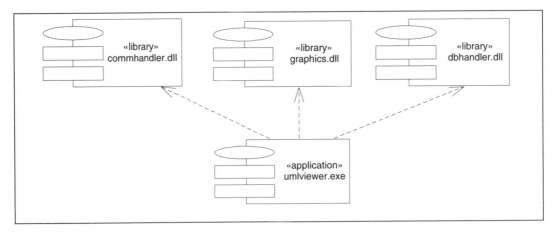

Figure 7.5 *Run-time components.*

Run-Time Components

A run-time component represents a component used when executing the system, as shown in Figure 7.5. It's generated from the link-time components (from object code and libraries) or in some cases directly from the compile-time components (in Java the "executable" bytecode is generated from the compile-time Java code). The stereotype «application» represents an executable program, and the stereotype «table» represents a database table that's also viewed as a component used at run time.

Only run-time components can have instances and are located on nodes (the units in the deployment diagram). A run-time instance of a component indicates that, from the component type, several processes are instantiated to run the application represented in the component file. The dependencies from a run-time component are other components needed for its execution: dynamic link libraries, image files, or database tables.

Deployment Diagram

The deployment diagram depicts the run-time architecture of processors, devices, and the software components that execute in this architecture. It is the ultimate physical description of the system topology, describing the structure of the hardware units and the software that execute on each unit. In such an architecture, it should be possible to look at a specific node in the topology, see which components are executing in that node, and which logical elements (classes, objects, collaborations, etc.) are implemented in the component, and finally trace those

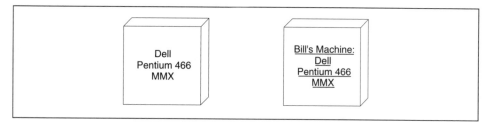

Figure 7.6 *The Dell Pentium 466 MMX is a node type, and Bill's Machine is an instance of that type.*

elements to the initial requirement analysis of the system (which could have been done through use-case modeling).

Nodes

Nodes are physical objects (devices) that have some kind of computational resource. This includes computers with processors, as well as devices such as printers, card readers, communication devices, and so on. The nodes are identified by looking at or deciding on the hardware resources necessary to implement the system, both in terms of capability (such as primary memory, computation power, and secondary storage) and of localization (that the system is available at all necessary geographical locations).

A node can be shown both as a type and an instance (a node is a class), where a type describes the characteristics of a processor or device type and an instance represents actual occurrences (machines) of that type (see Figure 7.6). The detailed definition of the capability of the system can be defined either as attributes or as properties defined for nodes. A node is drawn as a three-dimensional cube with the name inside it; and just as for the notation of classes and objects, if the symbol represents an instance, the name is underlined.

Devices in the system are also represented as nodes, typically with a stereotype that specifies the device type, or at least with a name that clearly defines it as a device node and not a processor node (see Figure 7.7).

Connections

Nodes are connected to each other by communication associations, as shown in Figure 7.8. They are drawn as normal associations with a straight line, indicating that there is some sort of communication path between them, and that the nodes exchange objects or send messages through that communication path. The communication type is represented by a stereotype that identifies the communication protocol or the network used.

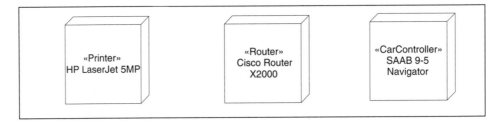

Figure 7.7 Device nodes and possible stereotypes.

Components

Executable component instances may be contained within node instance symbols, showing that they reside and execute on the node instance. From a node type, a dependency arrow with the stereotype «supports» may be drawn to a run-time component type, indicating that the node supports a specific component. When a node type supports a component type, it is possible to execute an instance of that component on an instance of that node type. For example, it is not possible to create a Windows program on an AS/400, so the node type AS/400 does not support that component type.

Components are connected to other components via dashed-arrow dependencies, as in the component diagram in Figure 7.9. Remember that in a deployment diagram, only run-time components are shown. This means that one component uses the services of another component.

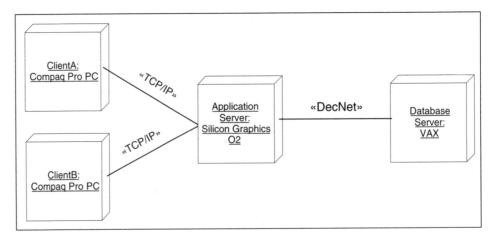

Figure 7.8 Communication associations between nodes.

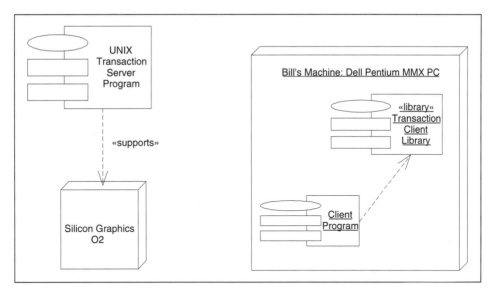

Figure 7.9 *A node type supporting a run-time component type, and a run-time component instance executing in a node instance.*

Objects

An object is placed inside a node instance to indicate where it resides on that instance. The object can either be active (with the stereotypes «process» or «thread», and drawn with a thick line), which executes on the node, or passive (see Figure 7.10). The object is contained within another object or within a component. This is depicted by nesting the symbols; or, if that gets too complicated, a location property can show where an object is located. For instance, a passive object can be contained within a process (an active object), and that process "lives" in a component allocated to a node.

An object can be drawn directly inside a node without showing the component in which it's implemented. The information about the component it belongs to is either defined through the location property or remains undefined in the deployment diagram.

In a distributed system, an object can move between different nodes during the life of the system, as shown in Figure 7.11. This is technically done through distributed objects systems such as OLE or CORBA, where objects can be transmitted through the network and can change their location in the system. An object that changes its location during the lifetime of the system can be included in all the nodes in which it can possibly exist. To show how the object may be distributed in

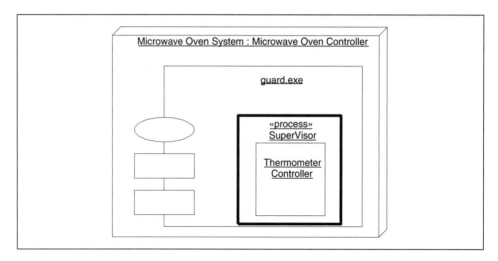

Figure 7.10 *A passive object (of class Thermometer Controller) within an active process object (of active class Supervisor) that lives within a component instance (of type guard.exe), which is allocated to the node Microwave Oven System (of type Microwave Oven Controller).*

the system, a dependency with the stereotype «becomes» is drawn between the different occurrences of the object. The dependency may contain properties that define the time or the condition that triggers the change in the object's location.

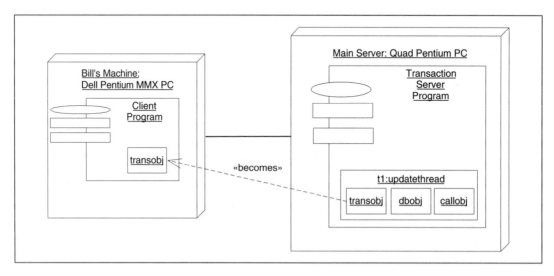

Figure 7.11 *Objects are allocated to nodes. The transobj object that originally exists in the Main Server node can be distributed to the Dell PC node (shown with the stereotype «becomes»).*

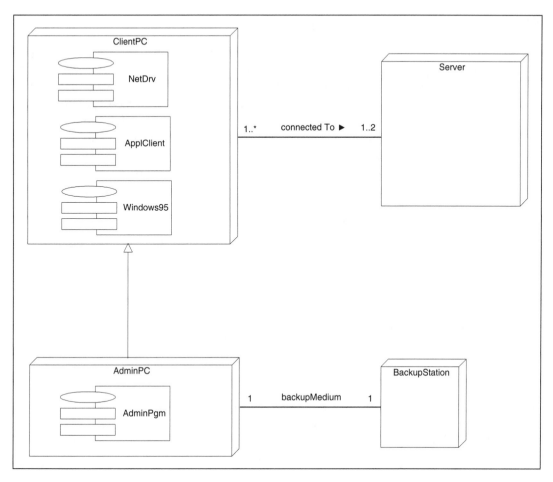

Figure 7.12 *A class diagram (using the node icon to represent node types) in which relationships between different node types have been modeled. The ClientPC node has an association to the Server node with a specified multiplicity. The AdminPC node is a specialization of ClientPC, which has some extra program. AdminPC also has an association to BackupStation.*

Complex Modeling of Nodes

Again, nodes are defined as classes in the UML; therefore, more complex relationships between nodes are described in a class diagram, as shown in Figure 7.12. This is used when describing a family of nodes, where generalization is used to define a general node configuration and specialization is used to capture special cases. A node can also be given a role in an association relationship and have an interface defined.

Allocating Components to Nodes

Classes and collaborations as defined in the logical design are allocated to components in which they are implemented. The allocation is driven by the programming language used. For example, C++ implements a class in two files: a header file (.h) containing the specification and an implementation file (.cpp) containing the implementation of the operations. Java implements a class in just one file, containing both the specification and the implementation. Some languages, such as Java, have a modular concept on larger scale than a class, which can be used to group classes. This can be mapped to implement the package mechanism in UML (it is also called a package in Java). The programming language defines the rules for allocating classes to components.

The processes are allocated to the components in which they execute. The allocation is driven by the need of active objects or by the need to geographically distribute the system. Identifying the need of parallel execution (i.e., active objects) and the division of a system into a number of active objects was discussed in Chapter 6.

Finally, components are allocated to nodes. A component instance executes on at least one node instance, and possibly on several. The allocation of components to nodes can also affect the actual topology, so that changes have to be made to the proposed configuration in terms of nodes. There are a number of aspects to consider when allocating components to nodes:

- *Resource usage*: One of the main goals when determining the physical architecture and the allocation of components is the resource usage of the hardware. Hardware should of course be utilized in an efficient manner, to the full capacity of each node (without overusing, which results in poor performance).

- *Geographical location*: Decisions have to be made regarding where specific functionality is required (on which nodes), and what functionality must be available locally (because of performance, or if it must be available even if other nodes are not operating).

- *Access to devices*: What are the needs for a specific device on a node? Can the printer be connected to the server, or does every client need a local printer?

- *Security*: Which architecture handles access rights and protection of information in an optimized and efficient way? Access control may concern both geographical location (having the server in a secure place) as well as the communication solutions (using secure hardware and software to communicate).

- *Performance*: The need for high performance will sometimes affect the location of a component. It is possible to improve performance by creating proxies on a local node, substituting for the real component available on another node.

- *Extensibility and portability*: When different nodes have different operating systems or machine architecture, you must consider which components can be dependent on a specific operating system and which must be portable to a number of operating systems. This affects the location of those components and perhaps the programming language for implementation as well.

Iterative design is required to produce the deployment diagram. Various solutions have to be tested, first by discussion during the modeling phase and later by implementing prototypes. Ideally the system will be flexible so that a specific component can be moved between different nodes. A distributed object system such as OLE or CORBA will enable the creation of such systems.

Summary

The system architecture can be divided into logical and physical categories. The logical architecture shows the classes and objects, along with their relationships and collaborations, which together make up the functional aspects of the system. The logical architecture is documented in use-case, class, state, sequence, collaboration, and activity diagrams.

The physical architecture deals with the structure of the code components and of the hardware that constitutes the system. It details the physical implementation of the concepts defined in the logical architecture. Classes are allocated to the components that implement them. These components can exist in different stages: compile time, link time, or run time. A run-time component is typically dependent on link-time components (which are linked either statically or dynamically), and a link-time component depends on one or more compile-time components (which are compiled to produce the link component). Components and their dependencies are shown in a component diagram in UML.

A deployment diagram depicts the hardware nodes and their connections to each other. A node is a physical object such as a computer or a device, and can be described both as a type and an instance. Stereotypes can be applied to nodes to show that they belong to a family of nodes with some specific capability, such as the stereotype «printer». Connections between nodes are represented by association, indicating that the nodes can communicate with each other. A stereotype on the association can identify the protocol or physical medium used, such as «TCP/IP». Executable components can be allocated to the nodes in which they execute, and objects (passive or active) can be allocated to the components in which they live. A deployment diagram can map all the way from the physical ap-

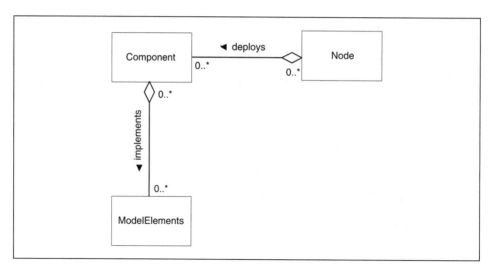

Figure 7.13 *Nodes deploy components that implement UML model elements. This allows for traceability in the models, from physical components executing in nodes to their logical equivalents.*

pearance of the system, via the components and objects that execute in the computers, to the logical design of the system, as shown in use-case, class, and interaction diagrams (see Figure 7.13).

8 *Extending the UML*

To avoid making the UML overly complex, the designers left out some definitions and mechanisms that are available in other modeling languages. Then they made the UML extendible, so that it can be adapted and extended to fit a specific method, organization, or user. Through these extension mechanisms, a user can define and use new elements. The intention is that CASE tools should support user-defined extensions as well as built-in elements.

The extension mechanisms are based on the existing UML elements, then add new semantics to the variants of those elements. New semantics could take the form of a redefinition, an addition, or some kind of constraint of an element's usage. UML has three types of mechanisms used for extending the core. These mechanisms have also been used to define a number of standard extensions, variants of existing elements. This chapter introduces all the standard UML extensions, then illustrates how UML can be extended with new user-defined mechanisms.

The three extension mechanisms are tagged values (properties), constraints, and stereotypes:

- *Tagged values* are properties attached to UML elements. Preconditions and postconditions attached to operations in a class are examples of standard tagged values.

- *Constraints* are rules that restrict the semantics of one or more elements in the UML. Constraints can be attached to classes or objects, and are often attached to relationships where they constrain the classes or objects that can participate in a relationship.

- A *stereotype* is the most sophisticated extension mechanism. It is a semantic attached to an existing model element. If a stereotype is attached to an element, the stereotype overrides the semantics defined for the element, which can then be seen as a new element based on an existing element. Typical stereotypes are metaclasses, which are defined for classes, and imports, which are defined for dependency relationships between packages. In both cases, the stereotypes add new or extra semantics to the element (the class or the dependency relationship).

There are a number of reasons to extend the UML. For example, the method being used might have some special concepts that are not directly supported in the UML, but that can be expressed by extending UML. The application domain or the organization might have some common concepts that are important enough to be defined in the modeling language. Alternatively, the modeler may want to create more precise and clear models, which is possible by extending the UML. All such extensions can be made through tagged values, constraints, and stereotypes.

Semantic Core Concept

In order to implement user-defined extensions, it is important to familiarize yourself with the UML's semantics or at least the core semantics. The extension mechanisms have been carefully defined so that the UML is a modeling language that essentially can extend itself. Both syntax and semantics are formally defined. Notation guidelines define the syntax in the UML reference manual (as in this book), and metamodels define the UML semantics. A metamodel describes other models; metamodels in the UML reference manual describe the UML. Furthermore, the metamodels in the reference manual are expressed in UML, which means that the UML is itself described with UML models. This can lead to confusion when approaching these metamodels, since they can seem very complex. The alternative is to have another modeling language (a metamodeling language) describe the UML, but this is also very confusing.

As an aid, this section provides a simplified description of the formal semantics given in the UML reference manual. Again, we recommend that you have a basic knowledge about the core semantics before you define your own extensions. This will also help you to understand the underlying model of the UML, and why it has been defined as it has.

An *element* is the abstract base class for most constituents in the UML. It acts as an anchor to which a number of mechanisms may be attached. An element is specialized to model elements, view elements, system, and model. A model element is an abstraction drawn from the system being modeled, such as a class, a message, nodes, an event, and so on. A view element is a projection—textual or graphical—of a single model element or a collection of model elements. The view elements are textual or graphical symbols, such as a rectangle symbol representing a class. This means that the model elements are the concepts and the view elements are the symbols used to build the models (diagrams). The view elements are also specialized to diagrams; they are use-case, component, class, deployment, state, activity, sequence, collaboration, and object diagrams. All elements can have names. The UML is modeled with the UML, and therefore, all the concepts used in the language are defined as classes. For example, an association is defined as a class with some attributes that describe what an association is.

A package "owns" elements and refers to them, as shown in Figure 8.1. A package is a grouping mechanism that can own or refer to elements (or to other packages). The elements within a package can be various kinds of elements, such as model elements, view elements, models, and systems. A package is thus a general grouping mechanism in the UML.

Model elements are specialized to artifacts that are useful when modeling systems. Most model elements have corresponding view elements that represent them. However, certain model elements exist without representation, such as the behavior in a model element, which cannot be visually depicted in a model. The class diagram in Figure 8.2 shows how the model elements are specialized to all the modeling concepts used in the UML. The model elements are specialized to the following subclasses:

- *Type*: A description of a set of instances that share the same operations, abstract attributes and relationships, and semantics. The type is specialized to primitive type, class, and use case. The class is specialized to active class, signal, component, and node. All type subclasses have a corresponding view element.

- *Instance*: An individual member described by a type. An instance of a class (the subclass to type) is an object. An object is similar to an instance (but normally used only for instances of classes).

- *Behavior instance*: An instance of a behavior.

- *Note*: A comment attached to an element or a collection of elements. A note has no semantics. The model element note has a corresponding view element.

- *Value*: An element of a type domain. The type domain is the domain specified for a certain type; for example, the number 42 is in the type domain of integer.

- *Stereotype*: A type of modeling element that extends the semantics of the UML. Stereotypes must be based on elements that are already defined in the UML. Stereotypes may extend the semantics, but not the structure of

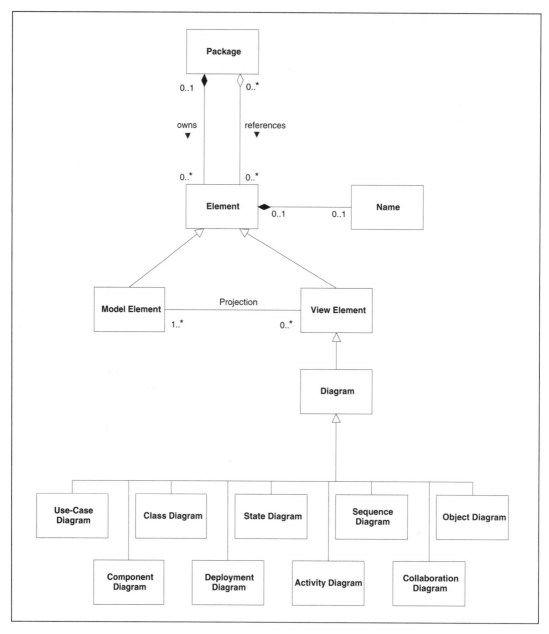

Figure 8.1 *A package owns and/or refers to elements, which can be model elements or view elements (or other elements such as system and model). View elements are projections of model elements. The view element projects a single model element or collections of model elements. The view elements are also specialized to nine different diagrams that are projections of collections of model elements.*

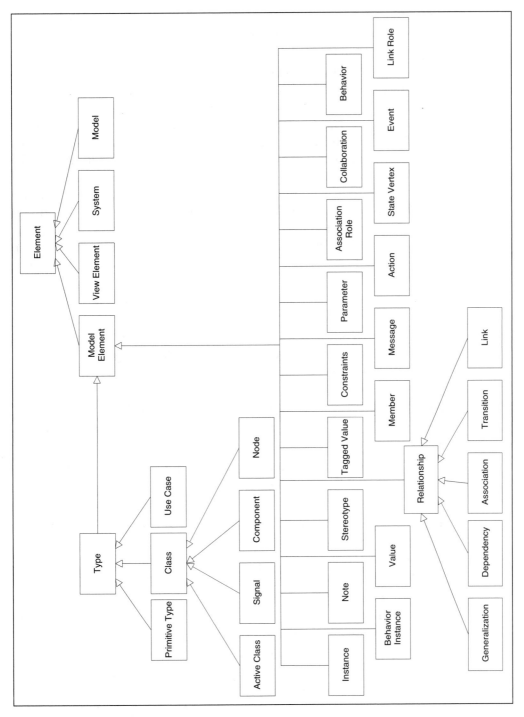

Figure 8.2 *The abstract class element is specialized to model element, view element, system, and model.*

preexisting elements. Certain stereotypes are predefined in UML; others may be user defined. Stereotypes have a corresponding view element, which is «name of the stereotype».

- *Relationship*: A semantic connection among model elements. The relationship is specialized to generalization, dependency, association, transition, and link. The generalization is a relationship between a more general and a more specific element. The more specific element is fully consistent with the more general element and contains additional information. An instance of the more specific element may be used where the more general element can be used. The dependency is a relationship between two model elements, in which a change to one model element (the independent model element) will affect the other model element (the dependent model element). An association is a relationship that describes a set of links. A link is a semantic connection among a tuple of objects. A transition is a relationship between two states that indicates that an object in the first state will perform certain specified actions and enter the second state when a specified event occurs and specified conditions are satisfied. There is a corresponding view element for each type of relationship.

- *Tagged value*: The explicit definition of a property as a name-value pair. In a tagged value, the name is referred to as the tag. Certain tags are predefined in the UML. The corresponding view element is a property-list. In UML, property is used in a general sense for any value connected to an element, including attributes in classes, associations, and tagged values.

- *Member*: A part of a type or class denoting either an attribute or an operation.

- *Constraints*: A semantic condition or restriction. Certain constraints are predefined in the UML. There are some corresponding view elements for constraints.

- *Messages*: A communication between objects that conveys information with the expectation that activity will ensue. The receipt of a message is normally considered an event. There are corresponding view elements of different types of messages.

- *Parameter*: The specification of a variable that can be changed, passed, or returned. A parameter may include a name, type, and direction. Parameters are used for operations, messages, and events.

- *Action*: An action is the invocation of a signal or an operation, representing a computational or algorithmic procedure.

- *Association role*: The role that a type or class plays in an association. There is a corresponding view element.

- *State vertex*: A source or target of a transition.

- *Collaboration*: A context that supports a set of interactions. An interaction is a specification that comprises a set of message exchanges among a set of objects within a particular context to accomplish a specific task.

- *Event*: A significant occurrence in time or space. An event has corresponding view elements.

- *Behavior*: A behavior is an observable effect, including its results.

- *Link role*: An instance of an association role.

All elements may have dependency relationships to other elements. The dependency relationship is also inherited by all the element subclasses, including the subclasses stereotype, constraint, and tagged value. The elements contain zero or one stereotype, zero or many tagged values, and have a derived dependency relationship to constraints. The derived dependency relationship between element and constraint has the multiplicity one at the element end and zero or more at the constraint end (see Figure 8.3).

Not all elements may be specialized or generalized; only generalizable elements may be specialized or generalized. The generalizable elements are stereotype, package, and type. Subclasses to generalizable elements are also generalizable. The type has the subclasses primitive type, class, and use-case. The class has the subclasses active class, signal, component, and node. Thus all these classes are specialized or generalized. Note that stereotypes can be specialized (see Figure 8.4).

Sometimes, it's useful to specialize or generalize associations, but this is not possible in the UML because association is not a generalizable element. However, the subset constraint between two or more associations can work as a surrogate.

If a tagged value, stereotype, or constraint is attached to a model element, a specialization to that model element will have the same tagged value, stereotype, or constraint. If a generalization has a stereotype, a specialization to that generalization may not have an additional stereotype. An element may have only zero or one stereotype, including any inherited stereotypes.

Core Semantics Summary

The element is the abstract base class for most constituents of the UML; it provides an anchor to which a number of mechanisms may be attached. The element is specialized to model elements, view elements, system, and model. A model element is

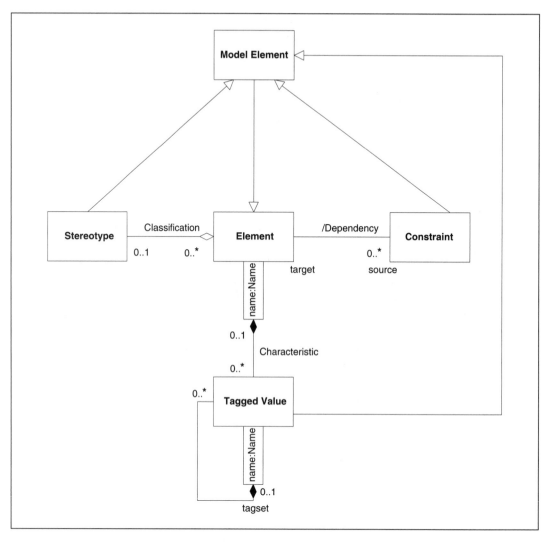

Figure 8.3 *An element may have zero or one stereotype, many constraints, and many tagged values. The tagged values may be a set of tagged values. Stereotype, constraint, and tagged value are all model elements, meaning that they are also elements.*

an abstraction drawn from the system being modeled. Some important model elements are type, relationship, stereotype, constraint, tagged values, state vertex, event, and message. The type and relationship model elements are both specialized into further subclasses. A view element is a projection (textual or graphical) of model elements. There is a view element (symbol) for single model elements, such

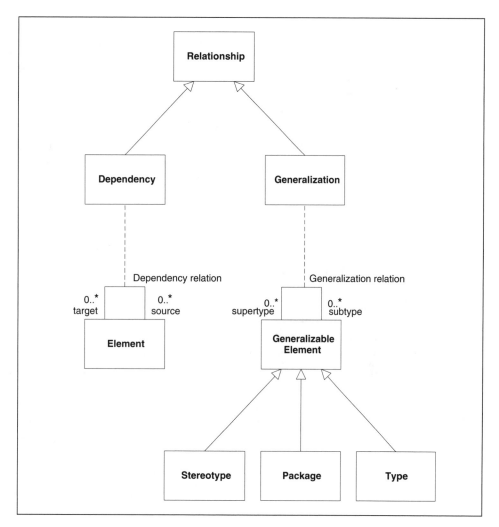

Figure 8.4 *Two of the relationships in UML are dependency and generalization. The dependency relationship may connect all kinds of model elements, but the generalization relationship may connect only generalizable elements, which are stereotype, package, and type (and their subclasses). The other relationships are association, transition, and link. Association may connect only types, and links may connect only instances of types. Transitions may connect only states (vertex).*

as class, node, state, and association, but there are also view elements for collections of model elements, what the UML calls diagrams. Again, the nine diagrams defined in the UML are: use-case, component, class, deployment, state, activity, sequence, collaboration, and object diagrams.

Elements may be grouped in packages; the packages may also contain other packages. Stereotype, package, and type (primitive type, class, active class, signal, component, node, and use-case) are generalizable elements, meaning that they may be specialized and generalized.

Stereotypes, constraints, and tagged values are mechanisms used to extend the UML. The UML has some predefined extensions, which are used to adapt or extend existing elements to become these extensions. An element may have only zero or one stereotype and many constraints and tagged values. If a tagged value, stereotype, or constraint is attached to an element, a specialization to that element will have the same tagged value, stereotype, or constraint. If a generalization has a stereotype, a specialization to that generalization may not have an additional stereotype.

Tagged Values and Properties

A property is used in a general sense for any value connected to an element. Properties are used to add information to model elements, and the information can be used both by humans and machines. Humans may use them to add administrative information about the models; for example, author of a model, time it was last modified, and so on. Machines may use them to process the models in a certain way; for example, code generation may be parameterized by properties in the model to tell the code generator what kind of code to generate. Note that properties are normally not present in the finished system. They contain information about the models and the elements *in the models*, not information that should be handled by the final system.

A tagged value is the explicit definition of a property as a name-value pair. In a tagged value, the name is referred to as the tag. Each tag represents a particular kind of property applicable to one or more kinds of elements. Both the tag and the value are encoded as strings. The notation for a property is:

```
{tag = value} or {tag1 = value1, tag2 = value2…} or {tag}
```

The property or properties are displayed inside braces, with a tag and a value. If the tag is a Boolean flag, then the default value is true if the value is omitted. Tags of types other than Boolean require explicit values. A value can be defined as uninterpreted (typically a string), which means that there is no formal definition of the syntax for the value. Such values are typically meant to be read by a human, who then interprets the value as a free text string; and where the tag name defines a context, that gives a meaning to the tagged value. For example:

```
{abstract}
{status = "under construction", system analyst = "Bob Smith"}
```

Properties (including tagged values) may be shown in the diagrams or be separately documented. When shown, properties are enclosed within braces inside or close to the element for which they are defined. Some CASE tools have a property window that can be revealed by executing a command on an element. This window lists all the properties of the element with their values. As noted, there are a number of predefined tagged values (standard tagged values) in the UML for elements, model elements, types, instances, operations, attributes, and components. In addition, a method or tool using the UML can add more tagged values to adapt UML to the method or the tool.

Tagged Values for Elements

Documentation is a tag for documenting the element instances to which they are attached. The value is just a string. This tagged value is typically shown separately (rather than in the diagram where the element is located); for example, in a tool, the value is shown in a property or documentation window. A value for a documentation tag attached to a class named Insurance Contract could be a description of the purpose of the class:

```
This class serves as a contract between the customer
(policyholder) and the insurer (insurance company).
```

Tagged Values for Types, Instances, Operations, and Attributes

There are nine tagged values that apply to types, instances, operations, and attributes. They are:

Invariant

Postcondition

Precondition

Responsibility

Abstract

Persistence

Semantics

Space semantics

Time semantics

Invariant applies to a type. It specifies a property that is preserved over the lifetime of an instance of the type. The property is usually some kind of condition that must be valid for the type instance. Some languages, such as Eiffel, have built-in support for invariants, and they can be directly implemented into the final code. The syntax of the value is uninterpreted, and usually not shown in the diagram.

A value for an invariant tag attached to a color attribute in a class named Car could be:

```
The value of the attribute color may not change during the
lifetime of the object.
```

A more formal invariant tag could be:

```
Car.Speed >= 0 (meaning that the speed may never be negative)
```

Postcondition applies to an operation. It is a condition that must be true after the completion of an operation. The value is uninterpreted, and usually not shown in the diagram.

A value for a postcondition tag attached to the operation sort(listOfElements : list) could be:

```
The list must be sorted after the completion of the sort
operation.
```

Precondition also applies to an operation. It is a condition that must be true before the operation is invoked. The value is uninterpreted, and typically not shown in the diagram.

A value for a precondition tag attached to the operation sort(listOfElements : list) could be:

```
The number of elements in list must be greater than one.
```

Invariants, preconditions, and postconditions are often used together to implement the technique known as *programming by contract*. An invariant is a condition that the *class implementor* guarantees to be true throughout the execution of the system. A precondition is one that the *caller* of an operation guarantees to be true before the operation is called; and the postcondition is one that the *operation implementor* guarantees to be true after the operation has been executed. Should anyone break any of these "contracts," the system may throw an exception (typically indicating an internal programming error in the system).

Responsibility is a tag that specifies the responsibility for a type; its value is a string. The responsibility is normally expressed in terms of obligations to other elements.

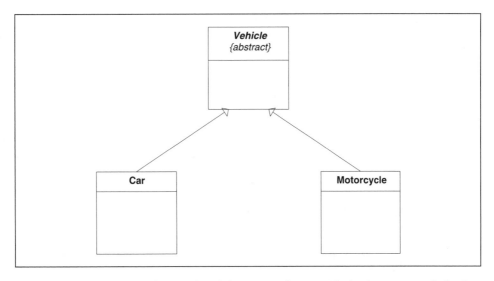

Figure 8.5 *Vehicle is an abstract class. This means that no Vehicle objects exist. Only Car and Motorcycle objects exist.*

Abstract is a tagged value that indicates that a class cannot have any objects, as shown in Figure 8.5. The class is there to be inherited and specialized into other, concrete, classes. The value is Boolean, which means that it's not necessary to show that the value is explicitly true since it's the default value. This tagged value is typically shown in class diagrams, within the class name compartment under the class name.

Persistence applies to a type. Defining a class as persistent means that objects of the class may be stored in a database or file, and that the object may retain its value (state) between different executions of the program. Attributes in the class can be specified as transitory or persistent (enumerated values), and only those attributes that are explicitly stated as being persistent will be part of the persistent state stored. The fact that a class is defined as persistent does not mean that all its objects must be stored as persistent (a specific instance can be defined as being transitory); it only indicates that the capability to be stored persistently exists. How the object is stored physically—for example, in a database table—is typically defined in the design phase. Persistence may be shown in the class diagram (e.g., {persistent} in the class name compartment).

Semantics, *space semantics*, and *time semantics* apply to types and operations. Semantics is the specification of the meaning of a type or operation. Space semantics is the specification of the meaning of the space complexity of the associated type or operation. Time semantics is the specification of the meaning of the time complexity of the associated type or operation. These tagged values are used only in specifying the UML (in the UML reference manual), and thus are not discussed in further detail here.

Tagged Values for Model Elements and Components

Location is a tagged value that applies to model elements and components. The location tells in which component (such as a source code file) a certain model element is located, or in which node (such as a computer) a certain component is located. The value of the location is either a component or a node.

Defining Your Own Tagged Values

A tagged value is composed of a name (the tag) and a value (of a type) and may be connected to all kinds of elements. A tagged value is used to add extra semantics to an attached element. Often, user-defined tagged values are used to add administrative information about the progress or status of a project, or information for further transformations of the models such as code or database generation. Tagged values are extra information needed about the models and the model elements, and are not directly visible in the final system (though they may be indirectly visible if they affected the implementation of the system).

To define a tagged value, follow these steps:

1. Investigate the purpose of the tagged value.
2. Define the elements it may be attached to.
3. Name the tagged value appropriately.
4. Define the type of the value.
5. Know who or what will interpret it, a machine or a human? If it is a machine, the value must be specified in a more formal syntax (e.g., in a formal language such as C++, algebraically, using predicate logic, etc.). If it is a human, the value can be more loosely specified (e.g., an uninterpreted string).
6. Document one or more examples on how to use the tagged value.

Two examples of possible user-defined tagged values are Standard algorithm and Author. The Standard algorithm should be attached to an operation within a class. The name of the tag is Standard algorithm and the value is a string. The value should be the name of the Standard algorithm. This tagged value could be used for CASE tools to generate code or as an instruction to a human. Examples of standard algorithms are quick sort and FFT. For example:

```
{Standard algorithm = "Quick sort"}
```

The Author tagged value can be attached to any element. It tells the name of the responsible author (the person who modeled an element; e.g., a class diagram, an operation, etc.). The value is a string. This tagged value can be used together with a configuration management tool to track responsible model authors and so on. For example:

```
{Author = "Peter Smith"}
```

Constraints

A constraint is a semantic condition or restriction on elements. Constraints are applied to elements; one constraint applies to one kind of element, thus, while a constraint can involve many elements, they must be of the same kind (e.g., many associations, as in the or-association). The constraints are displayed in braces ({constraint}), either directly in the diagrams or separately (typically available through a constraint window in a CASE tool). If a constraint is applied to a model element (e.g., a class) that has a corresponding view element (e.g., a rectangle with tree compartments), it can be displayed directly in the diagram next to the view element it constrains. If many elements of the same kind are involved in a constraint, the constraint should be displayed near a dashed line that crosses all the elements involved in the constraint (e.g., the or-constraint). In the UML, there are 14 standard constraints: association, global, local, parameter, self, complete, disjoint, incomplete, overlapping, implicit, or, ordered, vote, and broadcast. It is also possible to have user-defined constraints, which may be defined separately (like tagged values and stereotypes) or directly in a diagram near a view element (e.g., {person.boss.salary >= person.assistant.salary}).

Constraints for Generalization

Complete, disjoint, incomplete, and overlapping are four constraints that are applied to generalization; specifically, they are applicable only to generalizations with more than one specialization—subclasses. These constraints are semantic and are shown in braces (comma-separated) near the shared hollowed triangle, if several paths share a single hollowed triangle in the generalization. If the paths don't share a single hollowed triangle, a dashed line crosses through all inheritance lines, and the constraints are shown in braces near the dashed line (see Figure 8.6).

Overlapping inheritance means that any further subclasses inherited from the subclasses in the inheritance relationship can inherit more than one of the subclasses. In other words, it's possible to use multiple inheritance with a common superclass in the inheritance tree, as shown in Figure 8.7.

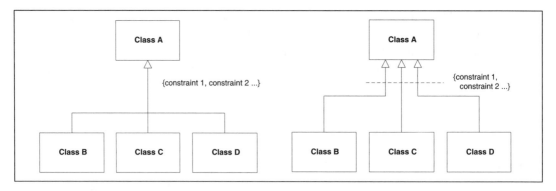

Figure 8.6 *Different ways of showing constraints on generalization.*

Disjoint inheritance is the default manner of inheritance. It's the opposite of overlapping inheritance. To have a disjoint inheritance, subclasses inheriting from a common superclass are not allowed to be specialized to one common subclass (through multiple inheritance).

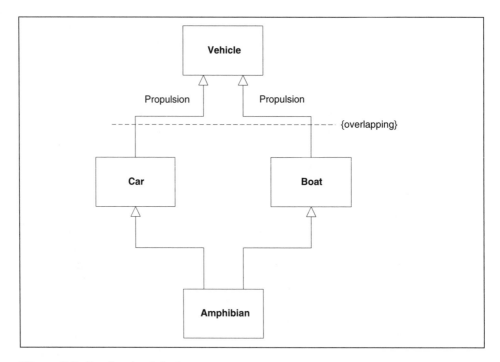

Figure 8.7 *Overlapping inheritance.*

In the constraint *complete generalization*, all subclasses in an inheritance relationship are specified; no additional subclasses can be added afterward. *Incomplete generalization* is the opposite of complete generalization, so additions can be added later. Incomplete generalization is the default.

Constraints for Associations

There are two default constraints applied to associations: *implicit* and *or*. The implicit constraint specifies that an association is conceptual, rather than physical. An implicit association connects classes, but the objects are not necessarily aware of each other. An implicit association is also an association in which objects don't have physical links to each other; instead, an object in the association becomes associated to the other object through some other mechanism, such as a global name of the object or a query object.

The or-constraint specifies that a set of associations has constraints on their links. The or-constraint is applied where an association connects a single class to a set of other classes. The or-constraint specifies that an object of the single class is connected (linked) only to one of the associated class objects (on the opposite side of the association). For instance, a person can have many (zero or more) insurance contracts and a company can have many insurance contracts, as shown in Figure 8.8. The model doesn't indicate whether an insurance contract can be owned by both a person and a company at the same time. To specify that an insurance con-

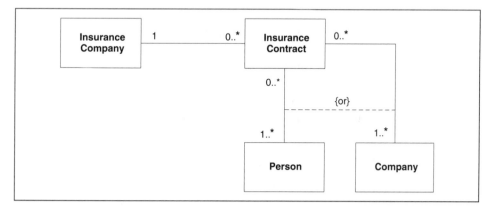

Figure 8.8 *A Person/Company can have zero or more Insurance Contracts. A contract can be owned by one or many Persons or by one or many Companies. Without the or-association, one or many Persons and one or many Companies can own the Insurance Contract. If multiplicity were changed at the Person or Company side (saying zero or more), this would affect the semantics, allowing an Insurance Contract to be owned by no one.*

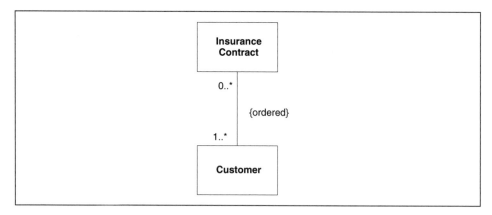

Figure 8.9 *The constraint {ordered} specifies that there is an explicit order between the links. The exact order may be shown inside the braces; for example, {ordered by increasing time}.*

tract can be owned only by either one person or one company, the or-constraint is used to restrict the associations between Insurance Contract and Person and between Insurance Contract and Company.

Constraints for Association Roles

The *ordered constraint* is the only standard constraint for association roles. An ordered association specifies that there is an implicit order between the links within the association. Windows are ordered on a screen, for example; one window is on top, one window is at the bottom, and so on. Therefore the association between the screen and the windows is ordered. The default value for an association is unordered, meaning the links may be in any order. The constraint is displayed in braces near the association, as shown in Figure 8.9. Both ordered and unordered constraints can be shown explicitly, though unordered is the default constraint for all associations, and doesn't have to be specified.

Constraints for Messages, Link Roles, and Objects

Nine constraints apply to interactions. Interactions can be viewed from the perspective of time, via sequence diagrams, space, via collaboration diagrams, or work, via activity diagrams. In all types of interaction diagrams (sequence, collaboration, and activity), messages, objects, and link roles are vital concepts. The objects are connected to each other via links (instances of associations). Each link has two link roles—instances of association roles. When objects interact, they play roles (the linked roles) and send messages among each other via the links.

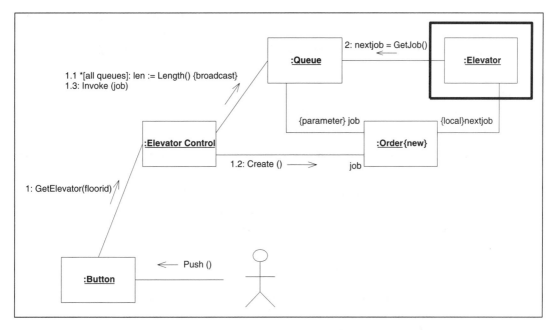

Figure 8.10 *The collaboration diagram shows how the objects collaborate to realize the push operation in the Button class. The objects in the collaboration diagram are instances in an elevator system. When a user hits the Push button (on a floor), the button sends a Push () message to the Elevator Control. The elevator control asks each Queue (one queue per Elevator) which one is the shortest, and then creates a job. It then sends the message Invoke (job) to the Elevator with the shortest queue. The Length message sent to each queue is a broadcast message. The invoke operation sends a job (which is a parameter to the Queue). The job is an object of the Order class created by the class Elevator Control objects. The Elevator asks its Queue for new jobs to perform.*

The constraints applied to these vital concepts are global, local, parameter, self, vote, broadcast, new, destroyed, and transient, as shown in Figure 8.10.

- *Global* is a constraint applied to a link role specifying that the corresponding instance is visible because it's in a global scope. The instance is available through a global name that is known throughout the system.
- *Local* is a constraint applied to a link role specifying that the corresponding instance is visible because it's a local variable in an operation.
- *Parameter* is a constraint applied to a link role specifying that the corresponding instance is visible because it's a parameter in an operation.
- *Self* is a constraint applied to a link role specifying that an object can send messages to itself (typically used in dispatchers).

- *Vote* is a constraint applied to a message, and restricts a collection of return messages. The vote constraint specifies that the return value is selected through a majority vote of all the return values in the collection.

- *Broadcast* is a constraint applied to messages specifying that the messages are not invoked in a certain order.

- *New* is a constraint that affects the life cycle of objects. The object is created during an execution of the interaction.

- *Destroyed* is a constraint that affects the life cycle of objects. The object is destroyed during an execution of an interaction.

- *Transient* is a constraint that affects the life cycle of objects. Transient objects are created and destroyed in the same execution of an operation. It is a combination of the new and destroyed constraints.

Defining Your Own Constraints

As noted, user-defined constraints are also permitted. A user-defined constraint is specified for the element to which it applies. The semantic impact—what it means to apply the constraint to an element—is also specified. Constraints are used to limit element semantics in terms of conditions or restrictions of the semantics. Consequently, when a user-defined constraint is specified, it's important to evaluate all the effects it might have. As with all types of specifications, it's useful to give examples on how the constraint can be used. Thus, to specify a constraint, it's necessary to describe:

- To which element the user-defined constraint applies.
- The semantic impact on the element of the user-defined constraint.
- One or more examples of how to apply the user-defined constraint.
- How the user-defined constraint can be implemented.

An example of a user-defined constraint, Singleton, (that can be applied to classes) is shown in Figure 8.11 and described in the following paragraphs.

A class with the Singleton constraint has a restriction on the number of objects it may have at the same time. The Singleton class can have only one object at a time. Singleton classes can be used for wrappers, where many coexisting objects can be problematic. For example, if you wrap legacy C code, the code might cause problems when executed in many simultaneous instances. Singleton classes, typically available throughout the system, can also be used for global configuration objects that should exist only in one instance.

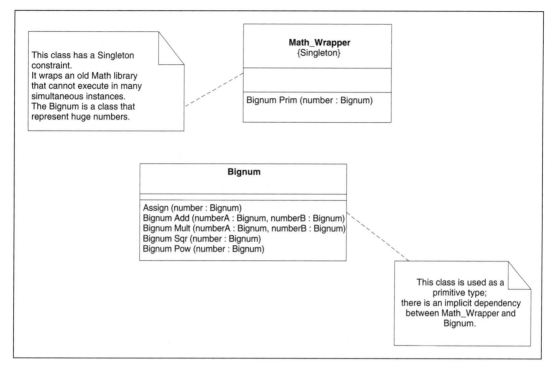

Figure 8.11 *An example with a Singleton class. The Math_Wrapper wraps an old Math library that cannot execute in many simultaneous instances. The Math_Wrapper class has a Singleton constraint.*

A Singleton class can be implemented with a class-scope attribute, which is used as an instance counter. The class constructor increments the class-scope attributes value every time it is called, that is, every time someone creates an object of the class. The destructor, which is in the class, decrements the class-scope attributes value every time it is called—every time someone destroys an object of the class. The default value of the class-scope attribute's value must be zero because no objects exist before the class; when the class-scope attribute's value is other than zero or one, an exception is thrown. A variant of this is to provide a class-scope operation to access the Singleton instance. When the instance counter is incremented to one from zero, this class-scope operation creates the only instance and returns it; and when called again, it returns the only existing instance repeatedly.

Generally the user-defined constraints are defined separately (like tagged values and stereotypes), but they can also be defined directly in a diagram near a view element. If the constraints are defined directly in a diagram, the navigation syntax is used. An example of constraints specified directly in a diagram are rules that constrain attributes or links.

Stereotypes

All model languages have their restrictions and limits, especially when it comes to semantics. When the semantics of a language are too general, it undermines the possibilities to make distinct and sharp statements about systems. Conversely, if the semantics are too specialized, this limits the possible statements. Specialized languages also tend to become very complex and extensive. C++ can be seen as a modeling language, but it is specialized for programming and is not that powerful for business modeling.

The stereotype mechanism is used to specialize semantics of elements already defined in the UML. Elements within the UML have general semantics, but with the possibility to be specialized and extended with stereotypes. Instead of adding properties or applying constraints to a model element, new semantics are added to an existing element. This can be seen as a kind of specialization of an existing model element type. Whenever a concept (any kind of element including relationships) is missing, it can be defined by, first, finding the existing model element that looks the most like the concept, and then adding or redefining the necessary semantics (a practical approach). Note that stereotypes may extend the semantics, but not the structure of preexisting elements.

Stereotypes are generalizable elements, which means that they can be specialized or generalized. If a generalizable element (type, package, or stereotype) has a stereotype attached to it and is specialized, the stereotype is also inherited by the specialization. This is also the case with tagged values and constraints.

There are more than 40 predefined stereotypes in the UML, and as with tagged values and constraints, it is possible to have user-defined stereotypes. Stereotypes always have a corresponding view element, which is the text string «name of the stereotype» (the characters used before and after the string are guillemets, « »). The view element (the stereotype string «name») is generally placed above or in front of the name of the element on which it is based. A stereotype is a semantic redefinition or extension to already defined element semantics. Stereotypes are typically applied to classes, types, relationships, nodes, components, and operations.

A graphical icon can be associated with a stereotype, but this is optional. The graphical icon can be colored. There are different ways of using icons together with stereotypes. The first is to display the icon inside the stereotyped element. If a

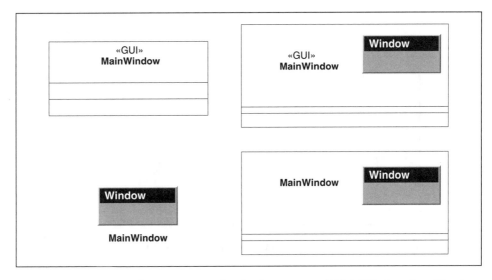

Figure 8.12 *Varieties of stereotype notation for the stereotyped MainWindow class. The class is of the stereotype «GUI» which has a graphical window icon as its visual representation.*

class is stereotyped, an icon can be attached to the name compartment in the class rectangle symbol (the view element). If the icon is displayed directly in an element, you can either display both the icon and the stereotype name or just the icon. The second way of displaying icons is to collapse the stereotyped element into the icon itself, with the name of the element above or below the icon (see Figure 8.12).

Stereotypes Applied to Type

Actor

An actor is a stereotyped type representing an abstraction that lies just outside the system being modeled. An actor lies outside the systems border but may still be of interest, especially when specifying how external actors interact with the system and which functions they require of the system. The actor stereotype is implemented in use-case modeling, as described in Chapter 3. Class is a subclass of type, and therefore the stereotype actor can be, and often is, applied to classes. Thus an actor in a use case is a class and can have attributes, operations, and relationships to other classes; but an actor is also of the stereotype «actor», which gives the class special semantics, as just described. The actor stereotype has the stickman icon (see Figure 8.13).

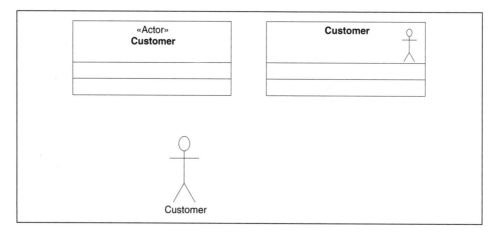

Figure 8.13 *The stereotype actor shown in different representations and with the stickman icon.*

Interface

An interface is a stereotyped type that publishes the behavior of types—classes, nodes, components, and so on. Interfaces can be connected to packages, components, and classes. When a package, component, or class has an interface connected to it, it is said to implement or support the specified interface (in that it supports the behavior defined in the interface). The interface is described as a class with the stereotype «interface» and usually consists only of abstract operations. An interface can be implemented (supported) in any number of components, packages, or classes, as shown in Figure 8.14.

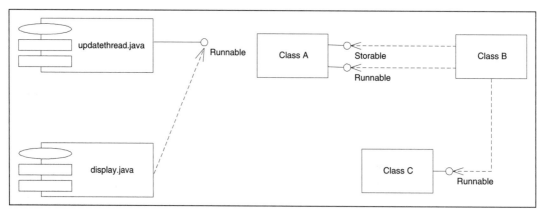

Figure 8.14 *Interfaces connected to classes and a component.*

Metaclass

A metaclass is a class whose instances are classes. Thus a metaclass is a class for classes. Metaclasses are useful in systems in which you need to declare classes at run-time. A metaclass is a stereotyped type, and is normally applied to classes (class is subclass to type, and therefore the stereotype metaclass may also be applied to classes). A metaclass may be applied to all kinds of types (i.e., subclasses to type) such as classes, primitive types, and use cases. The metaclass does not have an icon; it is just marked with the string «Metaclass». Metaclasses can be implemented in programming languages such as Smalltalk.

Powertype

When a generalization is specialized, a discriminator can be used to specify on what basis the inheritance is made. In a generalization structure where a superclass Purchase has the subclasses Purchase On Credit, Cash Purchase, and Hire Purchase, the discriminator could be payment, since that is what discriminates the instances of the subclasses.

The discriminator is used to separate instances; it works at the instance level. The discriminator type is called a *powertype*. A powertype works at the type level, and indicates on which basis the supertype (the generalized type) is specialized to subtypes. Thus, when we talk about instances, we use discriminators to specialize; and when we talk about types, we use powertypes to specialize.

Consider the following example. There are several methods of payment for purchases. One single purchase may be purchased on credit (credit payment). The instances of purchase can be classified and specialized by payment, and the purchase as concept (type) can be classified and specialized by method of payment. The discriminator is the payment and the powertype is the method of payment (see Figure 8.15).

A powertype is a stereotyped type, normally shown as a stereotyped class with the stereotype «Powertype» in a class diagram. Powertypes are optional; only a discriminator can be used (without showing the powertype of the discriminator).

Stereotypes Applied to Dependency

Becomes

Becomes is a stereotyped dependency whose source and target is the same instance, as shown in Figure 8.16. The becomes stereotype indicates that one instance will change state (in time/space) from one (the source instance state) to another (the

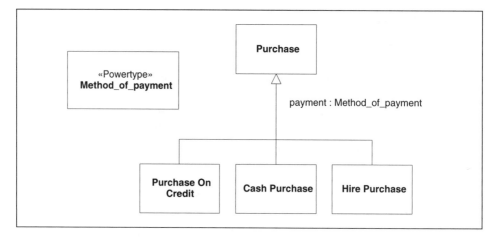

Figure 8.15 *A discriminator (Payment) and <<Powertype>> (Method_of_payment) used to specialize Purchase.*

target instance state). It can be used to show how objects move from one node to another—that is, where the location of an object changes in a distributed system— or in other situations where it might be useful to show explicitly how elements change their states.

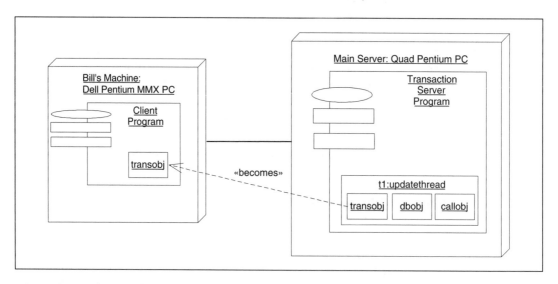

Figure 8.16 *The transobj in node Main Server becomes the transobj in node Bill's Machine.*

Call

Call is a stereotyped dependency connecting operations. If a class A has a call dependency to a class B, operations in class A may call any of the operations in class B.

Copy

A copy dependency connects two instances. If two instances are connected via a copy dependency, the source instance is an exact copy of the target instance (although they still have unique identities and are different instances).

Derived

The rules provided by the UML are either constraints or derivations. For example, an attribute can be derived from other attributes, as shown in Figure 8.17. The derivation is a stereotyped dependency.

Friend and Import

Friend is a stereotyped dependency from one package to another package. The friend dependency extends the visibility of an import between the packages. If the dependency is a friend, the source package can access elements in the target package with the public, protected, and private visibility but not with the implementation visibility. Thus a friend dependency gives special access for another package to elements that are defined as protected or private and normally should not be accessible to other packages.

The stereotyped import dependency between packages, which is the default, can only access elements within a package that has the public visibility.

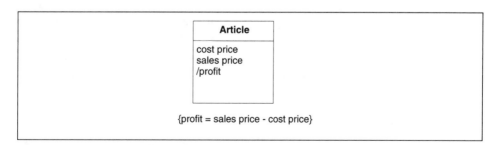

Figure 8.17 *The profit is a derived attribute. The formula (rule) for the derivation is shown within braces.*

Instance

The stereotyped instance dependency is a relationship between an instance and a corresponding type. The source is an instance and the target is a type. It can be used to explicitly show of which class an object is (with a stereotyped «instance» dependency from the object to the class).

Refinement

Refinement is a stereotyped dependency that has its own icon (which is also a view element in the UML). Refinement and its usage are described in more detail in Chapter 4. Refinement is a good example of how the UML is bootstrapped from a small kernel of model elements and how it is used to define and extend itself.

Role

The role is a stereotyped dependency between a type (class, node, etc.) and an association role. Roles are described in Chapter 4.

Send

Send is a stereotyped dependency where the source is an operation and the target is a signal (described as a class with the stereotype signal). The operation sends the signal.

Trace

A trace is a stereotyped dependency from one model element to another model element. The elements traced to each other may be in the same diagram or in different diagrams. The trace indicates that the source traces conceptually back to the target. The trace stereotype can be used to show that one diagram is a more detailed description of another diagram, or that a design diagram traces back to an analysis diagram of the same things.

Stereotypes Applied to Components

Several stereotypes can be applied to components. They are used to make the component diagram more precise and clear by defining what each component represents in the real world.

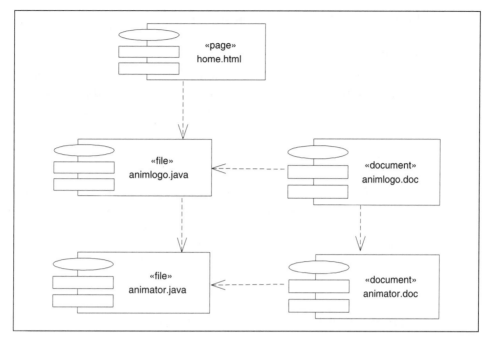

Figure 8.18 *Dependencies between source code components.*

- The stereotyped component «application» represents an executable program.

- The stereotyped component «document» is a representation of a document (containing documentation rather than source code that could be compiled).

- The stereotyped component «file» is a file containing source code (see Figure 8.18).

- The stereotyped component «library» can be used to show that a component is a static or dynamic library.

- The stereotyped component «page» is a representation of a Web page.

- The stereotyped component «table» represents a database table.

Stereotypes Applied to Note

A constraint is a stereotyped note that contains a constraint of the element to which the note is attached. A requirement is a stereotyped note that states a responsibility or obligation of the element to which the note is attached.

Stereotypes Applied to Primitive Type

Enumeration

An enumeration is a stereotyped primitive type, also known as a domain. It specifies a set of values, the allowed values, for the enumerated primitive type. Visibility is an enumeration in which the set of allowed values are public, protected, private, and implementation.

Utility

A utility is a stereotyped type that contains only class-scope operations and attributes. The utility doesn't have any instances; it's only a set of class-scope operations and attributes accessed through the type, not through any instance. A class-scope operation is called by specifying only the class name and the operation name, as in MathPack::sin(3.14). The utility is normally applied to classes, as shown in Figure 8.19.

Stereotypes Applied to Generalization

Extends

Extends is a stereotyped generalization between use cases implemented to specify that one use case inherits from another use case, and that parts of the inherited use case may be used when defining the specialized use case. Use case and the extends relationship are described in Chapter 3.

Uses

Uses is a stereotyped generalization between two use cases that describes that one use case is using another use case. The uses dependency is described in Chapter 3.

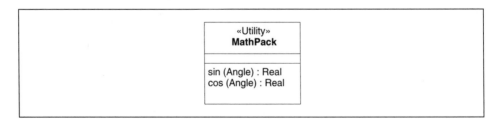

Figure 8.19 *A utility class for mathematical functions that are grouped together in a class and made available as class-scope operations.*

Stereotypes Applied to Packages

Façade

A *façade* is a stereotyped package that refers only to elements (imports, via friend dependency, etc.) from other packages. The façade does not own any elements (its contents are only referred to).

Stub

A *stub* is a stereotyped package that represents a package that is incompletely implemented; it presents a small piece of another system. You can have stubs for databases and so on.

Stereotypes Applied to Class

Signal

Signal is a stereotyped class that constrains the semantics of the objects of the class so that they can be sent only as signals, as shown in Figure 8.20. A signal is a named event that carries an object, and it's typically used in real-time systems where asynchronous messages are sent between different active objects. It's possible to build hierarchies of signals supporting polymorphism, so that if a state transition has an event-signature specifying a signal class, all the subclasses of that signal class will also be receivable and accepted in that case.

Control, Boundary, and Entity

Classes can be stereotyped to control, boundary, and entity. These stereotypes are used to increase the semantic meaning of the classes and their usage in modeling situations. They are based on the model-view-controller concept, where the entity is the model, the control is the controller, and the boundary is the view. The model-view-controller concept is a well-used solution (pattern) for building systems with an entity model, which is presented and manipulated via a graphical user interface (GUI), as shown in Figure 8.21. Since these stereotypes are based on the model-view-control concept, they are very useful when dealing with GUI-based systems. These stereotypes are also used in the Objectory process to analyze and realize use cases in more detail. In Objectory, they translate a use case described in plain text into the first level of analysis classes. The analysis classes are either an entity class (something to be stored in the system and implemented in many use cases), a boundary class (used to communicate with the external actors),

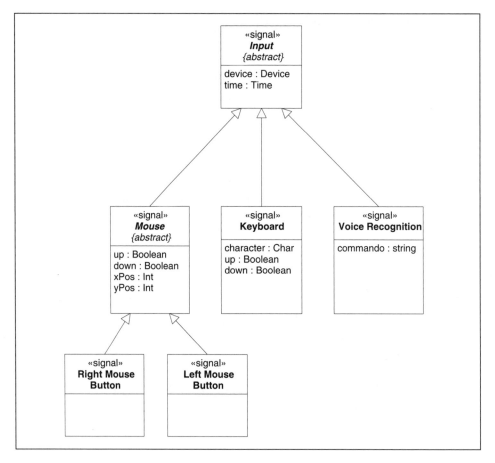

Figure 8.20 *A class hierarchy with signal stereotyped classes.*

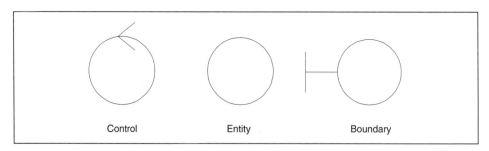

Figure 8.21 *The icons for the control, entity, and boundary stereotypes.*

or a control class (used to handle a specific use case or scenario, typically specialized to only one or a few use cases).

The *boundary* stereotype specializes in the usage of the class for presentation and manipulation. Boundary classes present and communicate the information in a system to another system, such as a human or a machine (i.e., actors). The boundary classes can also enable the manipulation of the information (through well-defined rules in the entity objects). Boundary classes are typically windows, dialogs, or communication classes, such as TCP/IP.

The *entity* stereotype is used to model business objects (the core concepts), such as debt, invoice, insurance contract, and so on. They are typically persistent so that they can be stored in the system.

The *control* stereotype is used to connect boundary objects with their entity objects and to handle a sequence of operations inside the system. The entity objects carry the information that should be presented and manipulated through boundary objects. Control objects typically handle the processing of the information in the entity objects, along with the functionality sequences that involve a number of entity objects.

By including these three simple stereotypes, a class diagram can be made more precise and easy to understand for the reader. The purpose and responsibility of a class is indicated by its stereotype and is immediately visible in the diagram. A more detailed description of the class can be accessed through the documentation and responsibility properties of the class. Furthermore, the relationships between classes are easily understood; for example, if a boundary class has an association to a entity class, it's usually the information in the entity class that is shown or manipulated through that boundary class.

User-defined stereotypes can define new stereotypes for classes, common class roles used in a specific application domain, where classes of a special type have their own icons and semantic meaning. For example, in the financial domain, possible stereotypes are «Asset», for describing classes that represent an item that has a price; or the stereotyped dependency «Affects», for showing that the price calculation of a instance of one class is affected by the price of an instance of another class—for example, the price of a stock option is affected by the price of the underlying stock. The organization that uses the stereotype decides how formal and extensive the semantics of a stereotype should be. However, the meaning of the stereotype should be well known by everyone reading the models in which the stereotype is used (see Figure 8.22).

Stereotypes Applied to Operations

A *constructor* is an operation that is called when objects are created; it may have arguments and may be explicitly called; it may have any name, but commonly it car-

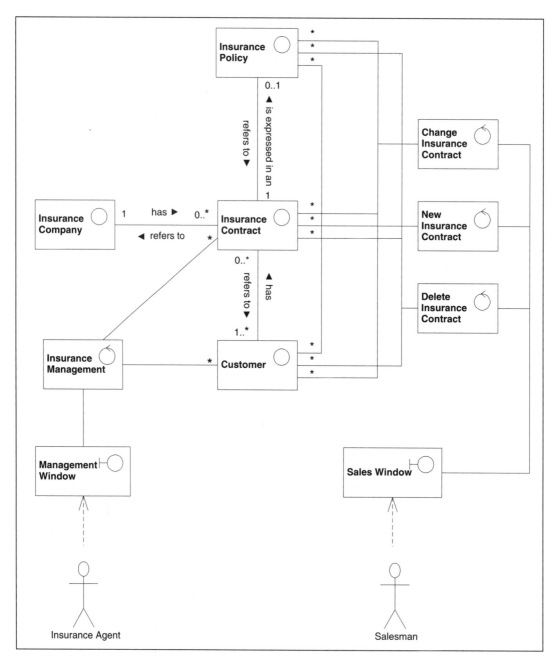

Figure 8.22 *The entity classes capture the core business, in this case, the insurance business. The entity classes are Insurance Policy, Insurance Contract, Customer, and Insurance Company. The control classes Change Insurance Contract, New Insurance Contract, and Delete Insurance Contract serve the boundary class Sales Window. The control class Insurance Management serves the Management Window with Customers and Insurance Contracts. This diagram was modeled with a touch of Objectory.*

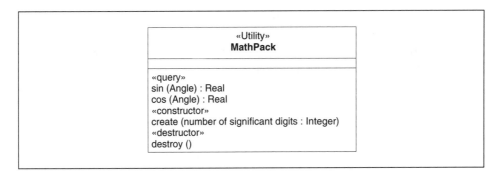

Figure 8.23 *A Mathpack class with constructor, destructor, and query operations.*

ries the name of the class (languages such as C++ or Java *require* the constructor to have the same name as the class) or simply the name "create (...)." For instance, the Invoice class may have a constructor called invoice with the arguments specification and amount. An explicit constructor call would look like this:

```
invoice ("A dell computer", 2000 $)
```

A destructor is an operation that is called implicitly when an object is no longer used or is actually destroyed. All object-oriented programming languages support both destructors and constructors.

A query operation doesn't affect the state of the owning object. Typically query operations are get and read operations of the attributes in the object. Constructor, destructor, and query are all stereotyped operations, as shown in Figure 8.23.

Stereotypes Applied to Active Classes

As discussed in detail in Chapter 6, there are two stereotypes applied to active classes: process and thread. A process is a stereotyped active class representing a heavyweight flow of control; a thread is a stereotyped active class representing a lightweight flow of control. The stereotypes are used to indicate how the active classes are implemented and mapped onto the underlying operating system.

Defining Your Own Stereotypes

In user-defined tagged values or constraints, value and semantics are added onto an element; a new type of element is defined, although it is always based on an existing element. A stereotype also has its own view element, and it can have an icon that represents the stereotype element in diagrams. The definition of stereotypes is typically supported by the CASE tool that allows this capability, along with an icon used as its view element.

User-defined stereotypes are often implemented when adapting UML to a specific method or to the application domain that an organization uses. Concepts used in the method, or common elements or relationships used in the application domain that are not supported in the standard UML, are usually defined as stereotypes. As noted earlier, stereotypes have been added to the UML to make it easier for the UML designers to answer the question: "Why isn't the concept X or Y defined in the UML?" They can always say: "Define a stereotype for it, and it's there!"

When defining stereotypes it is necessary to describe:

- On which element the user-defined stereotype should be based.
- The new semantics the stereotype adds or refines.
- One or more examples of how to implement the user-defined stereotype.

«Time», «Semaphore», and «GUI» are some examples of user-defined stereotypes. The time stereotype applies to associations, specifying that there is a time dependency. A time-stereotyped association must have the multiplicity one-to-many, where the many side is many over time. For instance, a shelf might be placed in many bookcases, but only one at a time.

The semaphore stereotype applies to classes. A semaphore class is one whose object guards a resource and allows access to only one or a specified number of users of that resource at a time. A printer should only be used by one thread in the system at a time, and thus could be guarded by a Printer Queue class with the stereotype «semaphore». The semaphore semantics indicate that only one thread at a time will gain access to the printer queue, thus preventing several threads from concurrently trying to write information to the printer.

The GUI stereotype is a specialization of the boundary stereotype. It has the same functionality and purpose as a boundary class, but concerns only graphical user interfaces (a boundary class also involves any other means of communication with users or other systems). Consequently a GUI class must be part of a graphical user interface, for example, a window or a message box. The GUI stereotype in Figure 8.24 is an example of a stereotype defined as a specialization of another stereotype (since stereotypes can inherit each other).

It is of course possible to extend elements other than model elements. The concept system (subclass to element) may be stereotyped to a set of different systems, (such as those mentioned in Chapter 1) and listed again here for convenience:

Information system
Technical system
Embedded real-time system

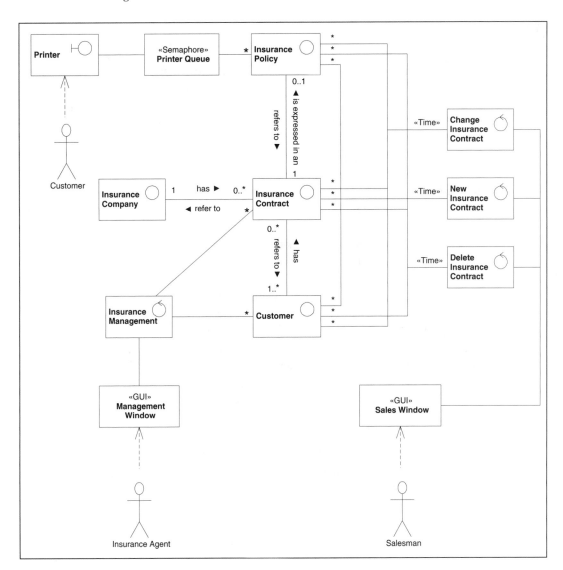

Figure 8.24 *An example of implementing user-defined stereotypes. The Printer Queue class is a sema-phore; it connects the Insurance Policy class with the Printer by controlling the access via the Printer Queue. The associations between the controller classes and the Insurance Contracts are stereotyped with time. The Management Window and Sales Window classes are GUI stereotyped.*

       Distributed system
       Business system
       Software system

Summary

All model languages have restrictions and limits. When a language is too general, it undermines the possibilities to make distinct and sharp statements; when it is too specialized, it limits the possible statements. C++ can be seen as a modeling language specialized for programming but not that powerful for business modeling. Therefore the UML is defined with a limited number of general elements and armed with extension mechanisms.

The UML has three kinds of extension mechanisms: tagged values, constraints, and stereotypes. These mechanisms are used to define a set of standard extensions included in the UML, to which new extensions may be added (user-defined extensions). Extensions are typically added to adapt UML to a method, an organization, or a specific application domain.

The extension mechanisms take elements as their starting point. In a meta-model describing UML, Element is the abstract base class for most constituents of the UML. Element provides an anchor to which a number of mechanisms may be attached; it is specialized to model element (the abstraction the element represents), view element (the symbol used to display the element), system, and model.

Tagged values are a mechanism by which to add extra information to the models and their elements. The information may be intended both for humans and for machines (such as code generators or CASE tools).

Constraints are used to restrict the semantics of the elements within the UML. A constraint may not add extra semantics, only limit the existing semantics of the elements.

Stereotypes are used for specializing semantics of the UML elements. They enable you to define and model with higher precision. Although it would be possible to substitute both tagged values and constraints with stereotypes, the division into three separate mechanisms—stereotype, tagged values, and constraints—is a more pragmatic way to handle extensions.

9 *Design Patterns and UML*

esign patterns have received a lot of attention in the object-oriented community in the last couple of years, for they represent a breakthrough in the development of software. Design patterns are smart, generic, well-proven, simple, reusable design solutions for object-oriented systems. Let's examine these characteristics individually:

- *Smart*: Design patterns are elegant solutions that a novice would not think of immediately.

- *Generic*: Design patterns are not normally dependent on a specific system type, programming language, or application domain. They are generic for a specific problem.

- *Well-proven*: Design patterns have been identified from real, object-oriented systems. They are not just the result of academic thinking, but have been successfully tested in several systems.

- *Simple*: Design patterns are usually quite small, involving only a handful of classes. To build more complex solutions, different design patterns are combined and intermixed with application code.

- *Reusable*: Design patterns are documented in such a manner that they are easy to reuse. As mentioned, they are generic, therefore they can be used in all kinds of systems. Note that the reuse is on the design level, not on the code level. Design patterns are not in class libraries; they are for the system architects.

- *Object-oriented*: Design patterns are built with the basic object-oriented mechanisms such as classes, objects, generalization, and polymorphism.

The core of a design pattern is a problem description and a solution. The *problem description* states when the pattern is used and which problem it tries to solve. The solution is described as a number of classes and objects, their structure, and dynamic collaboration. All patterns have names.

The documentation of a design pattern varies in different books and papers; sometimes it is only given in text and sometimes it is a combination of text and models in a modeling language. Patterns provide object-oriented software developers with:

- Reusable solutions to common problems based on experiences from the development of real systems.

- Names of abstractions above the class and object level. With design patterns, developers are able to discuss solutions at a higher level, for example: "I suggested that we use a Bridge or possibly an Adapter to solve that" (Bridge and Adapter are the names of two design patterns).

- Handling of both functional and nonfunctional aspects of development. Many patterns specifically address some of the areas that object-oriented programs are good at: separating interfaces and implementation, loose dependencies between parts, isolation between hardware and software platforms, and the potential for reuse of design and code.

- A base for developing frameworks and toolkits. Design patterns are the basic constructs used in designing reusable frameworks.

- Education and training support for those who are learning object-oriented programming and design. By studying design patterns, you can gain an understanding of the basic properties of good design, which you can then emulate in your own designs.

Design patterns in the software community were inspired by the work of the architect Christopher Alexander. Alexander has defined a "pattern language" to describe successful architecture in buildings and cities. His language describes how "good" buildings are constructed (a "good" building is one in which the visitor or inhabitant feels alive and whole); and although the patterns can appear in many variations, they are always present in successful architectures. Alexander's work has had a significant impact not only within his own discipline, but also on other disciplines where pattern languages are identified to describe general and good designs.

Many people in the software industry found Alexander's work very appealing, and this led to discussions about applying patterns in software in the early '90s. In August 1994, the Pattern Languages of Programs (PLoP) conference was held. It prompted a lot of work on producing patterns for software. Though the idea of patterns for software is not necessarily related to object orientation, it became clear that the modeling capability of objects enabled it to capture design abstractions; hence, most design patterns are related to object-oriented development. In the beginning of 1995, a group referred to as the "Gang of Four" (Erich Gamma, Richard Helm, Ralph Johnson, and John Vlissides) released the book *Design Patterns: Elements of Reusable Object-Oriented Software* that contained a basic catalog of design patterns and established patterns as a new research area for the software discipline. The pattern movement in the software industry is, however, still in its infancy, and not nearly as complete, mature, and consistent as Alexander's work in architecture.

The interest in patterns has since resulted in a number of other books applying patterns to a number of different areas, such as CORBA and project management. Some of the more interesting work is concerned with the move to pattern systems that attempt to identify patterns at different levels, where together they form a complete system of patterns. Of particular interest is the research into high-level patterns, such as the architectural patterns described by Buschmann (Buschmann et al., 1996). The architectural patterns describe fundamental schemas for organizing a system: subsystems, allocation of responsibility and rules, and guidelines for how subsystems communicate and cooperate. These top-level patterns are a very important step toward achieving a higher quality architecture of the systems produced.

The Gang of Four Patterns

The Gang of Four's patterns book defined a base catalog of 23 patterns, which are often referenced in other books; and the documentation style is used as a template for defining new patterns. The book defines these categories of patterns:

- *Creational patterns*: Handle the instantiation process (how, when, and what objects are created) and the configuration of classes and objects. Allow a system to work with "product" objects that vary in structure and functionality.

- *Structural patterns*: Handle the way classes and objects are used in larger structures, and separate interfaces from implementation.

- *Behavioral patterns*: Handles algorithms and the division of responsibility between objects, and dynamic interaction between classes and objects. Behavioral patterns handle the communication between objects, not only the structure.

The success of the *Design Patterns* book proved that there was a substantial need in the literature for this kind of design description. There were books on methodology (documenting notation, process, and tools) and on programming in specific languages, but these books were either too high-level or too low-level to show real design solutions that demonstrated how object-oriented development is achieved. The best way to understand design patterns is to actually study a pattern.

The Proxy Pattern

The proxy pattern is one of those given in the *Design Patterns* book. Proxy is a structural pattern that separates an interface from an implementation into different classes. The idea of the pattern is that a proxy object works as a surrogate object for another real object; the proxy controls access to this "real" object. Thus it solves the problem when an object (the real object) cannot always be instantiated directly due to performance, location, or access restrictions. It is a rather simple pattern, but it suits the purposes of describing and demonstrating patterns in UML. Figure 9.1 shows a class diagram for the Proxy pattern in UML.

There are three classes involved in the Proxy pattern: Subject, RealSubject, and Proxy. The Client class in the diagram shows the use of the pattern; in this case, the Client class always operates with the interface defined in the abstract class Subject. The interface in the Subject class is implemented in both the RealSubject class and in the Proxy class. The RealSubject class implements the operations in the interface, while the Proxy class only delegates any calls it receives to the RealSubject class. The Client class will always work against a Proxy object,

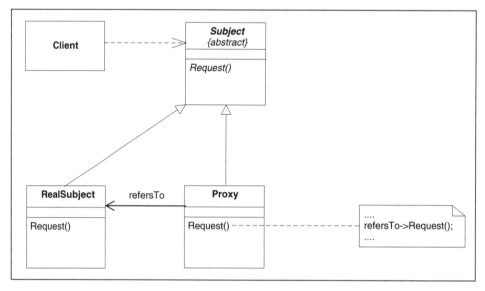

Figure 9.1 *The Proxy design pattern described as a UML class diagram.*

and thus the Proxy object controls the access to the RealSubject object. This is used in several ways, depending on the problem that needs to be solved:

- *Higher performance and efficiency*: A system can instantiate a cheap proxy until the real object is needed. When an operation is called in the proxy, it checks whether the RealSubject object is instantiated. If not, it instantiates it and then delegates the request to it. If it is instantiated, it immediately furthers the request. This is useful if the RealSubject object is "expensive" to create; that is, has to be read from a database, requires complex initialization, or has to be fetched from another system. By using proxies for all such objects, the system will instantiate only the objects necessary for a specific execution of the system. Many systems with lengthy start-up times can gain significant boosts in performance in terms of start-up time by using the Proxy pattern.

- *Authorization*: If it is necessary to check that the caller is authorized to call the RealSubject object, that check can be made by the Proxy. In that case, the caller has to identify itself, and the proxy has to communicate with some kind of authorization object to decide whether access is allowed.

- *Localization*: The RealSubject object is located on another system, and a local Proxy only "plays its role" in the system, and all requests are actually furthered to the other system. The local client is unaware of this and only sees the Proxy.

The Proxy pattern is varied in even more ways: It can contain additional functionality that it performs without delegating it to the RealSubject; it can change the types of parameters or the operation name (in which case, it becomes a lot like another pattern, an Adapter); or it can perform some preparation work to reduce the workload of RealSubject. All these variations demonstrate the idea behind patterns: the Pattern offers the core of a solution that can then be varied, adapted, or extended in a multitude of ways without removing the basic solution construction.

In the *Design Patterns* book, a pattern is documented with a class diagram, and occasionally with an object diagram and a message diagram (which looks like a sequence diagram in UML). Much of the documentation is in text describing different aspects, such as the intent, motivation, applicability, structure, collaboration, implementation, sample code, and consequences of the pattern. References to other names for the same pattern, other related patterns with similar properties, and known usage of the pattern are also included.

The code for the patterns is often very simple. The Java code for a Proxy class that instantiates the RealSubject on demand would simply look like this:

```
public class Proxy extends Object
{
    RealSubject refersTo;
    public void Request()
    {
        if (refersTo == null)
            refersTo = new RealSubject();
        refersTo.Request();
    }
}
```

Modeling Patterns in UML

A pattern is documented as a *collaboration* in UML. A collaboration describes both a context and an interaction. The context is a description of the objects involved in the collaboration, how they are related to each other, and of which classes they are instances. The interaction shows the communication that the objects perform in the collaboration (sending messages and calling each other). (Collaborations are described in Chapter 5.) A pattern has both a context and an interaction, and is suitably described as a collaboration (actually, as a *parameterized collaboration*, as described in the next section).

Figure 9.2 shows the symbol for a pattern in a collaboration (a dashed ellipse) with the pattern name inside it. As mentioned earlier, a pattern must always have a name. When using a tool for drawing the diagrams, the symbol can usually be expanded, in which case, the context and the interaction of the pattern collaboration are shown.

An object diagram for the Proxy pattern is shown in Figure 9.3. To fully understand the object diagram, a reference to the class diagram describing the classes of the objects must also be available. The object diagram for the Proxy pattern shows how the Client object has a link to the Proxy object, which in turn has a link to the RealSubject object.

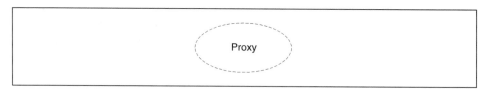

Figure 9.2 *A collaboration symbol representing a design pattern.*

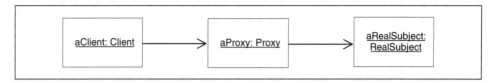

Figure 9.3 *The context of the Proxy pattern described as an object diagram.*

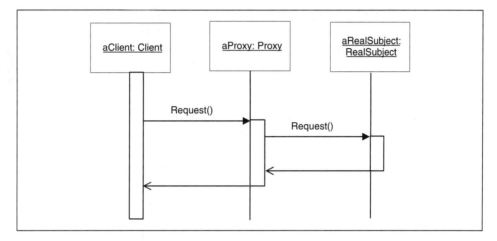

Figure 9.4 *The interaction in the Proxy pattern described as a sequence diagram.*

When describing the Proxy pattern, the interaction shows how the objects interact when the client makes a request. The sequence diagram in Figure 9.4 shows how the request is delegated to the RealSubject object and how the result is returned to the client.

A collaboration diagram can show both the context and the interaction in one diagram. The context from the object diagram in Figure 9.3 and the interaction shown in Figure 9.4 is condensed into one collaboration diagram in Figure 9.5. The decision to use a collaboration diagram or to divide it into an object diagram and a sequence diagram depends on the situation. (A discussion about the differ-

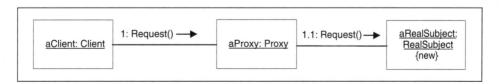

Figure 9.5 *The interaction in the Proxy pattern described as a collaboration diagram.*

ences between these diagrams is found in Chapter 5.) A more complex pattern may need to describe several interactions to show different behaviors of the pattern.

Parameterized Collaboration

As just noted, a pattern is actually defined as a parameterized collaboration, or a template collaboration. The parameters are types (such as classes), relationships, or operations specified when instantiating the template. In a parameterized collaboration, the parameters are called the *participants*, and are classes, relationships, or operations. The participants in a design pattern are the application elements that play the roles defined in the pattern; for example, in the Proxy pattern, the classes that act as the Subject, Proxy, or RealSubject class. The participants are illustrated by drawing dependencies from the pattern symbol to the elements that play the different roles in the patterns. The dependency is annotated with the participating role name, which describes which role the class "plays" in terms of the design pattern. Again, in the Proxy pattern, the participating roles are Subject, Proxy, and RealSubject.

If the collaboration is expanded in a tool, both the context and the interaction of the pattern are shown in terms of the participating classes. In Figure 9.6, the names of the classes that are participants are deliberately different from the roles they play, to illustrate that the role name of the dependency defines what its task is in the pattern. In practice, the classes are often named to suit the pattern; for example, the Sales class is called SalesProxy, the SaleStatistics class is called SalesStatisticsSubject, and so on. However, that is not possible if the classes are already defined or if they participate in several patterns. If the collaboration is expanded, the participants are shown "playing" their roles in the pattern, as shown in Figure 9.7.

Showing Patterns in Diagrams

By defining patterns as parameterized collaborations, we can use them as full-fledged design constructs, with their own names and where they represent a design construction on a higher abstraction level than the basic elements. They can be used repeatedly in designs, and as long as they are well established, they can simplify the models, because not all parts of the design have to be shown. The context and interaction in the pattern is implicit; therefore patterns can be seen as generators of design solutions, as shown in Figure 9.8.

When used in a tool, a developer sees a pattern in a diagram that he or she can expand to reveal the context and interaction that the pattern represents. The pat-

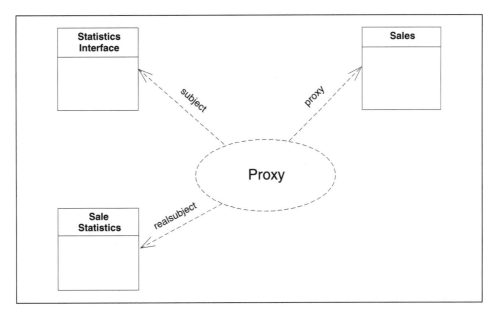

Figure 9.6 *The Proxy pattern used in a class diagram, where the Statistics Interface class has the participating role of subject, the Sales class has the participating role of proxy, and the Sale Statistics class has the role of realsubject.*

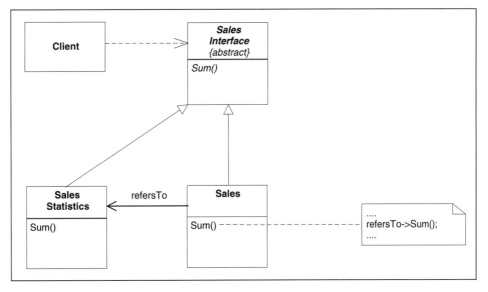

Figure 9.7 *The Proxy pattern expanded with participants from Figure 9.6.*

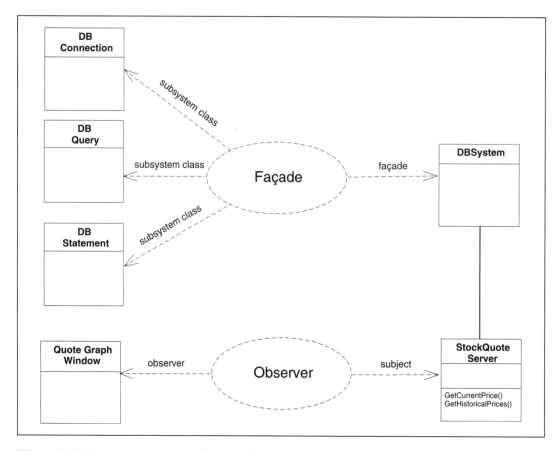

Figure 9.8 *Patterns as generators. The class diagram shows a number of classes, where parts of their context and collaboration are described by using patterns. In a tool, it's possible to access details about the patterns by expanding the parameterized collaborations.*

tern is viewed in terms of the participating classes, where they take their roles in the pattern. A tool can also be used to capture and document patterns in a repository, where new patterns are described, stored, and made available to other projects. The patterns are naturally described as parameterized collaborations in UML. Here are some suggestions for using design patterns:

- *The name of the pattern is important*: The name represents abstraction at a higher level than the design elements in the pattern, and the ability to communicate and discuss abstractions at a higher level is a very important property of design patterns.

- *Make sure everyone understands the patterns used in a project*: Some patterns are treacherously simple, and a developer may think he or she understands all the implications of using such a pattern, even when that is not the case. Good documentation and training are important activities when using patterns.

- *Adapt or modify patterns, but don't change their basic properties*: A pattern can be adapted or varied in a number of ways, but the fundamental core of the pattern should never be altered. The core is often the primary reason to use that specific pattern, and therefore it shouldn't be removed or changed.

- *Don't overuse patterns*: Patterns can be used in any system development, but they should never be regarded as a "silver bullet." Eager developers sometimes overuse patterns, so that everything is designed as patterns.

- *Emphasize patterns as reuse of design*: Many organizations try to transform patterns into reusable code (classes, libraries, and programs). That often means that a pattern has one specific implementation, and that none of its variations can be used. It also means that the documentation of the pattern transforms into detailed code documentation. A pattern is reused at the design level, not at the code level.

- *Have someone monitor the pattern community*: New patterns and new areas where patterns are applied are constantly appearing. Someone should be assigned to track what's happening by reading books and magazines, attending conferences, and searching the Internet.

Patterns and Use Cases

When examining patterns more closely, it's possible to see a resemblance between patterns and the realization of use cases. They have these characteristics in common:

- *Context*: Both are described as a network of objects related in some kind of structure.

- *Interaction*: Both have one primary interaction as to how the objects collaborate (their behavior in the pattern or the use case).

- *Participants*: Both are "instantiated" with a number of application classes that play a specific role in the pattern or use case.

Furthermore, use cases are realized and patterns are documented in the same way in UML. A parameterized collaboration can be either the documentation of a pattern or the description of how a use case is realized. The name of the collaboration

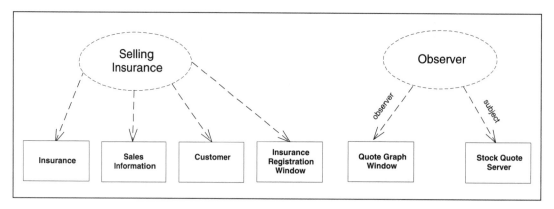

Figure 9.9 *A use-case collaboration and a pattern collaboration with dependencies to classes that are participants.*

is the name of the pattern or the use case, and the collaboration has dependencies to the participating classes. A pattern can be viewed as a generic collaboration that can be used in a number of systems, while a use case is an application-specific collaboration typically used in only one system (see Figure 9.9).

Summary

Design patterns are smart, generic, well-proven, and reusable design solutions that can be applied to common problems in object-oriented software development. A pattern describes the core of the solution, and that core can be varied or adapted in a multitude of ways without losing the basic idea and advantage of the pattern. Patterns have been available only for a couple of years in the software industry, but their importance and applicability will increase as new patterns are identified.

A pattern is described as a parameterized collaboration in UML. The collaboration describes both a context (a number of objects and their relationships to each other) and an interaction (a specific communication between the objects to achieve the behavior of the pattern). As a single element, a collaboration is represented by a dashed ellipse, and when expanded, as an object diagram and a sequence diagram, or as a collaboration diagram. When shown as the collaboration symbol, dependencies identify which classes in the system participate in the pattern. The participating classes take on the role of their corresponding classes, objects, or operations in the pattern.

A pattern and the realization of a use case are very similar constructs, in that they both have a context and an interaction. Classes in an application participate in a pattern or a use case, and that is demonstrated by dependencies to the parameterized collaboration that represents the pattern or use case. The difference between patterns and use cases is that a pattern represents a generic collaboration that can be used in a number of systems, while a use case is an application-specific collaboration, typically present in only one system.

10 *A Process for Using UML*

The UML contains notations and rules that make it possible to express object-oriented models. It does not, however, prescribe how the work should be done; that is, the process or method for working with the language. Instead, it was designed for use with many processes, different both in scope and purpose. Nevertheless, to use the UML successfully, some sort of process is necessary, especially when designing large models that require a team effort. Everyone's work must be coordinated and everyone must be aiming in the same direction. Using a process also makes it more efficient to measure progress and to control and improve the work. In addition, a process, particularly in the field of software engineering, will more fully enable reuse, both in terms of the process itself and parts (models, components, conclusions, etc.).

Simply, a process describes what to do, how to do it, when to do it, and why it should be done. It describes a number of activities that should be done in a certain order. As a result of the process, documentation (models and other descriptions) about the system being built is produced, and a product that solves the initial problems is introduced and delivered. As a modeling language needs tool support, a process needs tools to support its inherent activities. Unfortunately such tools are not as widely available as tools for modeling.

When the named activities of a process are complete, an explicit goal is achieved. A process should result in value for its customer (user). To that end, the process consumes resources in terms of humans, computers, tools, information, etc. There are rules for this resource utilization, and an important part of describing a process is to define these rules. A process is normally divided into nested subprocesses. At the bottom level, a process is atomic, meaning that it cannot be divided and broken down any further.

In contrast, a method is normally also considered as a set of related activities, but without explicit goals, resources, and rules. In software engineering, both methods and processes need a well-defined modeling language to express and communicate their results. A number of sources attempt to define the meaning of "process" and "method," including the differences between the terms. However, for our purposes, in this chapter, no significant differentiation will be made between the terms, though process will be used primarily. Some processes are of general interest, such as management processes, quality processes, manufacturing processes, and development processes. In this chapter, software development processes will be discussed, in particular, the development of software systems using the UML.

Defining and Understanding Software Engineering Processes

Defining a process for software engineering is not easy. It requires understanding the mechanisms behind the work of software development and knowledge of how the work *should* be done. At this juncture, some general aspects of processes for software engineering must be introduced. The ideas in this section have been derived from N. Jayaratna (1994) and his work on NIMSAD, which is a framework for defining and comparing processes. The terminology used here is also from NIMSAD. Certain object-oriented methods on the market today may be considered as processes, including OMT, Objectory, Booch, Fusion, and others.

Our intention in this section is to open the discussion of software engineering and process/method support. There will always be a need for structured ways of working and thinking, either explicitly as guided by a process or implicitly as guided by thought. With that in mind, a process can be viewed from the following aspects:

- *Process context*, which describes the problem domains in which the process can be used.

- *Process user*, which gives guidelines for how the process should be adopted and used.

- *Process steps*, which describes the steps (activities) to be taken during the process.

- *Process evaluation*, which describes how to evaluate the results (documents, products, experience, etc.).

Process Context

A process must describe its context, the problem domains in which it is applicable. Note that it may not be desirable (or even possible) to develop or choose a generic process that handles all potential problems. It is important only that the problems in a specific problem domain be properly handled by the process. However, this creates a dilemma, which is that often the problem domain is not completely known until *after* the process has been completed.

The problem domain, also called the process context, is part of an organizational or business context composed of people, power, politics, cultures, and more. The business has goals, and the information systems that are developed should support these goals. There are at least four reasons to regard a problem domain (related to an information system) as part of an organization or a business:

- Efficiency in an information system can be measured only by the contribution it makes to the business.

- To be able to develop information systems, the developers must interact with the people within the business.

- To solve a problem, the problem solver (the process user) must be introduced to the business and understand how it works.

- When a problem solver is introduced to a business, interpersonal relationships are formed between the people in the business and the problem solvers.

When defining a business, the term should be considered in a general sense, because there is no model or process that can capture all aspects of a business and this limitation must be documented within a process for software engineering. A well-known technique for describing a business is to describe it with metaphors such as machines, organisms, a rational control structure, social culture, political systems, psychic prisons, flux and transformations, instruments of domination, and others (Morgan, 1986).

Process User

A process for software engineering must include guidelines for its use. These guidelines should not refer only to the process itself, but also to the person or people using the process, the intended problem solver(s). We humans have mental constructs that affect how we think, including how we think about using tools such as a process. These mental constructs can be divided thusly:

- Perceptual process (how we pick up information)
- Values/ethics
- Motives and prejudices
- Reasoning ability
- Experiences

- Skills and knowledge sets
- Structuring ability
- Roles (played in our society and business)
- Patterns, models, and frameworks that are "in our heads"

All these constructs affect our interpretation of process descriptions. For instance, our experience of a process might affect the way we structure things even if the process gives us a different direction. Our values and ethics might restrict us from taking certain process steps, such as reorganizing or negotiating (especially in processes for developing and improving businesses). A well-defined process, then, must guide its users, in order to avoid misuse caused by mental constructs.

Process Steps

Most processes for software development consist of at least three basic phases (some processes might have more). They are *problem formulation, solution design,* and *implementation design.* The problem formulation phase helps to discover and formulate the problems; the solution design phase formulates a solution to the problems; and the implementation phase introduces and implements the solution, thereby (ideally) eliminating the problems. In a software engineering process for object-oriented systems, the steps could easily translate into *analysis, design,* and *implementation.*

Problem Formulation

Problem formulation consists of five general steps, which are all well-defined processes or methods for system engineering:

1. Understanding the domain of concern.
2. Completing the diagnosis.
3. Defining the prognosis outline.
4. Defining the problems.
5. Deriving notional systems.

The first step is to understand the problem domain; otherwise, it is difficult to describe the problems therein. It is important to investigate the nature of the problems to avoid a problem formulation that does not include the most important problems, which can happen if the problems are described just as they appear. Note that problems are related to each other, and consequently it is not always easy to capture the underlying issues that may be at the root of the obvious ones. Problems may be described within problem hierarchies. For example, a problem may be that the logistics in a company do not work. But the *underlying* problem might be that the actors that handle the logistics do not have sufficient knowledge, in which case, no information system will help solve the problem unless the actors are trained. The training can be done by means of information systems, but that software cannot be built until the real problem is discovered and described.

The second step is to complete a diagnosis, meaning that the present domain should be described in terms of what was discovered in the first step. Again, the previous step is to know and understand the domain of concern; this step is to summarize and document it. The documentation is called a diagnosis. A diagnosis might be that our systems are in some aspects not efficient compared to those of our competitors.

The third step is to formulate a prognosis outline, in which the desired future domain is described. This description should list where we want to be, why we want to be there, and when we want to be there. The prognosis outline might be that we need more efficient systems (in the aspects diagnosed in step 2) than our competitors, since we believe that such efficiency is a competitive strength. A prognosis should list which aspects in our systems should be improved, what advantages this will bring us, and when we want this achieved.

The fourth step is to describe how to go from the present domain to the desired future domain. This step normally requires itemizing steps and subgoals necessary to reach the final goal, the desired future domain. These steps and subgoals could, for instance, express functions to add or to improve in the system, and how to implement those functions as quickly as possible.

The final step is deriving the notional systems. A notional system is one that is formulated from our mental constructs, which, if designed and implemented, we believe would eliminate the identified problems within the problem domain.

Solution Design

The solution design normally consists of two main steps: to complete a conceptual/logical design, and to draw a physical design. The conceptual and logical design models (expresses) the notional system using a modeling language. The physical design is constructed of the nonfunctional aspects, such as performance, capability, and so on. The purpose of a conceptual and logical design is to create a model that is easy to implement; for example, with an object-oriented programming language. The purpose of the physical design is to create a model that captures nonfunctional aspects and leads to efficient use of our resources; for example, computers, printers, networks, and so on. The UML works perfectly for both these steps; the implementation is then straightforward.

Implementation Design

The last step is to implement the models produced in the solution design phase; in software engineering terms, they should be programmed. Implementation also means that the system should be introduced to the customer, so this step also covers documentation, online help, manuals, user training, converting parts of old systems and old data, and more.

Process Evaluation

It is important to evaluate everything that is done and everything that might affect our work. Only by evaluation can we learn from our work and continue to improve. Thus the process user, the process itself, and the process results should be continuously evaluated, because we never know whether the real problems have been captured (it is easier to capture the symptoms than the cause); furthermore, new problems might reveal themselves during the work. Often, after the customers or users describe the problem domain, an experienced developer will investigate whether their description really captures all of the problems (the customers' needs).

Both during and after projects, results should be evaluated. Results may be seen as the products delivered by the project (models, software components, etc.). The products are specified and developed to eliminate problems detected within the problem domain, so they must be evaluated in terms of how well they solve problems. In short, if the problem domain isn't carefully evaluated, the products cannot be evaluated; and if the products cannot be evaluated, then the customer/user might not be satisfied with the final system.

In order to improve our work, the process and the process user also need to be evaluated, in particular, under the current circumstances. Evaluating the results (the products) along with the reactions and experiences of the process users (the developers) can determine this. It is important to evaluate how the user actually uses the process. Ask questions such as these: Did the user follow all the process steps? Did the user follow the process intention? Were the results as expected? What problems did the user personally experience when implementing the process? Unfortunately, evaluating the process user is not done on a regular basis in many of today's software engineering processes.

The Basis for a UML Process

Although UML is considered generic for object-oriented modeling, its designers had to have some kind of process in mind when they designed it. Naturally the processes they had in mind were derived from the ideas in the Booch method,

OMT, and OOSE/Objectory. Currently they are working to define a new integrated process (which reportedly will be entitled Objectory), which will use UML. However, any object-oriented method or process can use UML as its modeling language. The basic characteristics that the designers had in mind for a process using UML are that it should be use-case-driven, architecture-centric, and iterative and incremental. These characteristics will now be studied in more detail one by one.

Use-Case-Driven Systems

In UML use cases capture the functional requirements of the system; they "drive" the development in all phases subsequent to the requirements analysis. Thus use cases are implemented to ensure that all functionality is realized in the system, and to verify and test the system. Because the use cases contain the descriptions of the functions, they affect all phases and all views, as shown in Figure 10.1. During analysis, they are used to capture the required functionality and to validate this

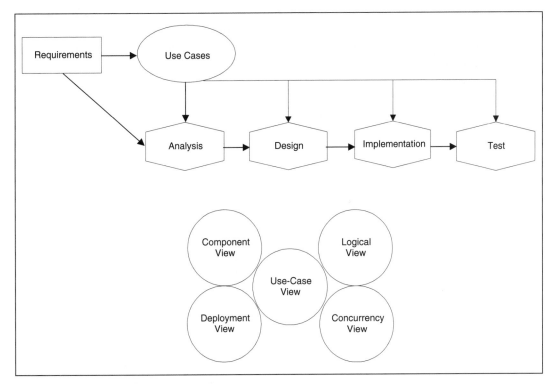

Figure 10.1 *Use cases affecting all phases and views.*

functionality with the customers. During design and implementation, the use cases must be realized in the construction. And, finally, during testing, the use cases verify the system; they become the bases for the test cases.

Processes in which use cases are the dominant concept, such as Objectory, also prescribe that the work organization be based around use cases. One person should be responsible for each use case, to follow it from its specification to its final test.

Architecture-centric

A process using UML is architecture-centric. This means that you consider a well-defined, basic system architecture important, and that you strive to establish such an architecture early in the process. A system architecture is reflected by the different views of the modeling language, and it's usually developed through several iterations. It is, however, important to define the basic architecture early in the project, then to prototype and evaluate it, and, finally, to refine it during the course of the project (see Figure 10.2).

The architecture works as a map of the system that defines the different parts of the system, their relationships and interactions, their communication mechanisms, and the overall rules for how parts may be added or changed. A good architecture addresses both functional and nonfunctional aspects. It is especially important to define a system that can be modified, that can be understood intuitively, and that enables reuse (either into or out of the system).

The most important aspect of creating a good architecture is to divide the system logically into subsystems (UML packages), in which the dependencies between

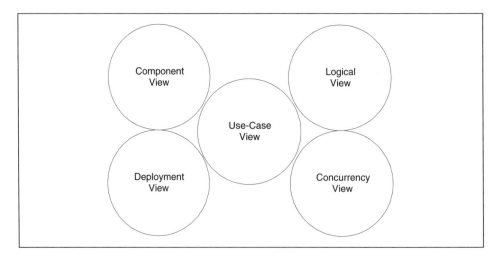

Figure 10.2 *The UML views reflect the system architecture.*

different packages are simple and sensible. Dependencies should usually be of the client/server type, where one package knows about the other, but not vice versa (if they both depend on each other, they are very hard to separate). Packages are also often organized in layers, where different layers handle the same thing but in various degrees of abstraction (a layer of business objects can be on top of a persistence handler layer, which in turn is on top of an SQL generation layer, etc.).

Iterative

Building models with UML is best done as a number of smaller iterations; that is, instead of trying to define all the details of a model or diagram at once, the development is a sequence of steps, whereby each iteration adds some new information or detail. Then each iteration is evaluated, either on paper or in a working prototype, and used to produce input for the next iteration. Thus a process that uses iterations provides continuous feedback that improves the process itself as well as the final product.

When deciding what to include in an iteration, focus on either the iteration that will have the greatest impact on the system or the highest level of risk. The iteration with the greatest impact gives the most "bang for the buck," meaning that a usable system can be delivered to an end user earlier; the iteration with the highest level of risk will handle the really tough problems early in the project, thereby reducing the *overall* risk of the project. Early iterations should tackle the big problems, not postpone them. Early iterations may also be considered prototypes, able to be thrown away if they do not produce the desired results.

Incremental

One iteration or a set of iterations can be treated as an increment of the system. An increment is a step in the evolution of the system, sometimes called a version of the system. When developing iteratively and incrementally, the development is based on the definition of a number of steps. A step is "delivered" and evaluated by its technical, economical, and process merits. When the system is delivered, it doesn't necessarily mean that the software is sent to a customer; in many cases, it is an internal release to the software department. When delivering, the development team should, however, hand over the system in its current state to someone who receives it (see Figure 10.3).

The delivered increment is then tested and evaluated, typically with the software team involved in the evaluation process. These questions are posed:

- Does the system have the functions that were supposed to be included in this step; and do they work as expected?

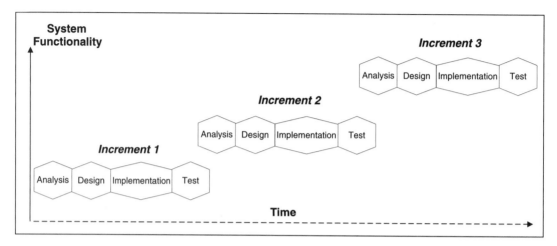

Figure 10.3 *Iterative and incremental development.*

- Does the system satisfy nonfunctional attributes such as adequate performance, reliability, and user-friendliness?
- Was this step developed within the time estimated; and was the resource budget adhered to—was the step developed within the economical constraints?
- Were there problems in the process/method during this step? Does the process/method have to be clarified, or do actions have to be taken, say to substitute or add new resources?

Other questions can be added. It is important that the steps be used to evaluate the entire development process—the functional and nonfunctional aspects of the product, as well as the process and the work of the software team. After each step, actions can be taken to correct any problems; and the experiences from each step can be input to the next step. Once a problem is identified, it doesn't necessarily lead to dramatic actions. It may simply indicate that overly optimistic and incorrect estimates were made, and they are the reasons for the failure of the increment. During the course of the project, the steps are meant to tune the product and the process so that the result is successful.

Every step should add new functionality or attributes to the product. Their contents should be planned; they shouldn't just be what the developers felt like including. As previously discussed, functions that have the greatest impact on the end user or pose the greatest risk should be put in first. An increment can also be delivered to the actual end users. The advantage of this action is that user opinions of the product and the interface are received early enough to be taken into account.

Opponents of iterative and incremental development often claim that this method makes it more difficult to plan and precludes long-term planning. But iterative and incremental development is more economical and predictive than the waterfall model, and when implemented correctly, creates a self-improving process of the overall software development.

The opposite of incremental development is the aforementioned waterfall model, in which each phase is performed only once and the system is released in what is called a "big bang." The entire system generation is analyzed in an analysis phase, designed in a single design phase, and implemented and tested in a construction phase. The risks posed by this model are apparent:

- Feedback and experiences during the development process can't be taken into account (at least not in an organized manner). Such experiences may concern both the product and the way it is being produced (the development process).

- A test to determine whether the analysis and design assumptions are correct is not done until very late in the project, when it might be too late to correct them.

- Maintaining the schedule might be very difficult because, during the construction phase, someone might realize that the plans are too optimistic, by which time it's too late to revamp the plans.

- The risks of the project are not pushed to the front, and thus they might reveal themselves late in the project as unpleasant surprises.

Some practical observations: Even though most proponents of object-oriented methods talk about and advocate incremental and iterative development, in practice, many use the waterfall method. Just because the system is being programmed in a number of releases (e.g., alpha, beta, pilot, etc.), doesn't mean that the development is incremental. Remember, each increment must add some new functional or nonfunctional aspects to the system, and not be just a set of bug fixes. Each step must be evaluated properly and used as input to the next step.

A Traditional Object-Oriented Method

This section looks at the different activities typically performed when using an object-oriented method, as shown in Figure 10.4. This is not an attempt to create a new method, nor to capture one specific method in detail. It's a generic description of the activities usually performed in a method. The methods referenced are Booch, OMT, Fusion, and so on. The main steps in these methods are analysis, design, construction, and test, usually called phases, although we refer to them as

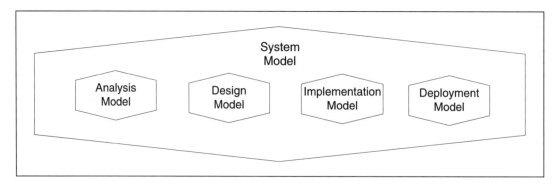

Figure 10.4 *The phases and models in a traditional method/process.*

activities. The next section introduces a macro process that contains phases; to avoid confusion, analysis, design, construction, and testing are called the *main activities*, each of which has a number of *subactivities*.

Each of the main activities produces its own model that consists of some diagrams. It's possible to introduce new functions by adding them to the analysis model and then to each of the other models as well. In addition to the main activities, other activities are present throughout the project, including walkthroughs and reviews, role specification for all roles of the software team, quality measurement, and so on. A process can also contain descriptions of how these vertical procedures are performed.

Requirements Analysis

The requirements analysis generates an agreement between a customer and a supplier of the system. The customer may be a user within the same organization as the supplier or separate companies where detailed business contracts are written based on the requirements documents. The requirements should be as detailed as possible, although it's usually impossible to define everything in such a document. When it's not possible to go into detail in the requirements analysis, the document should express an intention or an idea to be invoked when a conflict between the customer and supplier arises. The requirements analysis is often integrated with business modeling, where business resources, rules, goals, and actions are modeled. (Business modeling is discussed in Chapter 5.)

The requirements analysis implements use cases, business processes, or plain text to describe the functions required of the system. The system is viewed from the outside; it does not delve into how things are done technically. The practical work consists of discussions and negotiations between the customer and the supplier.

Along with the functional aspects, it is important to remember the nonfunctional requirements as well. Issues such as performance and reliability should be discussed, even though it is difficult at this early stage to write business contracts based on numbers here. Other constraints of the system should be made: size, technical environment, necessary integration with legacy systems, products and languages to use, and others. Estimates of the overall cost of development of the system must be made.

The requirements analysis results in a specification upon which the customer and supplier agree. To that end, a simple term catalog and/or conceptual model of the basic entities used in the system is helpful; and, naturally, if use cases have been used to capture the functionality requirements, they are included in the documentation as well.

The UML diagrams created in a requirements analysis include use-case diagrams, some simple class diagrams, and possibly some activity diagrams.

Analysis

The analysis generates models of the problem domain: classes, objects, and interactions that model the "real-world" entities. An analysis should be freed from any technical or implementation details, and contain an ideal model, for it is the formulation of the problem to be solved, and deals with acquiring the necessary knowledge about the domain.

Some typical activities in an analysis are:

- Domain knowledge is acquired from requirements specifications, models of the business processes, term catalog, descriptions of existing systems, and interviews with users and any other interested parties of the system. This is a research activity.

- If a formal requirements analysis has been done—use cases have already been defined for the system—it becomes part of the input to the analysis. If not, the definition of the system functions should be made with use cases or a similar formal technique.

- Finding candidates for suitable classes is typically done in a brainstorming session, during which possible classes are listed. When the session ends, a critical review of all candidates is given and certain classes are removed from the list for a number of reasons (e.g., they are functions; they are duplicate classes with different names; they don't have the characteristics of a class; they're not within the domain; they can't be defined in a concrete manner; etc.). The list of classes in the system typically changes throughout the development, as new experiences lead to the insertion or deletion of classes.

- The static relationships between classes are modeled in terms of associations, aggregations, generalizations, and dependencies. Class diagrams are used to document the classes, their specifications, and their relationships.

- The behavior and collaboration between objects of the classes are described using state, collaboration, sequence, activity, and collaboration diagrams. Typically the use cases (or scenarios of the use cases) are modeled in sequence or collaboration diagrams. Note that no technical solutions are modeled; that is, technical logic or factors such as database access are not described.

- When all diagrams have been developed (usually very iterative work where things constantly change), the overall model is verified by running the system "on paper." The entire model is presented to domain experts and discussed. The scenarios are "played," and the experts are asked whether this is a natural model for solving the problem.

- The basic user interface can be prototyped, though not necessarily in detail (e.g., finished window layouts). The overall structure—the navigation between windows, metaphors used, and the basic contents of the main windows—is prototyped, tested, and discussed with representatives of the users.

The analysis documentation consists of a model that describes the problem domain to be handled in the system, along with the necessary behavior of the domain classes to provide the necessary functionality. Again, the documentation should describe an "ideal" system, without taking the technical environment and its details into consideration.

The UML diagrams created in an analysis are class, sequence, collaboration, state, and activity diagrams, and their focus is on the problem domain, not on a specific technical solution.

Design

The design is a technical expansion and adaptation of the analysis result. The classes, relationships, and collaborations from the analysis are complemented with new elements, now focusing on how to implement the system in a computer. All the details of how things should work technically and the constraints of the implementation environment are taken into consideration. The results of the analysis are carried over to the design and maintained in the center of the system. The analysis classes (a.k.a. business objects) should not be tampered with unless absolutely necessary, to maintain their basic properties and behavior. Instead, the analysis classes should be embedded in a technical infrastructure, where technical classes help them to become persistent, to communicate, to present themselves in the user interface, and so on. By separating the analysis classes from the technical infrastructure, it is much easier to change or update either of them. In the design, the same diagram types are used as in the analyses, although new diagrams have to be created and modeled to show the technical solution.

Typical activities in a design are:

- An architectural phase, during which the analysis classes are divided into functional packages (if not already done in the analyses). New packages for technical areas such as the user interface, database handling, and communication are added. The analysis package might use technical services from these packages, but otherwise should remain as unaffected as possible. The communication mechanisms between different packages are established (striving for client/server relationships in which the functional analysis packages are servers).

- The concurrency needs are identified and modeled through active classes, asynchronous messages, and synchronization techniques for handling shared resources (as described in more detail in Chapter 6).

- The detailed format of the output from the system is specified: user interface, reports, and transactions sent to other systems. The user-interface design may be viewed as a separate design activity, considering its importance.

- Necessary class libraries and components that enhance the architecture and minimize implementation work are bought.

- If using a relational database, the classes in the system are mapped to tables in a traditional relational model. The mechanism for reading from the database is also established in the architecture design.

- Special consideration is taken to handle exceptions and faults in the system. This normally includes both "normal" error handling (errors that can be anticipated in the course of performing the system's functions) and abnormal errors (those that can't be anticipated and must be handled by some generic exception mechanism).

- The classes are allocated to source code components, and executable components are allocated to nodes, using component diagrams and deployment diagrams.

A detailed design activity should include specification of all classes, including the necessary implementation attributes, their detailed interfaces, and descriptions of the operations (in pseudo-code or plain text). The specifications should be detailed enough so that, together with the diagrams in the model, they provide all the necessary information for coding.

During the design phase, remember:

- *Traceability*: Document all decisions so it's apparent on what basis they were made and from where the original requirement was generated. Separate analysis, design, and construction models from each other.

- *Interfaces*: Create simple, complete, and consistent interfaces so that all component services can be easily understood and used.

- *Performance*: Do not overemphasize performance at an early stage (it's easier to increase performance in a working system than to improve a fast but non-working system).

- *Simplicity*: Strive to create simple constructions that are sure to be understood and used by all developers, rather than creating "ingenious" solutions that only a few can understand.

- *Documentation*: Keep notes about everything that happens in the development process so that all events are documented and all problems can be traced.

The UML diagrams created in a design phase are class, sequence, collaboration, state, activity, component, and deployment diagrams. Their focus is a detailed technical solution, to provide the basis for the implementation phase.

Implementation

The implementation activity is the actual writing of the code. If the design has been done correctly and with sufficient detail, the coding should be a simple task. This step involves making the final design decisions and translating the design diagrams and specifications into the syntax of the chosen programming language (which hopefully is an object-oriented language). It also involves the practical development process, to iteratively compile, link, and debug components.

The work is supported by programming rules that attempt to standardize code developed by different programmers, and to prevent dangerous or unsuitable constructions in the language. Code inspections or reviews, formal or informal, facilitate standards being followed and improve the overall quality of the code.

The implementation activity usually is very popular among programmers and managers. The programmers feel that this is the area with which they are familiar (making models is often regarded as abstract and unnecessary), and the managers feel that until the coding has started no real work has been done. When object-oriented analysis and design is introduced, it is not uncommon for managers to walk around saying, "Haven't you started coding yet?" or "Start coding!"

In most cases, the rush to start coding is a mistake. Obviously, the analysis and design decisions have to be made at some point; the choice is to make them using a well-composed team in a structured modeling process, or to have them made implicitly by a programmer during the coding. Wiser decisions usually are made in a structured manner. That said, remember to conduct the overall development process in an iterative manner: analyze a little, design a little, code a little, and then go back to analysis again. If any one of the activities takes too long (e.g., analyzing for months), it could lead to too much administration and documentation, followed by a decrease in the efficiency of the analysis.

Very few new diagrams are created in the implementation phase; rather, the diagrams created in the design phase are detailed or corrected when necessary.

Test

The aim of testing is to identify errors in the code. Finding an error is thus considered a success, not a failure. A test consists of a number of test cases, where different aspects of the part under test are checked. Each test case tells what to do, what data to use, and what result to expect. When conducting the test, the result—including any deviations from the planned test case—are noted in a test protocol. Normally a deviation indicates an error in the system (although sometimes the test case could be wrong and the system right). An error is noted and described in a test report, after which a responsible programmer is assigned to correct the bug for the next version of the system. Errors can be functional (e.g., a function is missing or incorrect), nonfunctional (e.g., performance is too slow), or logical (e.g., a user-interface detail is not considered logical).

The test process is becoming more and more automated, and often includes both tool support for specifying and doing the tests as well as administering the overall test process. There are a number of different types of tests. A unit test is one of a component or a set of components, often done by the developer of the components. An integration test is one of packages that are put together, where the interfaces of the packages and their collaboration are validated. The integration test is typically done by a special integration test team, whose members have good knowledge of the architecture of the system. A system test is a functional test of the entire system as viewed by end users, and is typically done with the requirements specification (with use cases) as the basis. The system test verifies that the system delivers the specified functionality to the end user. A variation of the system test is the acceptance test, which is done by the receiver of a system in order to determine whether to accept the delivered version.

A regression test is not a new test phase, but a technique to handle changes in systems. A regression test is run after changes have been made to the system; it is actually a series of tests run on the entire system to determine whether any other functionality has been incorrectly affected by the changes. It is very common that a change in one part of the system has unexpected effects on some other part (though the risk diminishes with object-oriented technology). Continuous regression tests will unveil such problems. Regression tests are often automated; they are run by a tool, and the tool signals any differences in relation to the expected result.

The use-case diagrams created during requirements analysis are used in the test phase to verify the system. The deployment, sequence, and collaboration diagrams created during analysis and design are typically used as the basis for integration tests.

Rational Objectory Process

Rational Software Corporation, the company where the designers of UML are employed, has for a long time been sketching ideas for a process called Rational Objectory Process. Because the current status and outcome of the work are unknown, the discussion here will just highlight some of the ideas and phases behind this anticipated process.

ROB is really a macro process for development, aimed at both managers and technicians. Microprocess activities such as analysis/design/construction/testing, are still present, but are placed in a larger framework for producing commercial software.

Here are the basic ideas behind the Rational Objectory Process:

- *Based on models of systems to be built*: The models reveal different views of the system, each detailing a specific aspect of the system. The views create a balance when defining the system, to prevent the developer from overemphasizing any one part of the system. Naturally, UML is the language used. The views and their purposes in UML are described in Chapter 2.

- *Process-oriented*: The work is done according to a well-defined set of activities that are repeatable by different teams in different projects. The work is not done individually, to preclude each project or participant from doing things in conflict.

- *Iterative and incremental*: The work is done as a number of iterations; the final product is developed incrementally.

- *Risk-driven*: The process focuses on eliminating risk, by calculating the risk of the activities and by pushing high-risk activities to early iterations.

- *Cyclical*: The development work is done in cycles; each cycle results in a generation of the system. A software product is thus developed in a number of cycles, each producing a commercial release of the product.

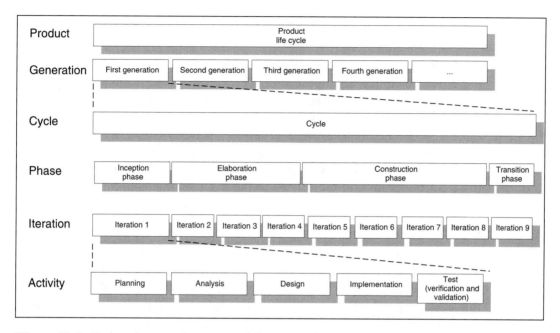

Figure 10.5 *Cycles, phases, and iterations of the Rational Objectory Process.*

The Life Cycle

The life cycle of the Rational Objectory Process governs the product life from conception to development completion. The life cycle consists of a number of cycles, each of which produces a generation, a release or version of the product. Every cycle consists of phases, and each phase consists of a number of iterations (see Figure 10.5).

The phases performed in every generation cycle are seen from a macro perspective—management. The work phases include the same activities found in object-oriented software development—analysis, design, implementation, and test—although they are performed in an iterative manner within the macro process.

The phases are:

- *Inception*: Defines the scope and goal of the project.

- *Elaboration*: Extends the vision defined in the inception phase. The feasibility of the project is investigated, the project is planned (in terms of activities and resources), and the basic functionality and architecture are defined.

- *Construction*: The product is developed in detail through a series of iterations. This involves more analysis and design, as well as actual programming.

- *Transition*: Delivers the system to end users (including activities such as marketing, packaging, support, documentation, and training).

Each phase in the cycle is performed as a series of iterations that can overlap each other. The amount of time spent in each phase depends on the project: Is it a contract job for subcontract, is it being done internally, and so on; the size of the project; how much new technology is used; and the general experience of the application domain. It also depends on which generation of the system is developed; the first generation will typically need more time in the inception and elaboration phases.

A number of milestones are defined at the end of a phase or an iteration, and these milestones are used to track the progress of the project.

Inception

The inception phase is when a vision of a product is created. If it is the first cycle, the inception phase contains the establishment of all the basic ideas about the product: its functionality and capability, its performance and other nonfunctional properties, and the technology to be used. In the second cycle and beyond, the inception phase is when the ideas to improve and enhance the product are formulated.

The inception phase is intended to result in a plan of what to build in this cycle, followed by a study determining whether it can be built and how it should be built (the feasibility of the project). The inception should also contain a basic domain analysis and architectural ideas. Typically the most primary functions and actors should be described in use cases. The plan must also include business arguments for the product, in terms of estimated development costs, market potential, risk analysis, and competitive products.

When the plan has been made, it is presented to the decision makers who, based on the product, the technical analysis, and the business arguments, make a decision whether or not to go ahead with the project.

The inception phase can be rather lengthy for the first cycle of a new product, but it is often not as extensive when new generations are produced.

Elaboration

The elaboration phase consists of a more detailed analysis of the system/generation to be built, along with a plan detailing the work to be done. Both the functionality and the problem domain are analyzed in more detail (using use cases, class diagrams, and dynamic diagrams), and a basic system architecture is defined. The architecture can usually be prototyped, and several ideas can be tested through those prototypes.

Next a project plan is drawn up to include an overall estimate of resources and a schedule. A preliminary draft itemizing how the work should be divided into iterations is also written, in which impact on the system and risk are the dominant factors for the assessment of the early iterations.

Following this phase, a more elaborate plan of the system/generation to be built is available, and a decision is made whether or not to further this cycle.

Construction

The construction phase is carried out as a series of iterations, where each iteration consists of analysis-design and programming activities. The inception and elaboration phase will only define a basic system architecture that is refined and detailed incrementally during the construction. This means that altering the architecture and ideas from earlier phases is allowed.

In this phase, the main activity is normally programming, but test specification and actual test work are also large parts of the construction phase. Another important construction activity is writing the documentation of the system, including both the development and use of the system.

The construction phase delivers a constructed system (in the current generation) in its final iteration, along with development and user documentation of the system.

Transition

The transition phase delivers the product to the end users; it takes the system from the development team and puts it into real use. The transition phase involves everything around that process, including:

- *Marketing*: Identifying the potential users and selling the product to them.

- *Packaging*: Giving the product an attractive package.

- *Installation*: Defining the correct installation procedures for all environments.

- *Configuration*: Defining all the possible configurations of the system.

- *Training*: Writing course materials and planning training of end users.

- *Support*: Organizing support around the product so that users can get their questions answered and their problems handled.

- *Maintenance*: Organizing the handling of problem reports, which will often be turned into error reports that must lead to bug-fix updates of the system (meaning that development resources must still be available in this phase).

The user manuals written in the construction phase are often expanded or complemented by materials from the marketing, installation, configuration, and support activities. These phases are also performed in iterations, where the marketing and support materials are continuously improved and bug-fix updates are released.

Comparison to a Traditional Process

Even though the Rational Objectory Process has different phases in its generation cycle, the activities normally done in object-oriented development are also present. They are, however, done in iterations that are part of the phases of the process. A mapping of the traditional activities would place them primarily in the following phases:

- *Inception*: Consists of project planning, analysis, and architectural design on a very high level, where the focus is on creating a vision of a product rather than on specifying any details.
- *Elaboration*: Consists of project planning, analysis, architectural design, and design work, where the vision is elaborated and the foundation for an actual implementation of the system is created.
- *Construction*: Consists of architectural design, design, implementation, integration, and testing. This is the actual construction work, when the final details are worked out and the system is programmed and integrated into a current generation and finally tested.
- *Transition*: Consists of implementation, integration, and testing in a delivered format, including the maintenance of reported bug fixes and release of maintenance versions of the system. This phase also accounts for activities not normally described in object-oriented software engineering methods, such as packaging, marketing, and training.

One very positive aspect of the Rational Objectory Process is that the iterative nature of the development process is clearly visible. Another advantage is that the cycles present one view for the managers (the inception, elaboration, construction, and transition phases) while another view, consistent with the first, is presented to the technicians in terms of a series of iterations containing analysis, design, construction, and testing.

Process Tools

Ideally, tools used in the development process should support the modeling language and the programming language, as well as the process. Today, most tools are based heavily on supporting a programming language, though new tools are being constructed to support visual modeling languages such as UML. Still, the support for the process is lacking in most tools (which can be explained by the fact that it is more difficult to define generic processes that can be used by everyone than to define generic programming and modeling languages).

With support for a process in a tool, the following features are envisaged:

- *Knowledge of the process phases*: The tool should know the phases of the process; and if the tool is used in more than one phase, it should adapt its behavior and provide support for the phase in which it is currently being used.

- *Online help and guidelines support*: The tool should be able to provide online support, citing a list of the activities to perform in the current phase, along with guidelines for how to do them.

- *Support for iterative development*: The tool should be able to iterate the work, where the tool supports a series of iterations. In a modeling tool, this could mean support for code generation and reverse engineering of modified code.

- *Team support*: The tool should support teamwork, enabling each team member to work on his or her part without disturbing the others.

- *A common system repository*: The tool should be able to share a common repository with other tools, so that all the tools have a shared global image of the system.

- *Integration with other tools*: It should be possible to integrate the tool easily with other tools.

Naturally some tools have a very specialized task and are involved in only one phase or in one activity. In that case, the tool doesn't need all the capabilities described here, but it should support how that one phase or activity is normally performed; for example, iteratively, with input from the previous phase, checking consistency, and so on. Figure 10.6 shows the tools that are usually involved in the development process. They are:

- *Language environment*: Editor, compiler, and debugger for the chosen programming language.

- *Configuration and version control*: Tools for handling different configurations and versions of the product, including support for handling concurrent development by several developers.

- *Documentation tools*: Support for automatic or easy production of development or user manuals.

- *Project management tools*: Help for the project manager to plan and track the development process.

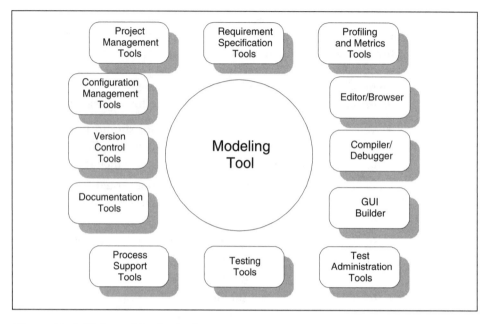

Figure 10.6 *Tools used in the development process.*

- *Test tools*: Support for different tests and for administration of the test process.
- *GUI builders*: Tools to build and prototype user interfaces and to deploy them in the system.
- *Requirement specification tools*: Support tools for capturing and describing the requirements of a system.

Summary

A process is a group of activities that, if done correctly, will achieve an explicit goal. There are many types of processes, such as management processes, manufacturing processes, sales processes, and so on. A process for developing software should be described along with the process context (when the process can be used), the process user (guidelines for how the user should use it), and the steps to take within the process. The basic steps in all processes are problem formulation (understanding and formulating the problem), solution design (creating a solution to the problem, both conceptually and physically), and implementation design (actual implementation of the solution).

The UML is designed for a process that is use-case-driven, architecture-centric, iterative, and incremental. A use-case-driven process means that use cases describing the overall functionality are used throughout the process as input to the work and to verify the models. Architecture-centric means that there is an emphasis on the definition of a well-defined architecture that is easy to modify, extend, and understand. An iterative and incremental process is one in which the product is developed in a series of iterations, and each iteration adds some incremental value to the product. Each increment is evaluated in terms of technology, economy, and process, and the result is used as feedback for the next step.

A traditional object-oriented method (process) is divided into requirements analysis, analysis, design, implementation, and testing. The requirements analysis captures the functional and nonfunctional requirements of the system to be produced. The analysis models the problem domain (classes, objects, and interactions that model the "real world") and creates an "ideal" model of the system without taking the technical environment into consideration. The design activity expands and adapts the analysis model into a technical environment, where the technical solutions are worked out in detail. The implementation consists of writing the actual programs; and the test activity tests the system on different levels (unit, integration, and system) to validate and verify the system that has been produced.

The Rational Objectory Process is a process under development at Rational Software Corporation, the professional base of the designers of UML. It consists of both a manager view and a technical view of the development. The technical view uses the traditional analysis, design, and implementation activities, while the manager view uses the following main phases in the development of each generation of a system:

- *Inception*: Defines the scope and goal of the project.
- *Elaboration*: Extends the vision defined in the inception phase. Planning for the overall project is done, amplified by a definition of the basic functionality and architecture.
- *Construction*: Develops the product in detail through a series of iterations. This involves more analysis and design, as well as the actual programming.
- *Transition*: Delivers the system to end users (including activities such as marketing, packaging, support, documentation, and training).

Each phase in the cycle is performed as a series of iterations that can overlap each other. Each iteration typically consists of traditional activities such as analysis and design, but in different proportions depending on the phase and which generation of the system is under development.

Modern tools should support not only the modeling or programming language used, but also the process used to develop a system. That includes knowledge of the phases in the process, online help, and guidelines for the activities in each phase, support for iterative development, team support, and easy integration with other tools.

11 *Getting Started*

To use the UML, you need more than just the knowledge of the modeling language; you need tools, techniques, and a method. And even if you are already familiar with these things from earlier projects, you may need to adjust them to UML. For example, a method you've used before may have to be adapted or upgraded to work successfully in the UML. Fortunately, it's easy to adapt the most common object-oriented methods such as OMT and Booch to the UML—it's primarily about changing the notation of the symbols and diagrams.

The tools you'll need to start your UML projects are not just CASE and computer-based drawing tools; you'll need practical modeling tools such as whiteboards, Post-it notes, plastic sheets, and others. The modeling techniques you'll implement will guide you through modeling sessions, voting, brainstorming, and so on.

This chapter explains how to adapt and upgrade from the most common object-oriented methods like the OMT and Booch methods. The chapter also describes a generic way of upgrading from any object-oriented method to enable its use with the UML. Concepts about modeling sessions, modeling techniques, and modeling tools are presented at the end of the chapter.

Converting to UML

Upgrading from Booch

Upgrading or adapting a method involves both the process and the notation. The process is the activities and the notation is the modeling language. The next section on process details how to adapt the Booch method for use with the UML.

The subsequent notation section highlights the graphical differences between the Booch method and the UML—for example, the different symbols used in each of the modeling languages.

Process

The Booch method (Booch, 1994) contains both a process and a notation (modeling language) for object-oriented development. It is an iterative and incremental approach whereby a number of different views are used during the development. It consists of three primary steps.

The initial step is *requirements analysis*, during which the customer's requirements are analyzed. The result of this step is a basic map describing the system's functions; it puts all the necessary information in place and creates a basic structure around it.

The second step is the *domain analysis*, whereby a number of object-oriented diagrams are produced. The diagrams model the piece of the real world that's relevant to the system under construction. The following steps are performed during the domain analysis:

1. Define classes.
2. Define aggregation relationships and associations between the defined classes.
3. Find attributes.
4. Define inheritance between classes.
5. Define operations.
6. Validate and iterate the model, which includes reviewing and testing the model until it's stable. Validation is an evaluation from the customer's point of view. Iteration is a repetition of the steps within the domain analysis until the model is complete and validated.

The diagrams produced in the domain analysis are class, state, object, and interaction. Class and state diagrams in Booch correspond to class and state-transition diagrams in UML. The object diagram is a simplified collaboration diagram, and an interaction diagram in Booch corresponds to a sequence diagram in UML.

The third and final step is the *design*, the process for determining an effective, efficient, and cost-effective physical implementation to carry out the functions and store and handle the data (information) defined in the domain analysis. In the design, strategies, policies, and other documents affecting the physical design are evaluated. As in the domain analysis, the design process is highly iterative and incremental. In other words, the steps are repeated until the design model is deemed satisfactory. The design starts with the model from the analysis, which is refined and extended throughout the following activities:

1. Determine the initial architecture. The system is divided into class categories (groups of classes) and allocated to processes and threads. Decisions about prototypes are made.

2. Determine the logical design, which includes the specification of all data types, data structure, operations, and decisions about visibility (public, protected, private, etc.).

3. Map to the physical implementation. The logical design is mapped to the physical design. The physical design is reflected in module diagrams and process diagrams, in which the classes are distributed.

4. Refine the design to incorporate what is learned from the prototypes under construction. This step also includes necessary refinement of the system to meet the performance requirements.

Again, the design model is a refined and extended analysis model, using these diagrams: category, module, and process. The category diagram is used to divide the system into smaller parts such as class categories that correspond to packages in the UML. A package is drawn in a class diagram or other diagrams, such as the component or use-case diagrams. Grouping of parts is done in the normal UML diagrams. A module diagram is very similar to a component diagram in UML; a process diagram is similar to a deployment diagram in UML. Directly mapping from the Booch diagrams and notation to the UML is very easy.

Notation

Figures 11.1 through 11.27 form a mapping of the primary Booch symbols to their UML equivalents. In all the figures, the Booch symbols are on the left and the corresponding UML symbols are on the right.

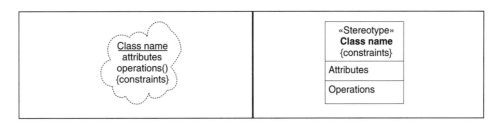

Figure 11.1 *Class.*

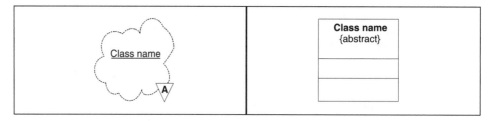

Figure 11.2 *Abstract class.*

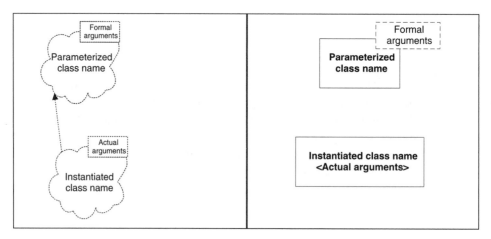

Figure 11.3 *Parameterized class.*

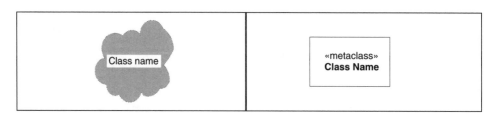

Figure 11.4 *Metaclass.*

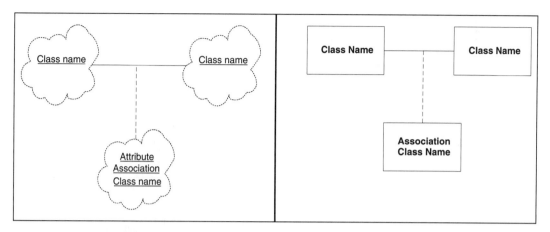

Figure 11.5 *Attributed association class.*

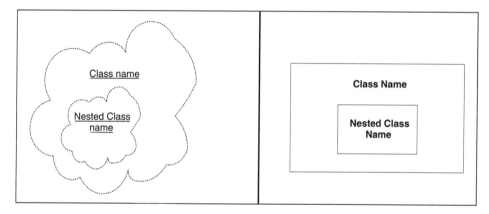

Figure 11.6 *Nested classes.*

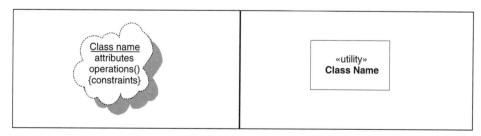

Figure 11.7 *Utility.*

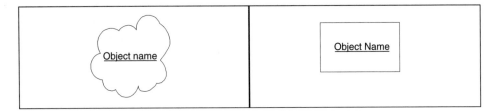

Figure 11.8 *Object.*

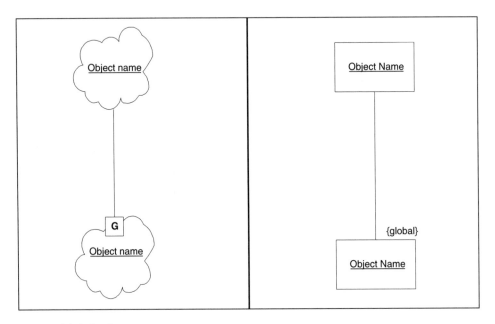

Figure 11.9 *Link.*

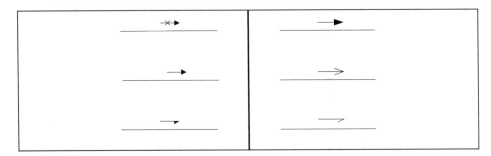

Figure 11.10 *Synchronization.*

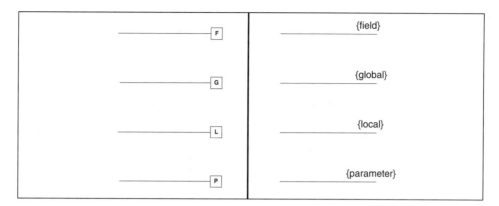

Figure 11.11 *Object visibility.*

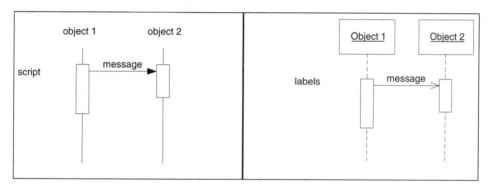

Figure 11.12 *Interactions (sequences in UML).*

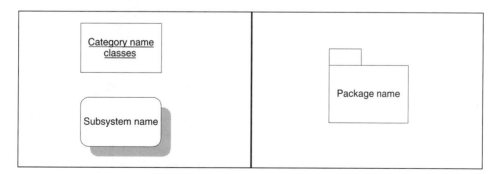

Figure 11.13 *Category and subsystem (package in UML).*

Figure 11.14 *Association, cardinality (multiplicity in UML), label, constraint, and role.*

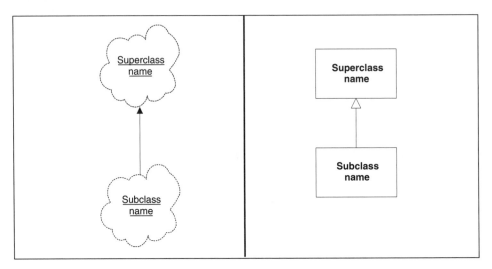

Figure 11.15 *Inheritance (generalization in UML).*

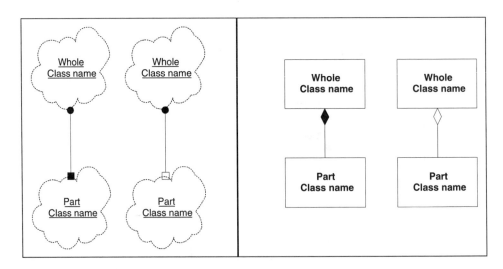

Figure 11.16 *Has (aggregate in UML).*

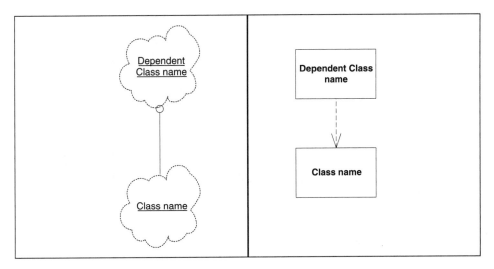

Figure 11.17 *Using (dependency in UML).*

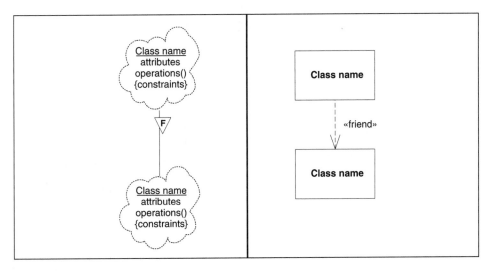

Figure 11.18 *Friend.*

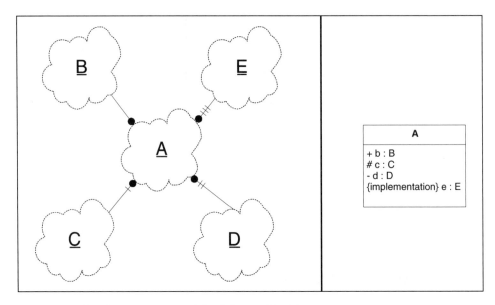

Figure 11.19 *Class export control (visibility in UML).*

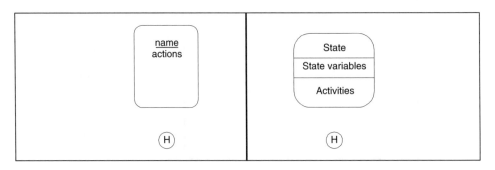

Figure 11.20 *Notes.*

Figure 11.21 *State.*

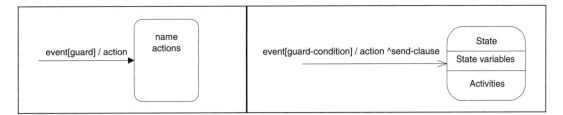

Figure 11.22 *State transition.*

Figure 11.23 *Start and end points in state transition diagrams.*

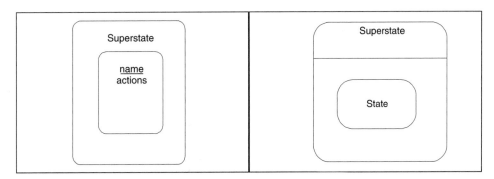

Figure 11.24 *Nested substates.*

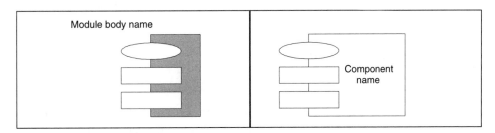

Figure 11.25 *Module (component in UML).*

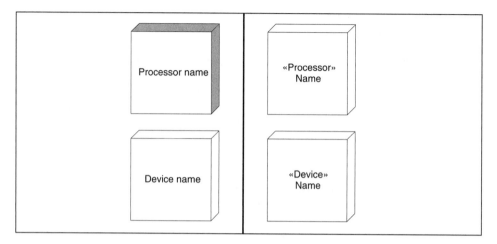

Figure 11.26 *Device and processor (node in UML).*

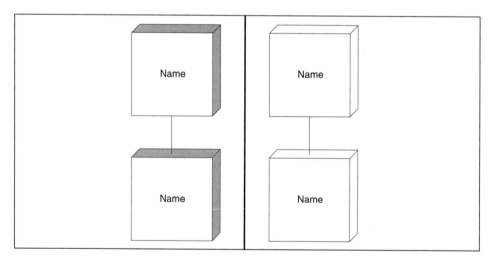

Figure 11.27 *Connection between nodes (association in UML).*

Upgrading from OMT

Process

The Object Modeling Technique (Rumbaugh et al., 1991) is also a process and a notation (modeling language) for object-oriented development. A preparation step is to write or obtain the problem statement and describe the problems to be solved. When the problem statement is written, the OMT provides three primary steps for defining and building a system: analysis, system design, and object design. After the object design step, the models can be implemented with programming code and, in some cases, a database schema.

The first step, analysis, is the modeling of the key concepts within the problem domain. The key concepts are found, or should be found, in the problem statement. The analysis is a blueprint used for the next two steps: system and object design. The analysis provides three different views/models of the system: an object model, a dynamic model, and a functional model. The results from the analysis are object-model diagrams, state diagrams, event-flow diagrams, and data-flow diagrams. The steps in the analysis are:

1. Write or obtain the problem statement.
2. Build an object model (object-model diagram).
3. Develop a dynamic model (state diagrams and event-flow diagrams).
4. Construct a functional model (data-flow diagram).
5. Verify, iterate, and refine the three models (object, dynamic, and functional).

In OMT, the object-model diagram and the state diagram correspond to the class and state diagram in UML. The data-flow diagram has no corresponding diagram in UML, but the activity diagram can be used for similar, though not exactly the same types of models. An event-flow diagram corresponds to a sequence diagram in UML.

After the analysis step is complete, the system design begins and concentrates on the overall architecture of the system. The steps are:

1. Organize the system into subsystems. Divide the models into packages. The UML subsystem does this.
2. Identify concurrency inherent in the problems. The UML handles concurrency within the collaboration diagrams.
3. Allocate the subsystems to processors and tasks. The deployment diagram and the component diagram within the UML are used to model processors and tasks.
4. Choose basic strategies for implementing data stores.
5. Determine mechanisms for controlling access to global resources.
6. Implement software control.
7. Handle boundary situations.
8. Establish trade-off priorities.

Stereotypes are used to indicate that some classes are used to handle global resources, data stores, and so on.

The final step is object design, when all the models are fully specified and the basis for the programming is created. The steps are:

1. Extract operations from the dynamic models and the functional models. From a UML perspective, the operations are identified from the interactions that are or may be expressed in sequence diagrams (event-flow diagrams in the OMT), collaboration diagrams, or activity diagrams (which are similar to the data-flow diagrams within the OMT).

2. Design algorithms to implement the operations.

3. Optimize the paths to data.

4. Implement software control.

5. Adjust class structure to increase inheritance.

6. Design implementation of associations and aggregates.

7. Determine the representation of attributes such as types, default values, and so on.

8. Package classes and associations into modules. UML does this with component diagrams.

As outlined, everything expressed with the OMT notation can also be expressed with UML. However, some of the OMT concepts that lack notation have notations in the UML, such as components and nodes. Data flow diagrams are not part of the UML, but similar specifications are handled with an activity diagram. The main difference between the OMT and UML notation is how interactions are illustrated. The OMT shows interactions with two focal points: data and events; the UML shows interactions with three focal points: time (sequence diagram), space (collaboration diagram), and work (activity diagram). OMT has a principle whereby operations are identified and defined through the interaction models (data-flow and event). This principle is maintained in the UML albeit with a different perspective on interactions. In short, this difference is not significant, as data-flow descriptions are regarded as part of workflow descriptions in an activity diagram.

Notation

Figures 11.28 through 11.46 show the graphical differences between the OMT and the UML notation. As in the previous figures, the OMT symbols are on the left and the corresponding UML symbols are on the right.

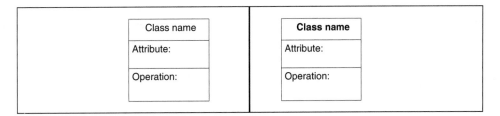

Figure 11.28 *Class.*

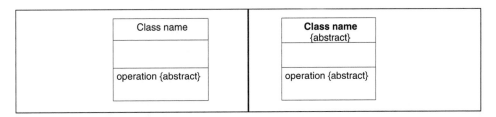

Figure 11.29 *Abstract operation.*

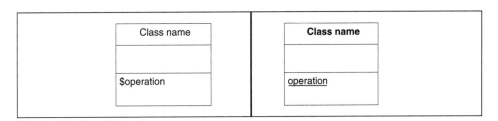

Figure 11.30 *Static member (class-scope attribute in UML).*

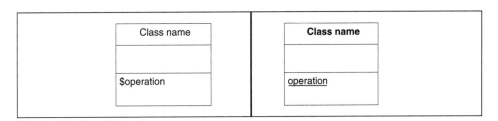

Figure 11.31 *Object.*

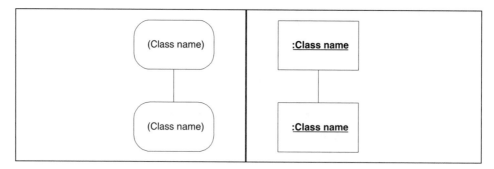

Figure 11.32 *Link.*

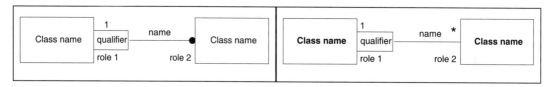

Figure 11.33 *Association, multiplicity, name, qualifier, and role.*

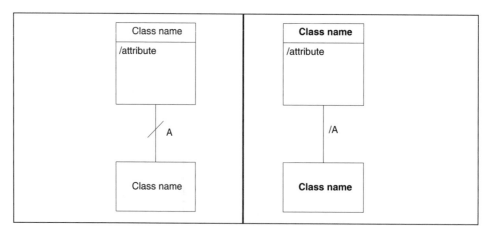

Figure 11.34 *Derived association and attribute.*

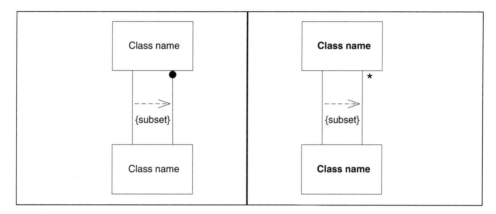

Figure 11.35 *Subset of an association.*

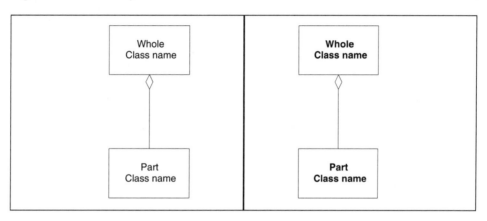

Figure 11.36 *Aggregate.*

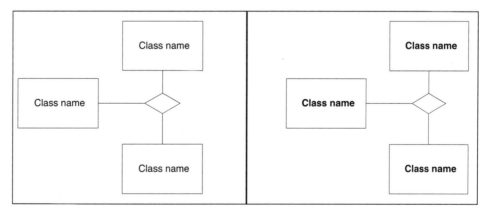

Figure 11.37 *Ternary.*

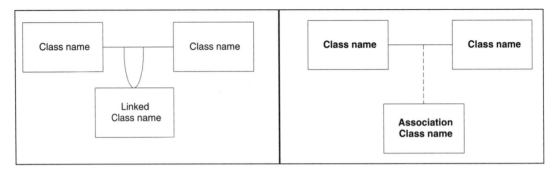

Figure 11.38 *Linked object (association class in UML).*

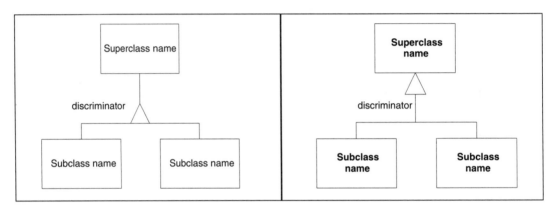

Figure 11.39 *Discriminator and generalization.*

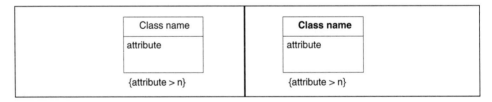

Figure 11.40 *Constraints on objects.*

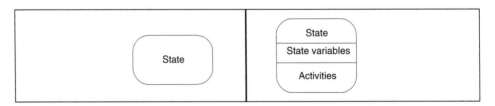

Figure 11.41 *State.*

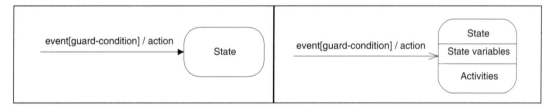

Figure 11.42 *State transition.*

Figure 11.43 *Start and end points in state transition diagrams.*

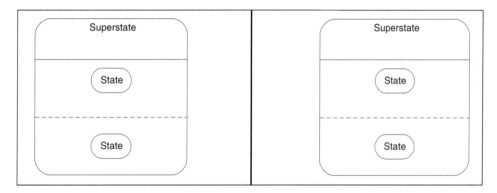

Figure 11.44 *Concurrent substates (and-state in UML).*

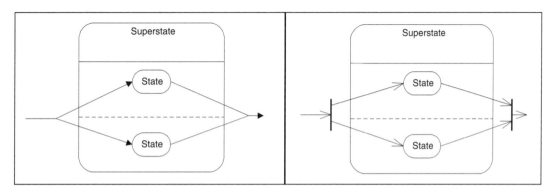

Figure 11.45 *Split of control.*

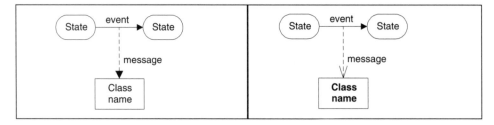

Figure 11.46 *Message between state diagrams.*

A Generic Approach to Upgrading

Let's assume you want to use the UML but that you already have a method that satisfies your needs and that you feel comfortable with. There are two ways for adapting the UML. First, you can revise your current method to fit the UML, or you can revise or adapt UML to fit the existing method. However, be aware that the second way may cause problems with CASE tools, and can be confusing for people who know the UML. Therefore we recommend the first as the most practical way of handling an adaptation. Here are the general steps to take to adapt a method to the UML:

1. Define the diagrams included in your method.
2. Revise the diagrams and the method description concerning the diagrams in order to fit the UML. This activity can generate more fundamental changes if the views are different.
3. Define the model elements within your method; classify them and describe them textually and visually.
4. Try to find corresponding model elements in the UML. If necessary, define stereotypes that adapt the model elements in UML to the elements in your method.
5. Define a visual and textual translation list for the model elements within your method; revise the method description, if necessary—it may be fine with just a translation list.
6. Finally, make additions to the method. Typically this includes real-time adaptations and advanced concepts, such as powertypes, refinement, stereotypes, signals, and so on. Don't introduce something to your method just because it is available in the UML. Introduce only the concepts you need in your modeling.

A more scientific way of adapting a method and its notation is to define a metalanguage. Then you can express both the UML as metamodels and the metamodels for your method in the metalanguage; finally, you can compare and adjust any mismatch. Note that this technique is very time-consuming and more appropriate for language theorists than for ordinary users. Metamodeling is a science of its own.

Modeling Sessions, Tools, and Techniques

We use modeling language development processes or methods to express our models. A method or process is a defined and explicit way of structuring work; the result of this kind of work is expressed in models. A model is used to say something about something else (Nilson, 1979). A modeling language has syntax, semantics, and pragmatics. The syntax states how the symbols within the language combine; the semantics provide the meaning of the symbols; and the pragmatic rules form the intention from the modeling language.

Methods and modeling languages, however, are not sufficient. We must produce models of high (or exacting) quality, otherwise the projects will fail. For example, a system might be built that implements the system models as specified, but that doesn't always mean it solves the problem. If well-composed teams made up of both modeling experts (analysts) and customers with knowledge about the problem domain produce the models, the chances are better of capturing the essence of the problem domain and of the results being of higher quality. Efficiency improves even further when the team members are given the power to make decisions, not only those decisions concerning the system under construction, but also those involving requirements of that system.

A modeling session takes place when a modeling team is prepared to target a certain domain of concerns. A modeling team is typically composed of 5 to 12 people, one of whom is the modeling leader. It is important that the team be formed for a certain purpose such as an early analysis or an overall improvement of the architecture. Modeling sessions are usually done in 5 to 12-hour periods, with regular breaks and free days. The modeling session is driven by the leader, who does not necessarily possess expert knowledge in the problem domain. It is more important that he or she be very familiar with the modeling language used and with various analysis techniques and tools. Most important is that the leader must have social competence, that is, the ability, talent, and experience to deal with people and interpersonal relationships in many different circumstances, under high levels of stress. The modeling leader should be able to inspire the team members with enthusiasm, to know when to stimulate the discussion and when to keep silent, and to keep some distance in order to drive the process in a positive direction. It's not necessary that the customer have experience or knowledge of object-oriented modeling and modeling languages. A modeling session can start with a brief presentation of the modeling language chosen during which a skilled modeling leader can teach the necessary basic concepts in less than an hour. Then the team can get going. The domain experts are there to contribute their knowledge about the problem domain, the language syntax, and rules.

The modeling leader may decide to use a set of modeling techniques during the modeling sessions. Conventional techniques and tools include computer-based drawing tools; more creative and practical tools include Post-it notes, plastic sheets, and digital cameras. Computers are used to document already established facts after most of the creative work is done. Informal tools, such as Post-it notes, support creativity and ensure no technical problems get in the way of expressing ideas.

During the early phases, when the problem situation is defined, it may be difficult to verify and validate the models under construction. One approach is to form a group whose members have all the required competence and knowledge. But even an expert team can fail if they aren't talking about the same problems and the same models. To avoid misunderstandings, hang sheets of paper on a wall where all the models can be drawn and redrawn. Be careful not to put the models into CASE or drawing tools before they are consolidated and everyone agrees on them. "Modeling on the wall" enables everyone to see the progress and agree or disagree immediately. Another advantage of this technique is that the models can be taken away afterward, documented, and detailed in a CASE or drawing tool. Although whiteboards can be used as an alternative, they are usually too heavy to move easily.

The sheets should be large enough to accommodate the models—usually a width of 50 to 80 inches and a length of 80 to 120 inches is sufficient. The sheets should be made of transparent plastic (PVC, for instance) or paper. The models can be drawn with whiteboard markers and highlighted with Post-it notes or regular slips of paper attached with spray adhesive.

If you use Post-it notes or slips of paper, use colored paper to add an extra dimension to the models. Different colors can be assigned to highlight specific elements such as problems, important aspects or purposes, or semantics of the model elements within the models. For instance, if you cannot agree on a certain solution, mark it with a slip of red paper to indicate that it's incomplete or a tricky problem not yet solved. Model important elements green, and so on. The colors will help you and your team to move forward.

Diagrams that require a more creative process include class diagrams, use-case diagrams, and interaction diagrams (sequences diagrams, collaboration diagrams, and activity diagrams). When modeling class diagrams consider the following conventions:

- Beige Post-it notes or slips of paper represent classes on which all compartments are drawn (name, attributes, and operations).

- Lines drawn with colored whiteboard markers represent relationships. Small, yellow slips of paper or Post-it notes represent optional, relation-names, constraints, or roles.
- Red slips of paper or Post-it notes connected to the problem elements represent problems within the model.
- Blue slips of paper or Post-it notes represent goals connected to problems. Remember, a problem always has a goal, otherwise it is not a problem.
- Green paper represents very important model elements.
- Colored icons printed on slips represent stereotypes.

If you are unable to solve a problem because of differing opinions or interpersonal conflicts, take a vote! One technique for voting is to give every team member five stickers that they assign to those elements they consider most important. The modeling leader then removes the model elements with the fewest stickers, and the model work can move on from there. A vote doesn't have to be final. Some of the removed elements can be returned to the model later if it's discovered they are needed. A vote is used to break a standstill and get the work back on track.

If you conduct a series of modeling sessions, it's necessary to document each of them. A practical approach is to take photographs after every modeling session with a digital camera that can produce printouts of the models immediately after the session—one copy per team member. Another approach is to assign one person to put the session's results into a CASE tool and print out the documentation for everyone. It is most efficient when the team members can take the documentation with them after every modeling session, to give them the time and opportunity for reflection.

Other useful techniques are to draw up problem lists, conduct brainstorming sessions, "walk" the model, and use patterns. Problem lists are begun as soon as problems appear. As noted, problems can be represented by red slips of paper on the models or as separate lists. The problem lists enable teams to move on even if not all the problems have been solved.

In a brainstorming session, ideas about the situation of concern are generated and documented. *All* ideas are noted regardless of their quality. Criticism or opposition is not allowed. It's important to maintain a creative and open atmosphere in a brainstorming session, otherwise, the number of ideas may be reduced. After brainstorming, the ideas are evaluated. Some of the ideas may require that you take the process further.

Patterns are useful for creating a foundation upon which to build. For instance, business, analysis, and design patterns are used at the beginning of a modeling session to help focus attention on the core of the problems.

Walking the model is a new approach most appropriate for process and use-case models. When we describe the present situation or the desired situation (in a business), the models are validated by actually following the use cases or processes in real life to see what effect they have and whether the purposes and goals of the models have been satisfied. We actually study ("walk") the processes as they occur. This is a much more efficient way of validating business models than just showing them to a customer.

Modeling is about communication among people. We make contracts in terms of drawings, textual descriptions, oral statements, and so on. This section provided some concepts to consider for the modeling process. As in love and war, all is fair as long as a result is achieved.

12 *Case Study*

This chapter presents a case study to demonstrate how UML is used in an application. As discussed throughout this book, an application is analyzed and described in an analysis model with use cases and a domain analysis. It's then expanded into a design model that describes a technical solution; finally, it is programmed in Java to create an application that is ready to run. Most case studies discuss an application and include a few examples, but don't include all the models and diagrams; however, on the CD-ROM accompanying this book, the complete analysis and design models are supplied, along with the code for the application.

This case study is an application that handles the borrowing and reserving of books and magazines in a library. Although, it's not a very large application, at the conclusion, a number of exercises are provided to enable you to extend the system in more advanced directions. The purpose of the case study is threefold:

- To show the usage of UML in a complete application, tracing the models from an analysis via a design model to the actual code and into a running application.

- To illustrate the use of tools when modeling with UML by supplying the demo version of Rational Rose.

- To give you an opportunity to invoke UML in an existing model by going through the exercises at the end of this chapter that contain extensions and improvements to the application. You can choose to do the exercises only in analysis and/or design; or if you know how to program in Java, the actual code can also be substituted to incorporate the changes.

The initial models are available on the CD-ROM that accompany this book, along with the demo version of Rational Rose 4.0. A 15-day trial version of Symantec Visual Café (for the editing and compiling of Java code) can be found at

319

www.symantec.com/trialware/dlvcafewin10.html. This chapter discusses only certain of the diagrams from the case study, but the entire model is on the CD-ROM and can be studied and printed out from Rational Rose. You are encouraged to examine and experiment with the models, to learn about both the tools and the more practical uses for UML. Instructions to install and run the software on the CD-ROM are provided on the CD-ROM in the file *readme.txt* on the root catalog of the CD-ROM.

The Rational Rose 4.0 demo version can be used to view the models. Unfortunately, the demo version doesn't allow saving the large models included in this case study. To change the models and save them, you must buy the commercial version of Rational Rose. Also, be aware that Rational Rose 4.0 doesn't support UML in full. Some parts of diagrams are not correctly shown as they are defined in the UML definition, and activity diagrams aren't supported at all in the tool. No doubt this will change in future versions of Rational Rose, but in case you are confused when viewing some of the diagrams, remember that the tool doesn't show everything in correct UML notation. When differences are noted between the UML notation as described in this book and as shown in Rational Rose 4.0, assume the book contains the correct notation.

Throughout this chapter and on the CD-ROM, remember that what's shown is only *one* possible solution. There are plenty of others, and there is no "right" solution for all circumstances. If you feel like making some changes to the initial models, feel free to do so. The goal is to produce a system that satisfies the requirements and that works well, not to produce diagrams that are "perfect" in all their details. Of course, some solutions will prove better than others, but only experience and hard work will result in that knowledge.

Requirements

A typical text requirement specification for the first version of the library application written by a representative for the end user of the system and/or the customer (who will pay for the system) looks like this:

- It is a support system for a library.
- A library lends books and magazines to borrowers, who are registered in the system, as are the books and magazines.
- A library handles the purchase of new titles for the library. Popular titles are bought in multiple copies. Old books and magazines are removed when they are out of date or in poor condition.
- The librarian is an employee of the library who interacts with the customers (borrowers) and whose work is supported by the system.

- A borrower can reserve a book or magazine that is not currently available in the library, so that when it's returned or purchased by the library, that person is notified. The reservation is canceled when the borrower checks out the book or magazine or through an explicit canceling procedure.
- The library can easily create, update, and delete information about the titles, borrowers, loans, and reservations in the system.
- The system can run on all popular technical environments (UNIX, Windows, OS/2, etc.) and has a modern graphical user interface (GUI).
- The system is easy to extend with new functionality.

The first version of the system doesn't have to handle the message that is sent to the borrower when a reserved title becomes available, nor does it have to check that a title has become overdue. Additional requirements for future versions are available in the exercises at the end of this chapter.

Analysis

The analysis is intended to capture and describe all the requirements of the system, and to make a model that defines the key domain classes in the system (*what* is handled in the system). The purpose is to provide an understanding and to enable a communication about the system between the developers and the people establishing the requirements (user/customer), therefore the analysis is typically conducted in cooperation with the user or customer.

The analysis is not restricted by technical solutions or details. The developer shouldn't think in terms of code or programs during this phase; it is the first step toward really understanding the requirements and the reality of the system under design.

Requirements Analysis

The first step in the analysis is to define the use cases, which describe what the library system provides in terms of functionality—the functional requirements of the system. A use-case analysis involves reading and analyzing the specifications, as well as discussing the system with potential users (customers) of the system.

The actors in the library are identified as the librarians and the borrowers. The librarians are the users of the system and the borrowers are the customers, the people who check out and reserve books and magazines, although occasionally a librarian or another library may be a borrower. The borrower is not intended to directly interact with the system; the borrower's functions are done on behalf of the borrower by the librarian.

The use cases in the library system are:

- Lend Item
- Return Item
- Make Reservation
- Remove Reservation
- Add Title
- Update or Remove Title
- Add Item
- Remove Item
- Add Borrower
- Update or Remove Borrower

Not included on the list is Maintenance, which is a more general use case that uses other use cases. It can be argued whether this really is a use case of its own, but to clearly separate the maintenance tasks from the key functions in the system it's defined as such.

Also note in the list the concepts of "title" and "item." Because a library often has several copies of a popular title, the system must separate the concept of the title, which can be the name of a book, the book's author, or other item, which represents a physical copy of a specific title. The items are borrowed from the library. It's also possible to add a title to the system before the library has a copy (an item), to enable the borrowers to make reservations.

The library system analysis is documented in a UML use-case diagram as shown in Figure 12.1. Each of the use cases is documented with text, describing the use case and its interaction with the actor in more detail. The text is defined through discussions with the user/customer. The use case Lending Item is described as:

1. If the borrower has no reservation:

   a. A title is identified.

   b. An available item of the title is identified.

   c. The borrower is identified.

   d. The library lends the item.

   e. A new loan is registered.

2. If the borrower has a reservation:

   a. The borrower is identified.

   b. The title is identified.

   c. An available item of the title is identified.

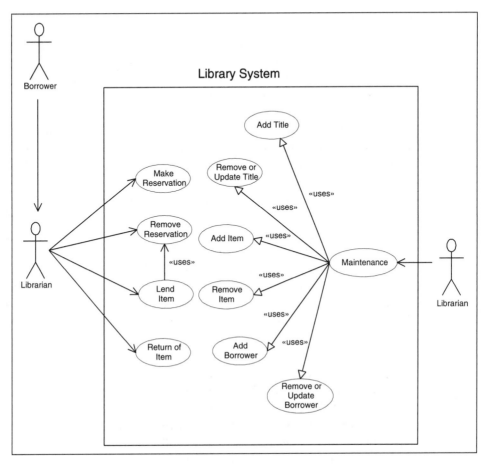

Figure 12.1 *A use-case diagram for the library system.*

- d. The library lends the corresponding item.
- e. A new loan is registered.
- f. The reservation is removed.

The descriptions of all the use cases are included in the analysis model on the CD-ROM. The use cases are implemented throughout the development of the system to provide descriptions of the functional requirements of the system. They are used in the analysis to check whether the appropriate domain classes have been defined, and they can be used during the design process to confirm that the technical solution is sufficient to handle the required functionality. The use cases can be visualized in sequence diagrams, which detail their realization.

Domain Analysis

An analysis also itemizes the domain, the key classes in the system. To conduct a domain analysis, read the specifications and the use cases and look at which "concepts" should be handled by the system. Or organize a brainstorming session with users and domain experts to try to identify all the key concepts that must be handled, along with their relationships to each other.

The domain classes in the library system are: Borrower (named BorrowerInformation here to separate it from the actor Borrower in the use-case diagram), Title, Book Title, Magazine Title, Item, Reservation, and Loan. They are documented in a class diagram along with their relationships, as shown in Figure 12.2. The domain classes are defined with the stereotype «Business Object», which is a user-defined stereotype specifying that objects of the class are part of the key domain and should be stored persistently in the system. A more formal specification could be made, but it is not relevant for this system.

We emphasize that the domain classes are being "sketched" at this stage. The operations and attributes defined are not the final ones; they are those that seem appropriate for these classes at this point. Some of the operations have been defined by sketching sequence diagrams over the use cases (described later in this chapter).

Certain of the classes have UML state diagrams to show the different states that objects of those classes can have, along with the events that will make them change their state. The classes that have state diagrams are Item and Title. The state diagram for the Title class is shown in Figure 12.3.

To describe the dynamic behavior of the domain classes, any of the dynamic UML diagrams can be used: sequence, collaboration, or activity. Since Rational Rose 4.0 doesn't support activity diagrams and offers only limited support for collaboration diagrams (in full UML notation), we use sequence diagrams. The basis for the sequence diagrams are the use cases, where each use case has been described with its impact on the domain classes, to illustrate how the domain classes collaborate to perform the use case inside the system. Naturally, when modeling these sequence diagrams, you will discover new operations and add them to the classes (the class diagram in Figure 12.2 shows the result of the modeling of sequence diagrams). Again, the operations are only sketches and as such don't have to be described in detail with signatures and so on. The goals of this analysis are to achieve a communication between the user/customer and create an understanding of the system being built; it is not a detailed design solution.

A sequence diagram for the use case Lend Item (the borrower does not have a reservation) is shown in Figure 12.4. Sequence diagrams for all the use cases are included in the model on the CD-ROM.

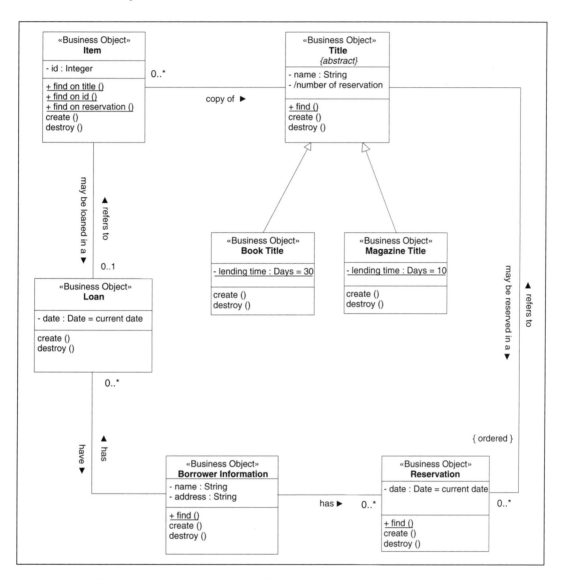

Figure 12.2 *The domain class structure for the library system.*

When modeling the sequence diagrams, it becomes obvious that windows or dialogs are needed to provide an interface to the actors. In Figure 12.4 a window for lending items is present. In the analysis, it is sufficient to be aware that interface windows are needed and to identify the basic interfaces. Windows that can be identified are for lending, reserving, and returning items; a window for maintenance is

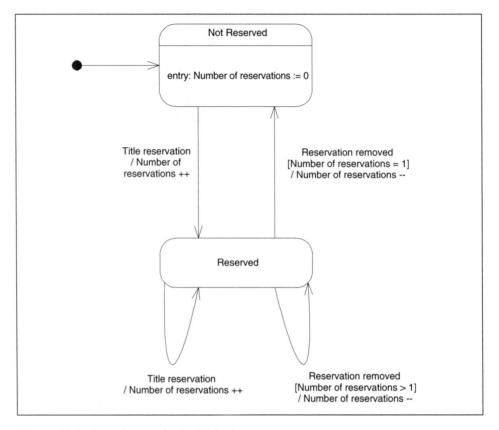

Figure 12.3 *State diagram for the Title class.*

also necessary. The detailed user interface is not specified at this point; again, this is only a sketch of what the user interfaces include. Be aware, however, that there are processes/methods that advocate doing a detailed user interface design or a prototype at this stage, but this case study does not use that technique due to the simplicity of the application. A detailed user interface is part of the design phase.

To separate the window classes in the analysis from the domain classes, the window classes are grouped into a GUI package named GUI Package, and the domain classes are grouped into a package named Business Package. At this point, the application is also given a name, the Unified Library Application.

Design

The design phase and the resulting UML model expands and details the analysis model by taking into account all technical implications and restrictions. The pur-

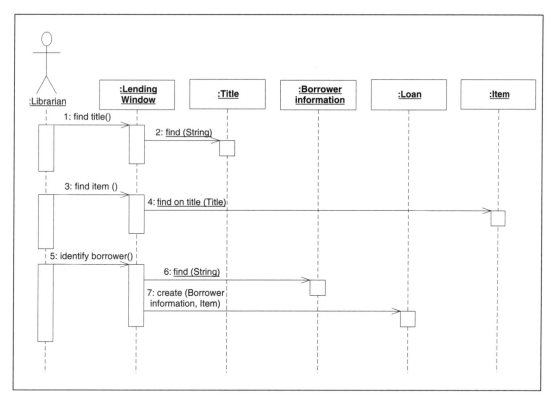

Figure 12.4 *A sequence diagram for the use case Lend Item (the borrower does not have a reservation for the title).*

pose of the design is to specify a working solution that can be easily translated into programming code. The classes defined in the analysis are detailed, and new classes are added to handle technical areas such as a database, a user interface, communication, devices, and more.

The design can be divided into two segments:

- *Architectural design*: This is the high-level design where the packages (subsystems) are defined, including the dependencies and primary communication mechanisms between the packages. Naturally, a clear and simple architecture is the goal, where the dependencies are few and bidirectional dependencies are avoided if at all possible.

- *Detailed design*: This part details the contents in the packages, so that all classes are described in enough detail to give clear specifications to the programmer who will code the class. Dynamic models from the UML are used to demonstrate how objects of the classes behave in specific situations.

Architecture Design

A well-designed architecture is the foundation for an extensible and changeable system. The packages can concern either handling of a specific functional area or a specific technical area. It is vital to separate the application logic (the domain classes) from the technical logic so that changes in either of these segments can be done easily without too much impact on the other part. Key issues to address when defining the architecture are to identify and set up rules for dependencies between the packages (e.g., "subsystems") so that no bidirectional dependencies are created between packages (avoiding packages becoming too tightly integrated with each other), and to identify the need for standard libraries and to find libraries to use. Libraries available on the market today address technical areas such as the user interface, the database, or communication, but more application-specific libraries are expected to emerge as well.

The packages, or subsystems, or layers in the case study are:

- *User interface package*: Classes for the entire user interface, to enable the user to view data from the system and to enter new data. These classes are based on the Java AWT package, which is a standard library in Java for writing user-interface applications. This package cooperates with the business objects package, which contains the classes where the data is actually stored. The UI package calls operations on the business objects to retrieve and insert data into them.

- *Business objects package*: This includes the domain classes from the analysis model such as BorrowerInformation, Title, Item, Loan, and so on. These classes are detailed in the design so that their operations are completely defined, and support for persistence is added. The business object package cooperates with the database package in that all Business object classes must inherit from the Persistent class in the database package.

- *Database package*: The database package supplies services to other classes in the Business object package so that they can be stored persistently. In the current version, the Persistent class will store objects of its subclasses to files in the file system.

- *Utility package*: The utility package contains services that are used in other packages in the system. Currently the ObjId class is the only one in the package. It is used to refer to persistent objects throughout the system and is used in both the user-interface, business object, and database packages.

The internal design of these packages is shown in Figure 12.5.

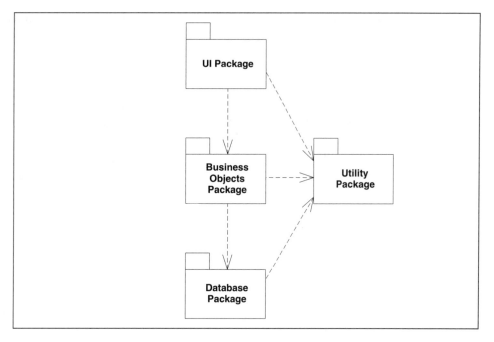

Figure 12.5 *A class diagram showing an architectural overview with the application packages and their dependencies.*

Detailed Design

The purpose of the detailed design is to describe the new technical classes—classes in the user-interface and database packages—and to expand and detail the descriptions of the business object classes, which already have been sketched in the analysis. This is done by creating new class diagrams, state diagrams, and dynamic diagrams (such as sequence, collaboration, and activity diagrams). These are the same diagrams that are used in the analysis; but here, they are defined on a more detailed and technical level. The use-case descriptions from the analysis are used to verify that the use cases are handled in the design; and sequence diagrams are used to illustrate how each use case is technically realized in the system.

Database Package

The application must have objects stored persistently, therefore a database layer must be added to provide this service. The natural solution in a full-fledged application would be to use a commercial database, either a true object-oriented database or a traditional relational database with an object-to-table translation layer. But because our case study application is intended to be portable and does not require licenses from a specific vendor, we have chosen a simpler solution. The objects are simply stored in files on the disk. However, details about the storage are hidden from the application, which has to call only common operations such as store(), update(), delete(), find(), and so on on the objects. All the implementation of the persistent storage handling is done in a class called Persistent, which all classes that need persistent objects must inherit. The Persistent class, which is abstract, requires the subclasses to implement the operations write() and read() with code for how to write its attributes to a file object and how to read the attributes from a file object. The subclasses can also choose to implement class-scope operations to find objects of the class; such an implementation would call the more generic operations in the Persistent superclass.

An important factor in the persistence handling is the ObjId class, whose objects are used to refer to any persistent object in the system (regardless of whether the object is on disk or has been read into the application). ObjId, short for object identity, is a well-known technique for handling object references elegantly in an application. By using object identifiers, an object ID can be passed to the generic Persistent.getObject() operation and the object will be retrieved from persistent storage and returned. Usually this is not done directly, but through a getObject operation in each persistent class, which also performs necessary type checks and conversions. An object identifier can also be passed easily as a parameter between operations (e.g., a search window that looks for a specific object can pass its result to another window through an object ID).

The ObjId is a general class used by all packages in the system (user interface, business objects, and database) so it has been placed in a utility package in the design (it is currently the only utility in that package). Actually, it is most closely related to the database package, but placing it there would mean that the user-interface package would have a dependency directly on the database package, which should be avoided (the user interface should be dependent only on the business objects package).

The current implementation of the Persistent class could be improved. When an object is updated, its current record is simply marked as deleted, and the new version of the object is added to the end of the file. The reason the old record can't be overwritten is that the object may have changed its length (if it has a vector of unlimited size used for storing one-to-many or many-to-many associations). Also, searching for objects currently is done sequentially, by searching the file from start to finish (ignoring deleted records). Some simple improvements could be to reclaim deleted storage in the file and to add an index file that optimizes the searching for objects.

The interface to the Persistent class has been defined so that it should be easy to change the implementation of persistent storage. Some alternatives might be to store the objects in a relational database or in an object-oriented database, or to store them using persistent object support in Java 1.1. There is nothing in the current design that prevents this; only the internal implementation of the Persistent class would have to be changed.

Business Objects Package

The business objects package in the design is based on the corresponding package in the analysis, the domain classes. The classes, their relationships, and behavior are preserved; only the classes are described in more detail, including how their relationships and behavior are implemented. Among these implementation specifications is the fact that all business object classes inherit the Persistent class from the database package and implement the necessary read and write operations.

The operations from the analysis have been detailed, which means some of them have been translated into several operations in the design model and some have changed names. This is considered normal, since the analysis is a sketch of the capabilities of each class while the design is a detailed description of the system. Consequently all operations in the design model must have well-defined signatures and return values (they are not shown in Figure 12.6 due to space restrictions, but they are present in the model on the CD-ROM). Note these changes between the design and the analysis:

- The current version of the system does not have to handle checks on whether an item is returned in time, nor does the system have to handle the ordering of reservations. Therefore the date attribute in the Loan and Reservation classes has not been implemented.

- The handling of magazine and book titles is identical, except for the maximum lending period, which doesn't have to be handled. The subclasses Magazine and Book Title in the analysis has thus been deemed as unnecessary and only a type attribute in the Title class specifies whether the title refers to a book or magazine. There's nothing in object-oriented design that says the design can't simplify the analysis!

Both of these simplifications could be removed easily if deemed necessary in future versions of the application.

The state diagrams from the analysis are also detailed in the design, showing how the states are represented and handled in the working system. The design state diagram for the Title class is shown in Figure 12.7. The states are implemented in the design by using a vector called reservations, which contains the object identifiers

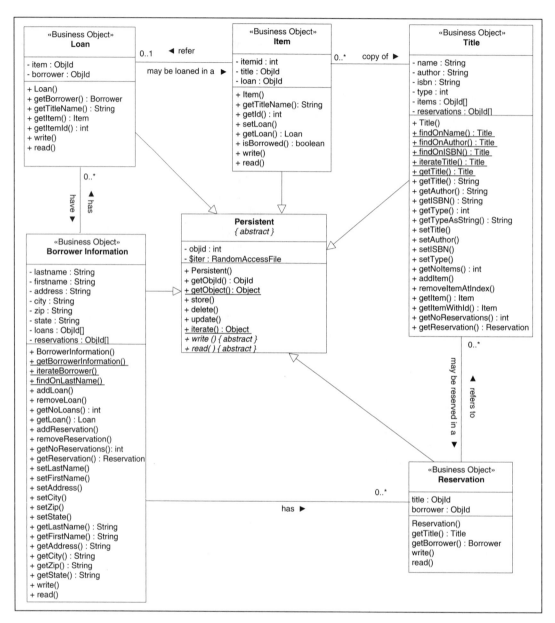

Figure 12.6 *The business objects in the design model.*

of the attached reservation objects (see the association from Title to Reservation in the class diagram). When the vector has a size of zero elements (i.e., it is empty), the Title object is in the state Not Reserved; when the size is one or more, the state

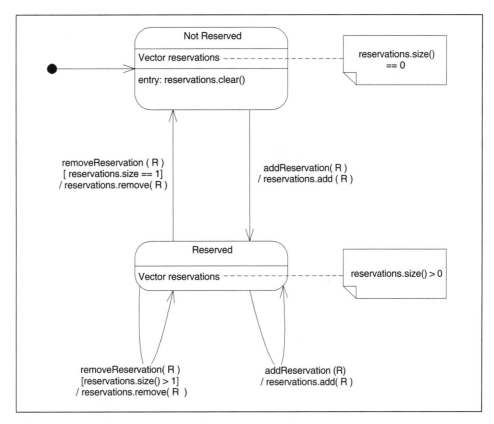

Figure 12.7 *A design state diagram for Title showing the implementation.*

is Reserved. Other objects can change the state of the Title object by calling the operations addReservation() and removeReservation(), as shown in the diagram. Compare the analysis diagram previously shown in Figure 12.3 to the design diagram in Figure 12.7 to see how an analysis state diagram can be translated into a corresponding design diagram showing the implementation of the states.

User-Interface Package

The user interface package is "on top" of the other packages. It presents the services and information in the system to a user. As noted, this package is based on the standard Java AWT (Abstract Window Toolkit) class library for writing user-interface applications in Java, and can be executed on all Java platforms. The classes in the AWT library are not shown in the design model, though they could have been shown in a package of their own (a Java version of Rational Rose to read and show the structure of Java classes would have simplified that). The AWT library has classes for different types of windows (frames, dialogs, etc.) and for different types of interface components such as labels, buttons, edit fields, list boxes, and so on. The AWT library also manages event handling when the user generates events such as mouse clicks or keypresses.

The dynamic models in the design model have been allocated to the GUI package, since all interactions with the user are initiated through the user interface. Again, sequence diagrams have been chosen to show the dynamic models, although some of the sequence diagrams have been converted to collaboration diagrams. The basis for the sequence diagrams is like that in the analysis of the use cases, except that the realizations of the use cases are shown in exact detail in the design model (including the actual operations on the classes; the analysis of the interaction was more of an overview). The sequence diagrams are not drawn as they appear here or in the model, but are drawn in iterations, whereby the final design is slowly generated. Furthermore, other modifications in the sequence diagrams were generated by discoveries made in the implementation (coding) phase. The sequence diagrams in the design model are the result of these iterations. Figure 12.8 shows the design sequence diagram for Add Title. The operations and signatures are exactly as they appear in the code.

Collaboration diagrams can be used as an alternative to sequence diagrams, as shown in Figure 12.9. Note, however, that Rational Rose 4.0 doesn't use the full UML notation for collaboration diagrams. Among other things, the message numbering scheme is simpler; each message is given a sequential number: 1, 2, 3, and so on. The collaboration diagrams shown in the Rational Rose design model are therefore simplified versions of the sequence diagrams, and do not show all the actual advantages of UML collaboration diagrams. A complex sequence diagram is very hard to translate to the collaboration diagrams in Rational Rose 4.0, while a UML collaboration diagram would not have any problem covering the same sequence diagram. The more complex sequence diagrams in the design model have therefore not been translated into collaborations diagram in the Rational Rose model.

User-Interface Design

A special activity carried out during the design phase is the creation of the user interface—its "look and feel." Initiated during the analysis phase, this is done separately, but in parallel to the other design work. (Creating a successful user interface is beyond the scope of this book, however, and other sources devoted to that topic should be consulted for more information.)

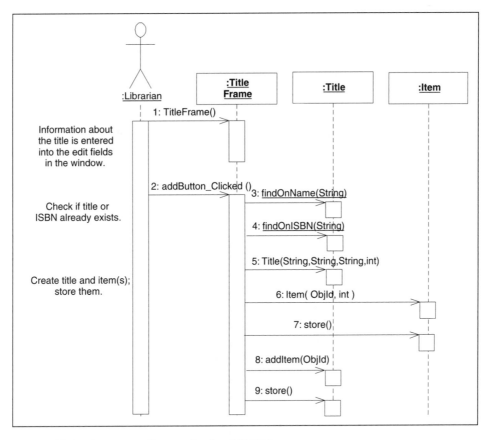

Figure 12.8 *A sequence diagram for the Add Title use case.*

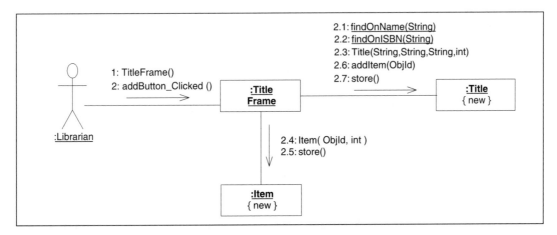

Figure 12.9 *A collaboration diagram for the Add Title use case using correct UML syntax.*

The user interface in the library application is based on the use cases, and has been divided into the following sections, each of which has been given a separate menu bar in the main window menu:

- *Functions*: Windows for the primary functions in the system, that is, lending and returning items and making reservations of titles.

- *Information*: Windows for viewing the information in the system, the collected information about titles and borrowers.

- *Maintenance*: Windows for maintaining the system, that is, adding, updating, and removing titles, borrowers, and items.

The windows have been drawn in the Symantec Visual Café environment, where components such as buttons and edit fields can be visually and interactively incorporated into a window. The environment then generates the necessary code for creating a window with that appearance, including the addition of attributes that map to the components in the window; for example, adding an attribute ok-Button to the AWT Button class, which corresponds to the OK button in the window. The attributes are automatically generated, so their default names are of the sort: label1, label2, textField1, and so on.

In the Visual Café environment, it is also easy to add event handlers for user-generated events such as mouse clicks and menu choices, by selecting a specific component such as the okButton and then selecting an event on that button that needs to be handled such as the Clicked event. The environment then generates an okButton_Clicked method that will be called when the OK button is clicked, an event that itself was generated by code added to a standard handleEvent method (the details of which are not necessary to understand here). When studying classes in the user interface package, it is important to know the principle that says, for example, that an operation findTitleButton_Clicked will be called when the user presses the findTitleButton in the window, that itemList_Selected will be called when an item is selected in the listbox named itemList, and that LendingItem_Action will be called when the menu choice Lending Item is selected. Figure 12.10 shows an example of one of the class diagrams in the user interface package where these types of event handlers can be found. The attributes for buttons, labels, edit fields are not shown.

The resulting application user interface is composed of a main window featuring a menu bar and an appropriate graphic, from which all the other windows in the system can be reached (see Figure 12.11). The other windows typically present a service of the system and are mapped to an initial use case (although not all user interfaces must map from a use case). Note that the windows are small and simple and do not feature a lot of bells and whistles.

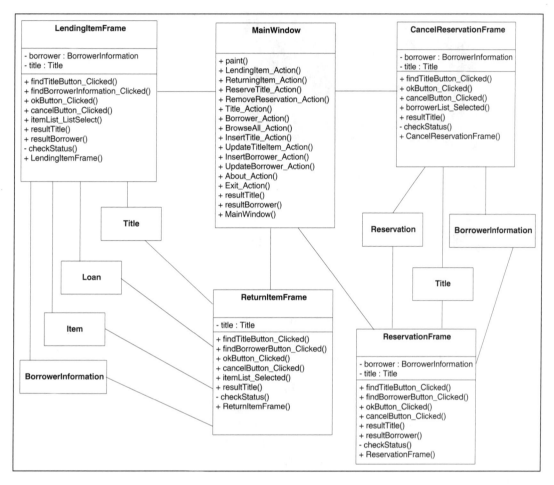

Figure 12.10 *User-interface classes in the Functions menu (shown in the Functions class diagram in the model). All the associations are typically one-to-one, and all imply that the associated window class at some point is created or that the associated business object class at some point is accessed. The associations are not detailed further.*

Implementation

The construction or implementation phase is when the classes are programmed. The requirements specify that the system be able to run on a number of different processors and operating systems, so Java was chosen to implement the system. But note, for this application, Java is being used as a general-purpose programming language. It has not been implemented as a Java applet because no Java applet is per-

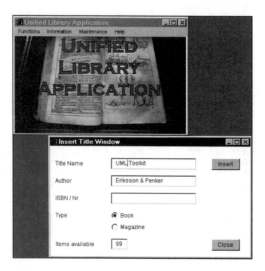

Figure 12.11 *Sample user-interface windows from the library application.*

mitted to access the file system on the client side. Java makes mapping the logical classes to the code components easy, because there is a one-to-one mapping of a class to a Java code file (and a one-to-one mapping to a Java executable .class file). Java also specifies that the name of the file be the same as that of the class it contains.

Figure 12.12 illustrates that the component diagrams in the design model contain (in this case) a simple mapping of the classes in the logical view to components in the component view. The packages in the logical view are also mapped to corresponding packages in the component view, so there is a UI Package in the component view containing the components that implement the classes in the UI Package in the logical view. Each component contains a link to the class description in the logical view making it easy to navigate between the different views (even if, as in this case, it is just as simple to use only the filename). The dependencies between the components are not shown in the component diagrams (except for the business objects package) because the dependencies can be derived from the class diagrams in the logical view.

For coding, the specifications were fetched from the following diagrams in the design model:

- *Class specifications*: The specification of each class, showing in detail the necessary attributes and operations.
- *Class diagrams*: The class diagrams in which the class is present, showing its static structure and relationship to other classes.

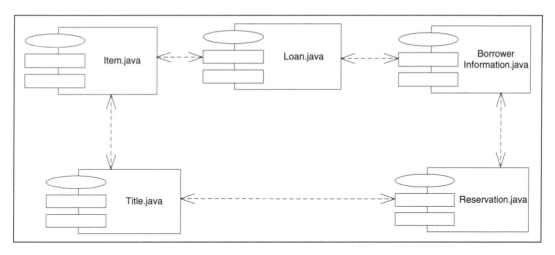

Figure 12.12 *A component diagram identifying the components that implement the domain class. The associations of these classes are bidirectional, therefore dependencies go in both directions between the classes involved in the association.*

- *State diagram*: A state diagram for the class, showing the possible states and the transitions that need to be handled (along with the operations that trigger the transitions).
- *Dynamic diagrams (sequence, collaboration, and activity) in which objects of the class are involved*: Diagrams showing the implementation of a specific method in the class or how other objects are using objects of the class.
- *Use-case diagrams and specifications*: Diagrams that show the result of the system are used when the developer needs more information regarding how the system will be used (when the developer feels he or she is getting lost in details—losing sight of the overall context).

Naturally, deficiencies will be uncovered in the design model during the coding phase. The need for new or modified operations may be identified, meaning that the developer will have to change the design model. This happens in all projects. What's important is to synchronize the design model and the code so that the model can be used as final documentation of the system.

The Java code examples given here are for the Loan class and the TitleFrame class. The Java code for the entire application is available on the accompanying CD-ROM. When studying the code, read it with the UML models in mind and try to see how the UML constructs have been transferred to code. Consider these points:

- The Java package specification is the code equivalent for specifying to which package in the component or logical view the class belongs.
- The private attributes correspond to the attributes specified in the model; and, naturally, the Java methods correspond to the operations in the model.
- The ObjId class (object identifiers) is invoked to implement associations, meaning that associations normally are saved along with the class (since the ObjId class is persistent).

The first code example is from the Loan class, which is a business object class used for storing information about a loan. The implementation is straightforward and the code is simple since the class is mainly a storage place for information. Most of the functionality is inherited from the Persistent class in the database package. The only attributes in the class are the object identifiers for the associations to the Item and BorrowerInformation class, and these association attributes are also stored in the write() and read() operations.

```java
//
//  Loan.java: represents a loan. The loan refers to one
//   title and one borrower.

package bo;
import util.ObjId;
import db.*;
import java.io.*;
import java.util.*;

public class Loan extends Persistent
{
    private ObjId item;
    private ObjId borrower;
    public Loan()
    {
    }
    public Loan(ObjId it, ObjId b)
    {
        item = it;
        borrower = b;
    }
    public BorrowerInformation getBorrower()
    {
        BorrowerInformation ret =
            (BorrowerInformation) Persistent.getObject(borrower);
```

```
            return ret;
        }
        public String getTitleName()
        {
            Item it = (Item) Persistent.getObject(item);
            return it.getTitleName();
        }
        public Item getItem()
        {
            Item it =
                (Item) Persistent.getObject(item);
            return it;
        }
        public int getItemId()
        {
            Item it = (Item) Persistent.getObject(item);
            return it.getId();
        }
        public void write(RandomAccessFile out)
            throws IOException
        {
            item.write(out);
            borrower.write(out);

        }
        public void read(RandomAccessFile in)
            throws IOException
        {
            item = new ObjId();
            item.read(in);
            borrower = new ObjId();
            borrower.read(in);
        }
    }
```

TitleFrame is a user-interface class implementing the window frame where new titles can be added to the system. This class is based on the Java AWT library. The class also contains automatically generated Java code from the Symantec Visual Café environment that determines the layout and look of the window. As previously mentioned, the Visual Café environment allows the user to add and position buttons or edit fields on a window; it also automatically generates the Java code that results in the window's run-time appearance. The automatically generated Java code occurs at the end of the class, and involves the declaration of controls such as

buttons, labels, and edit fields; some standard operations such as show() and han-
dleEvent(); and the creation and initialization of controls in the constructor of the
class. And keep in mind that automatically generated code should not be modified
manually, and is not part of the design model of the class. Only the "real" operations and attributes are modeled, and they occur at the beginning of the class.

You can examine the code in the addButton_Clicked() operation in the context of the Add Title sequence diagram previously shown, as it is the code that implements that sequence diagram. Read the code together with the sequence
diagram to see that it is just another, more detailed description of the same collaboration described by the diagram. The code for all the sequence diagrams in the
design model is included in the source code on the CD-ROM (the operation and
class names are shown in the sequence diagrams).

```java
//
//  TitleFrame.java
//
package ui;
import bo.*;
import util.*;
import java.awt.*;

public class TitleFrame extends Frame {
    private Title current;

    void addButton_Clicked(Event event) {
        if (Title.findOnName(titleField.getText()) != null)
        {
            new MessageBox(this,
                "A Title with that name already exists!");
            return;
        }
        if (Title.findOnISBN(isbnField.getText()) != null)
        {
            new MessageBox(this,
                "A title with the same isbn/nr field already exists!");
            return;
        }
        int type = 0;
        if (bookButton.getState() == true)
            type = Title.TYPE_BOOK;
        else
            if (magazineButton.getState() == true)
                type = Title.TYPE_MAGAZINE;
```

```
        else
        {
            new MessageBox(this,
                "Please specify type of title!");
            return;
        }
    current =
        new Title(
            titleField.getText(),
            authorField.getText(),
            isbnField.getText()
            type);
    int itemno;
    if (itemsField.getText().equals(""))
        itemno = 0;
    else
        itemno = Integer.valueOf(itemsField.getText()).intValue();
    if (itemno > 25)
    {
        new MessageBox(this,
            "Maximum number of items is 25!");
        return;
    }
    for (int i = 0; i < itemno; i++)
    {
        Item it = new Item(current.getObjId(),i+1);
        it.store();
        current.addItem(it.getObjId());
    }
    current.store();
    titleField.setText("");
    authorField.setText("");
    isbnField.setText("");
    itemsField.setText("");
    bookButton.setState(false);
    magazineButton.setState(false);
}

void cancelButton_Clicked(Event event) {
    dispose();
}

public TitleFrame() {
```

```
//{{INIT_CONTROLS
setLayout(null);
addNotify();
resize(insets().left + insets().right + 430,
    insets().top + insets().bottom + 229);
titleLabel = new java.awt.Label("Title Name");
titleLabel.reshape(insets().left + 12,insets().top +
    24,84,24);
add(titleLabel);
titleField = new java.awt.TextField();
titleField.reshape(insets().left + 132,insets().top + 24,
    183,24);
add(titleField);
authorField = new java.awt.TextField();
authorField.reshape(insets().left + 132,insets().top + 60,183,24);
add(authorField);
isbnField = new java.awt.TextField();
isbnField.reshape(insets().left + 132,insets().top + 96,183,24);
add(isbnField);
label1 = new java.awt.Label("ISBN / Nr");
label1.reshape(insets().left + 12,insets().top + 96,84,24);
add(label1);
label2 = new java.awt.Label("Author");
label2.reshape(insets().left + 12,insets().top + 60,84,24);
add(label2);
addButton = new java.awt.Button("Insert");
addButton.reshape(insets().left + 348,insets().top + 24,60,24);
add(addButton);
cancelButton = new java.awt.Button("Close");
cancelButton.reshape(insets().left + 348,insets().top + 192,
    60,24);
add(cancelButton);
label3 = new java.awt.Label("Items available");
label3.reshape(insets().left + 12,insets().top + 192,108,24);
add(label3);
itemsField = new java.awt.TextField();
itemsField.reshape(insets().left + 132,insets().top + 192,36,23);
add(itemsField);
Group1 = new CheckboxGroup();
bookButton = new java.awt.Checkbox("Book", Group1, false);
bookButton.reshape(insets().left + 132,
```

```
        insets().top + 132,108,24);
    add(bookButton);
    magazineButton = new java.awt.Checkbox("Magazine",
        Group1, false);
    magazineButton.reshape(insets().left + 132,
        insets().top + 156,108,24);
    add(magazineButton);
    label4 = new java.awt.Label("Type");
    label4.reshape(insets().left + 12,insets().top + 132,108,24);
    add(label4);
    setTitle("Insert Title Window");
    //}
    bookButton.setState(true);
    titleField.requestFocus();

    //{{INIT_MENUS
    //}}
}

public TitleFrame(String title) {
    this();
    setTitle(title);
}

public synchronized void show() {
    move(50, 50);
    super.show();
}

public boolean handleEvent(Event event) {
    if (event.id == Event.WINDOW_DESTROY) {
        dispose();
        return true;
    }
    if (event.target == addButton &&
        event.id == Event.ACTION_EVENT) {
        addButton_Clicked(event);
        return true;
    }
    if (event.target == cancelButton &&
        event.id == Event.ACTION_EVENT) {
```

```
            cancelButton_Clicked(event);
            return true;
    }
        return super.handleEvent(event);
    }


//{{DECLARE_CONTROLS
java.awt.Label titleLabel;
java.awt.TextField titleField;
java.awt.TextField authorField;
java.awt.TextField isbnField;
java.awt.Label label1;
java.awt.Label label2;
java.awt.Button addButton;
java.awt.Button cancelButton;
java.awt.Label label3;
java.awt.TextField itemsField;
java.awt.Checkbox bookButton;
CheckboxGroup Group1;
java.awt.Checkbox magazineButton;
java.awt.Label label4;
//}}

//{{DECLARE_MENUS
//}}
    }
```

Test and Deployment

The application, of course, has to be tested. For this example, the original use cases were tried in the finished application to determine whether they were supported by the application and could be performed as defined in the use-case descriptions. The application was also tested in a more informal way by putting it into the hands of a user. A larger-scale application would require more formal specifications and an errors-report system.

The deployment of the system is the actual delivery, including the documentation, which in this case comprises the models and this chapter. In a real-life project, user manuals and marketing descriptions would typically be part of the documentation work. A deployment diagram should also be drawn of the physical architecture, as shown in Figure 12.13. This system can be deployed in any computer with Java support; and note, some of the exercises require a printer.

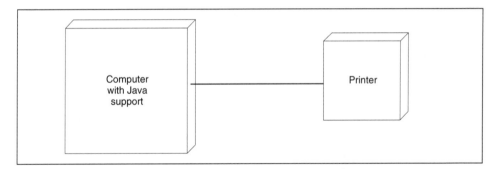

Figure 12.13 *A deployment diagram for the library system. Components could have been allocated to the computer, but because all of these execute on the same computer, it was unnecessary in this case.*

Summary

The case study demonstrated how a short text specification of a system can be modeled in an analysis model, expanded and detailed into a design model, and finally implemented and programmed in Java. The various parts of this case study were designed by a group of people who made every effort to work in the same manner they would have used on an actual project. And though the different phases and activities might seem separate and to have been conducted in a strict sequence, the work is more iterative in practice. The lessons and conclusions resulting from the design were fed back into the analysis model, and discoveries made in the implementation were updated and changed in the design model. This is the normal way to build object-oriented systems.

Exercises

The exercises presented here will enable you to immediately begin to apply the UML. They are divided into analysis and design/construction categories. The first category lists new requirements on the system that have to be analyzed, designed, and implemented in the system. The second category contains technical changes and improvements that primarily affect design and implementation. You can decide to what the extent to implement the solutions to the exercises, but note that some can only be made in the analysis and design models. If you are proficient in Java, you can code and test the solutions in the final application.

The initial exercise is provided to familiarize you with Rational Rose 4.0. Start the tool, open the analysis or design model, and start playing around with the model. Look at the different views, the different diagrams, and the specifications; then print out the complete model.

Analysis Exercises

Exercise 1: Introduce functionality to inform a customer with a reservation when an item of the reserved title is returned to the library. The customer with the oldest reservation should be informed first.

Exercise 2: Introduce functionality to inform a person when a loan is due.

Exercise 3: Extend the system so that reservations are removed after a specified amount of time.

Exercise 4: Extend the handling of titles so that they can be placed in different categories, and to add user-defined information to each title (e.g., a review of a book).

Exercise 5: Extend the system to administrate the purchases of new items.

Exercise 6: Introduce rules in the library model to constrain the loans. For example, restrict borrowers to no more than five reservations at the same time, or to no more than 10 loans at the same time. Make it easy to define such new rules.

Exercise 7: Insert a general class for printing lists and letters; for example, lists of titles and items for an inventory, and letters to borrowers about reservations and loans.

Exercise 8: Extend the model with an Internet connection to enable a borrower to search for titles and items on a World Wide Web site.

Exercise 9: In the current model, the administration of services is handled from the user-interface objects that perform operations on the business objects. Change the architecture so that control object classes (classes that handle a specific service from start to finish) are supported. An example of a control object class is one that collects statistics about the current situation in the library—the number of borrowers, titles, items, and current loans—and displays the results in a window.

Exercise 10: Rebuild the library model to support integration of other libraries using the same system. This means that one library should be able to search for a title or an item in another library. A library should be able to lend an item in another library by sending a message to that specific library, which then performs the loan procedure and sends the item by mail to the lending library. Show a deployment diagram for this new system.

Design and Construction Exercises

Exercise 11: Add the Book Title and Magazine Title classes to the design, and add some new appropriate attributes to each of these classes. Make the existing Title class abstract and make sure the new classes can be stored persistently.

Exercise 12: Change the "Browse All" window so that a user can double-click on a title or a borrower in the list-boxes and immediately enter the correct Update window.

Exercise 13: Change the design of the search facility of objects, so that "wild card" characters can be used when searching for titles, authors, or borrowers (e.g., "UML★" searches for all titles starting with "UML").

Exercise 14: Change the design of the search facility of objects, so that multiple search results are handled (currently only the first match will be returned). The number of "hits" should be reported and the user should be able to choose among the result records.

Exercise 15: Add support in the user interface for a toolbar with buttons to choose a function from.

Exercise 16: Improve the performance of the database by adding support for reusing deleted records in a file, and support for an index file where a more efficient search for a specific object can be done (the current search is sequential).

Exercise 17: Change the design of the database package so a relational database is used instead of the current file solution. This will require new classes in the database package. Try not to change the interface to the Persistent class, so that the rest of the application will remain unaffected by the change.

Exercise 18: Change the user interface so that the application becomes a "one-window" application, where the main window changes according to what function is currently used.

Exercise 19: Add a new utility class for creating a log which all parts of the application can use to log either debug or trace messages of its operation. The type of information actually saved in the log should be configurable from the user interface.

Exercise 20: Remove the need for the write() and read() operations in a persistent class. Instead, use a solution where persistent classes maintain metadata (data about itself, i.e., a description of its attributes), so that a database class can query an unknown persistent object about what kind of attributes it has and the values of these attributes, and then store them in the database. A new class Metadata should be defined, and a meta-data object should be aggregated by all persistent classes.

Visual Glossary

Activity diagram

Action state:

Action

Start state:

Stop state:

Action state transition:

transition specification

Decision:

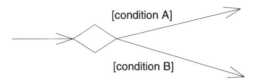

[condition A]

[condition B]

Concurrent actions:

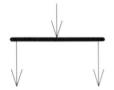

Swimlanes:

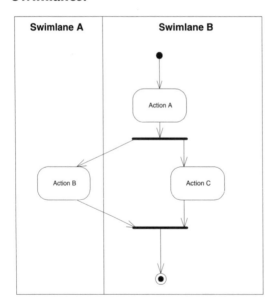

Object as input or output:

Signal sending:

Signal receiving:

Class diagram

Class:

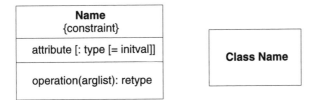

Association:

Multiplicity:

Role names in association:

Qualified association:

Or-constraint (between associations):

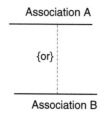

Association class:

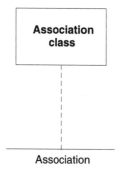

Ternary association:

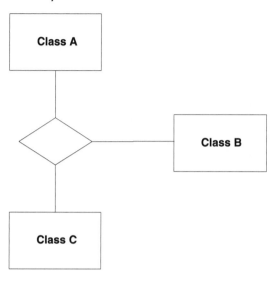

Aggregation:

Composite aggregation:

Aggregation (alternative):

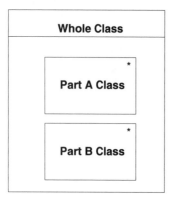

Generalization:

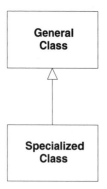

Abstract class:

<table>
<tr><td>Class
{abstract}</td></tr>
</table>

Dependency:

Refinement:

Interface:

Interface name

Parameterized class (template):

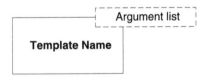

Instantiated parameterized class:

Template Name
<parameters>

Object:

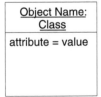

Collaboration diagram

Object:

Link (between objects):

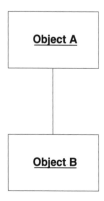

Communication between linked objects:

message label
⟶

Synchronous message:

⟶

Asynchronous message:

⟶

Simple message:

⟶

Creation and destruction of object:

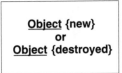

Active class or object:

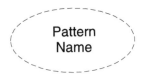

Pattern (parameterized collaboration):

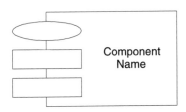

Component diagram

Component:

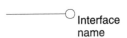

Interface:

Dependency:

Deployment diagram

Node:

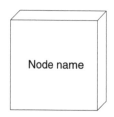

Communication association:

«Communication Type»
_____

Dependency (from node to component or between components/objects):

General mechanims

Note:

Package:

Nested packages and dependency between packages:

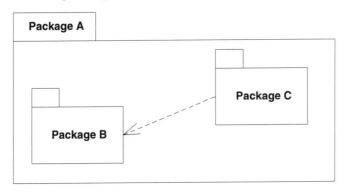

Stereotype (different representations):

Constraint:

{constraint}

Property:

{tag = value}

Sequence diagram

Object instance with lifeline:

Activation of object:

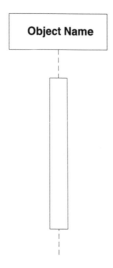

Synchronous message:

Asynchronous message:

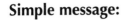

Simple message:

Synchronous message with immediate return:

Condition:

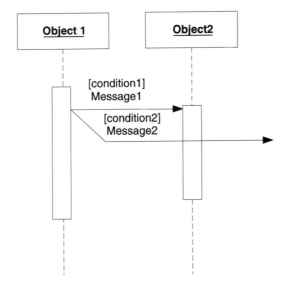

Message with transmission time:

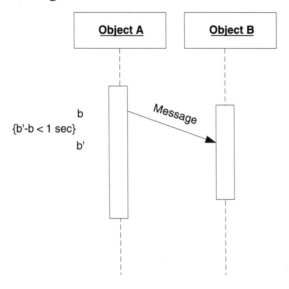

Script:

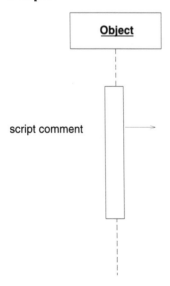

Creation of object:

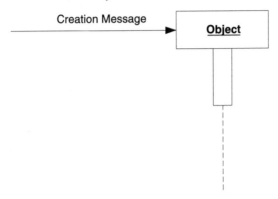

Destruction of object:

Recursion:

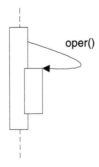

State diagram

State:

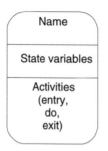

State transition:

Start state:

Stop state:

Substates:

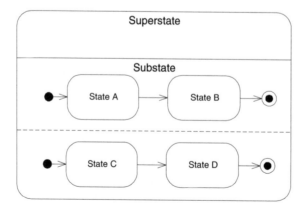

History indicator:

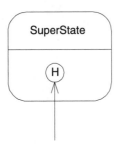

Use-case diagram

System:

Actor:

Use case:

Association:

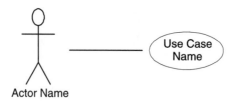

Actor Name

Generalization:

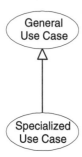

Glossary

Abstract class   a class with no instances. An abstract class is used only to inherit from.

Action   a procedure of executable statements. An action may be attached to state transitions or used when specifying activities.

Action expression   an expression that results in actions.

Action state   a state with internal actions that are executed while in the state. An action state typically has an automatic state transition to another action state when its actions have been performed.

Activation   the execution of an action. An object is said to be activated while it is executing.

Active class   a class whose objects execute concurrently and have their own thread of control.

Active object   an object that has its own thread of control.

Activity diagram   shows interactions, focusing on the work performed. The activity diagram displays a sequence of actions including alternative execution and objects involved in performing the work.

Actor   something external that interacts with the system. An actor can be a human being or other systems.

Aggregate   a relationship in which one class consists of another class. The relationship indicates a whole-part connection. Aggregate is a special case of association.

Analysis   used to examine a problem and produce a hypothesis or diagnosis of a solution. In object-oriented analysis, a model is created of all the real-world entities, including their relationships and collaboration, without consideration of a technical solution.

And-state   substates (within another state) that may exist at the same time.

Application   the stereotyped component «application» represents an executable program.

Architecture   ". . . a description of the subsystems and components of a software system and the relationships between them. Subsystems and components are typically specified in different views to show the relevant functional and non-functional properties of a software system. The software architecture of a system is an artifact. It is the result of the software design activity" (Buschmann, 1996).

Argument   values that are parsed to parameters within an operation's signature.

Association   a relationship that describes a set of links between classes (their objects). Used to describe that objects of the involved classes have some sort of connection to each other.

Association class   a class attached to an association to provide extra information about the connection. The association class is just like a normal class; it can have attributes, operations, and other associations.

Association role   an association can have roles connected to each class involved in the association. The role-name indicates the role played by the class (and its objects) in terms of the association. Role-names are part of the association, not of the classes.

Asynchronous message   asynchronous flow-of-control occurs when there is no explicit return to the caller and the sender continues to execute after sending the message without waiting for it to be handled.

Attribute   a member within a class to store data. The attribute has a name and a type and may have a default value.

Becomes   a stereotyped dependency whose source and target are the same instance. The stereotype «becomes» means that one instance will change state (in time/space) from one state (the source instance state) to another (the target instance state). Typically used to show how one object is moved to another location in the physical architecture (transferred from one node to another).

Behavior   an observable effect, including its results.

Bind   a stereotyped dependency. The dependency connects types or collaborations and has arguments to match properties of the source to the target. A bind dependency specifies that the source is a binding of the target, where parameters are used to make the source definition complete. Typically used to show the instantiaton of a parameterized class (template).

Boundary object   a stereotyped class whose objects are used to communicate with actors.

Broadcast   a constraint applied to a set of messages. Broadcast specifies that the messages are not invoked in a certain order.

Call   a stereotyped dependency connecting operations in classes. If class A has a call dependency to class B, operations in class A may call any of the operations in class B.

Class   a model element used to model things, both intellectual and physical. A class is a type (*see* Type) and may be instantiated to objects that are individual entities (objects) of the same class. A class is described with members that are attributes, operations, and relationships to other classes. The members are reflected in objects of the class. A class can be generalized and specialized; extension mechanisms may be attached to the class.

Class diagram   shows a static structure with classes and their definitions and relationships.

Collaboration   describes how a set of objects interact to perform some specific function. A collaboration describes both a context and an interaction. The context shows the set of objects involved in the collaboration along with their links to each other. The interaction shows the communication that the objects perform in the collaboration.

Collaboration diagram   describes how objects interact, and focuses on the collaboration in space, which means that the relationships (links) between the objects are explicitly shown.

Complete inheritance   the complete generalization constraint says that all subclasses in an inheritance relationship have been specified. No additional subclasses may be added.

Component   a physical implementation that uses logical model elements as defined in class or interaction diagrams. A component can be viewed at different stages of the development such as compile time, link time, or run time.

Component diagram   describes software components (source, link, and executable) and their dependencies to each other, representing the structure of the code. The components are distributed to nodes in deployment diagrams.

Composite state   a state that consists of substates (and-substates or or-substates).

Composition   a composition aggregation is an aggregation where the whole owns its parts (strong ownership). The parts live inside the whole and will be destroyed together with its whole.

Concrete class   a class that can have instances (objects). The opposite of an abstract class.

Concurrency   when two or more activities execute simultaneously (in parallel).

Concurrent substate   *see* And-state.

Constraint   a semantic condition or restriction. Certain constraints are predefined in the UML; others may be user-defined. For example, a constraint could restrict which objects may be part of a specific association.

Context   a description of a set of objects involved in collaboration, including their links to each other.

Control object   a stereotyped class whose objects typically handle the processing and operational sequence of entity objects. A control object often controls the realization of a use case.

Copy   a copy dependency connects two instances, which means that the source instance is an exact copy of the target instance (but that they still have unique and different identities and are thus different instances).

Deadlock   occurs when a number of threads are all waiting for each other.

Dependency   a relationship between two model elements, in which a change to the independent model element will affect the dependent model element.

Deployment diagram   shows the run-time architecture of processors, devices, and the software components that execute in the architecture. It is the ultimate physical description of the system topology, including the structure of the hardware units and the software that executes on each unit.

Design   used to describe how an analysis model may be implemented within a technical environment. A design model should provide enough detail so that the system can be implemented in a programming language.

Destroyed   a constraint that affects the life cycle of objects. The constrained object is destroyed during the execution of an interaction.

Diagram   a view element that shows (projects) a set of model elements. There are nine diagrams within the UML: use-case, component, class, deployment, state, activity, sequence, collaboration, and object.

Discriminator   *see* Powertype.

Disjoint inheritance   subclasses inheriting from a common superclass cannot be specialized to one common subclass (using multiple inheritance). Disjoint inheritance is the default, and is the opposite of overlapping inheritance.

Document   the stereotyped component «document» is a representation of a document (containing documentation rather than source code that could be compiled).

Element   the abstract base class for most constituents in the UML. The element class provides an anchor upon which a number of mechanisms may be attached. Element is specialized to model elements, view elements, system, and model. A model element is an abstraction drawn from the system being modeled (e.g., a class, message, nodes, event, etc.). A view element is a projection (textual or graphical) of a single model element or a collection of model elements (when the view element is a diagram). The view elements are textual or graphical symbols (e.g., a rectangle symbol representing a class).

Entity object   the entity stereotype is used to model objects that hold information, typically business objects such as debt, invoice, insurance contract, and so on. Usually, they are persistently stored in the system.

Enumeration   a stereotyped primitive type, specifying a set of values (a domain) that are the allowed values for the enumerated primitive type.

Event   a significant occurrence in time or space.

Event-Signature   consists of an event-name and parameters.

Export   a package may export its contents (the elements) so that the contents may be referred to and used in other packages.

Extends   a generalization relationship between use cases where one use case extends another by adding actions to a general use case. The extending use case may include behavior from the use case being extended (depending on conditions in the extension). Described by the stereotyped generalization «extends».

Façade   a stereotyped package that refers only to elements from other packages (imports, via friend dependency, etc.). The façade does not own any elements, but typically presents an interface to the services provided by a package.

File   the stereotyped component «file» is a file containing source code.

Fire   a state transition is said to fire when the attached event specification occurs.

Friend   the stereotyped friend dependency between packages or classes means that the friend element may access elements that have the protected and private visibility (which normally it can't). The friend construct is directly available in the C++ programming language.

Generalizable element   not all elements may be specialized or generalized, only generalizable elements. The generalizable elements are stereotype, package, and type (including subtypes to type, including class).

Generalization   a relationship between a general element and a more specific element. The more specific element is fully consistent with the more general element and contains additional information or behavior. An instance of the more specific element may be used wherever the more general element can be used.

Global   a constraint applied to a link role specifying that the corresponding instance is visible because it is in global scope (the instance is available through a global name that is known throughout the system).

Guard-condition   a Boolean expression of a state transition. If the guard-condition is combined with an event-signature, the event must occur and the guard-condition must be true for the state to change. However, only a guard-condition can be attached to a state transition, meaning that the state will change when the condition becomes true.

History indicator   used to memorize internal states.

Import   the stereotyped import dependency between packages means that a package imports and can access elements within another package that has the public visibility.

Incomplete inheritance   an incomplete generalization indicates that new subclasses may be added in the future. Incomplete generalization is the opposite of complete generalization and is the default.

Inheritance   *see* Generalization.

Instance   an individual member described by a type. An instance of a class (the subclass to type) is an object.

Interaction   shows how the classes/objects interact to perform a specific functionality.

Interaction diagram   a generic term for sequence, collaboration, and activity diagrams.

Interface publishes classes, packages, and components. An interface describes the externally visible and accessible behavior of a class, a package, or a component.

Interface inheritance generalization and specialization among interfaces (since interfaces don't have implementation, only the interface is inherited).

Invariant applies to a type and specifies a property (i.e., condition) that must be preserved over the lifetime of an instance of the type.

Label used in the margins of sequence diagrams to specify iterations, loops, time constraints, and so on. Labels may also be used on messages in collaboration and sequence diagrams to specify details about the communication (message labels).

Library the stereotyped component «library» shows that a component is a static or dynamic library.

Link a semantic connection between instances; an instantiation of an association, the actual connection between two (or more) objects.

Link role an instance of an association role.

Local a constraint applied to a link role, specifying that the corresponding instance is visible because it is a local variable in an operation.

Member a part of a type or a class denoting either an attribute or an operation.

Message a communication between objects that conveys information with the expectation that activity will ensue. The receipt of a message is normally considered an event.

Metaclass a class that can be instantiated to other classes (a class for classes).

Metamodel a model that describes other models, expressed in a metalanguage. Metamodels are used to describe UML. UML is both a modeling language and a metalanguage since it is expressed using itself.

Metatype a type whose instances are types.

Method the implementation of an operation.

Model an abstract description of a system, expressed with diagrams.

Model coordination different models of the same thing must be able to be integrated and related to each other. Models should be coordinated on each level of abstraction (e.g., structure and behavior) and between the different levels of abstraction (e.g., system versus subsystem and analysis versus design).

Model element   the concepts within the UML, for example, class, object, node, and state. Most model elements have a corresponding view element that shows their graphical appearance; they may, therefore, be projected within diagrams.

Model integration   if a set of models have the same purpose and represent the same thing, it should be possible to put them together without inconsistencies.

Model quality   (high) model quality means that all models must have an explicit and clear purpose, and that they capture the essence of what is being studied and modeled. All models should be easy to communicate, verify, validate, and maintain.

Modeling language   a language used to express models, defined with syntax and semantics. Some modeling languages also have pragmatic rules.

Multiple inheritance   when a type is specialized from more than one supertype.

Multiplicity   the range of allowed links and how they combine the objects at each end of the link. There is a range of nonnegative integers on each role in an association or aggregation, specifying the number of objects allowed in each role.

Name   a string used to identify a model element.

New   a constraint that affects the life cycle of objects. Describes that an object is created during the execution of the interaction.

Node   physical objects (devices) that have some kind of computational resource. Includes computers with processors, but also devices such as printers, card readers, communication devices, and so on.

Note   a comment attached to an element or a collection of elements. A note has no semantics.

Object   a unique instance of a class.

Object diagram   a snapshot of a system execution, showing objects and their links.

Object lifeline   a line in a sequence diagram that represents the existence of an object.

Operation   a member of a class. An operation is defined as a function with a signature and an implementation.

Or-constraint   applied to a set of associations that have constraints on their links. The or-constraint may be applied where an association connects a single class with a set of other classes. The or-constraint specifies that an object of the single class may be connected to only one of the associated classes objects (on the opposite side of the association).

Or-state   substates that cannot exist at the same time.

Overlapping inheritance   subclasses inheriting from a common superclass can be specialized to one common subclass using multiple inheritance. The opposite of disjoint inheritance.

Package   a grouping mechanism to link elements; for example, to create groups of diagrams, classes, nodes, and so on.

Page   the stereotyped component «page» is a representation of a Web page.

Parameter   the specification of a variable that can be changed, passed, or returned. A parameter can include a name, type, and direction. Parameters are used for operations, messages, and events.

Parameterized class   an incomplete class that needs to be bound with a parameter (typically a type) to become complete. It is used to express generic classes that are filled with types (such as classes and primitive types) to instantiate other, more specialized classes. Parameterized classes are often an alternative to using inheritance. In C++, a parameterized class is called a template.

Pattern   smart, generic, well-proven, simple, and reusable solutions used to design object-oriented systems. A pattern is documented as a collaboration in UML.

Persistence   applies to a type. Defining a class as persistent means that objects of the class may be stored in a database or a file, and that the object can retain its value (state) between different executions of the program.

Postcondition   a condition that must be true after the completion of an operation.

Powertype   when a generalization is specialized, a discriminator can be used to specify on what basis the inheritance is made. The discriminator is used to separate instances. The discriminator type is called a powertype. A powertype works at the type level, while the discriminator works at the instance level.

Precondition   a condition that must be true before the operation is invoked.

Primitive type   a nonclass, such as an integer or an enumeration. There are no predefined primitive types in UML.

Process (activities)   a description of a set of related activities that, correctly performed, will satisfy an explicit goal.

Process (program execution)   a "heavyweight" thread of control, in contrast to a thread, which is a "lightweight" thread of control. The important difference between process and thread is that a process normally encapsulates all its internal structure and executes in its own memory space, while a thread executes in a memory space shared with other threads.

Process user   the user of a process; in the case of a software engineering process, normally the developer.

Projection   model elements are projected in diagrams via view elements; for example, a class is a model element, its view element is a rectangle and a diagram where it might be projected is a class diagram.

Property   a general description for built-in properties, such as names on elements. A property may also be predefined and user-defined tagged values attached to model elements. Property-lists specify the value domain for attributes.

Qualifier   qualified associations are used together with one-to-many or many-to-many associations. The qualifier distinguishes among the set of objects at the many end of an association (e.g., works as a key in navigation among the objects in the association).

Recursion   when an operation calls itself (until a condition becomes true).

Refinement   a relationship between two descriptions of the same thing, but at different levels of abstraction. The refinement is a stereotyped dependency relationship that can be used to connect an analysis description with the design description of the same thing.

Relationship   a semantic connection among model elements. A relationship is specialized to generalization, dependency, association, transition, and link.

Role   an association (or aggregate) can have roles connected to each class involved, indicating the role played by the class in terms of the association. Roles are a useful technique to specify the context for a class and its objects. Role names are part of the association, not part of the classes.

Scheduling   a part of the synchronization between active objects is handled through the scheduling of active objects. Scheduling determines which thread should run next where a number of threads are conceivable.

Self   a constraint applied to a link role, specifying that an object can send messages to itself (typically used in dispatchers).

Semantics used to describe the meaning of something. Semantics may be seen as the link between a concept and the symbol for that concept, and must be known when communicating about the concept, otherwise misunderstandings will arise.

Send-clause a variant on an action; an explicit syntax for sending a message during the transition between two states in a state diagram.

Sequence diagram describes how objects interact with each other. Sequence diagrams focus on time, meaning they display when messages are sent and received.

Signal a stereotyped class whose objects are sent as messages.

Signature normally considered the name of an operation, including a list of parameters and a return-type.

Simple message represents a flat flow of control, illustrating how the control is passed from one object to another without describing any details about the communication. This message type is used when details about the communication are not known or not considered relevant in the diagram.

Starvation when one thread (active object) never is able to run. The problem occurs when the priorities of the threads are defined in such a way that it is impossible or very difficult for one thread to gain control.

State an object state is determined by its attribute values and links to other objects. A state is a result of previous activities in the object.

State diagram captures object life cycles (also the life cycles of subsystems and systems). State diagrams illustrate how events (messages, time, errors, and state changes affect object states over time.

State vertex a source or target of a state transition.

Stereotype a type of modeling element that extends the semantics of the UML. Stereotypes must be based on elements that already are defined in the UML. Stereotypes may extend the semantics but not the structure of preexisting elements. Certain stereotypes are predefined in UML, others may be user-defined.

Stub a stereotyped package that represents a package that is incompletely implemented. The stub presents a small piece of another system.

Subclass a class that is a specialization of another class.

Substate a state within another state.

Subsystem   a part of a system. The representation of a subsystem in UML is a package.

Subtype   a type that is a specialization of another type.

Superclass   a class that is a generalization of another class.

Superstate   a state that contains other states and substates.

Supertype   a type that is a generalization of another type.

Swimlane   groups activities in an activity diagram according to their responsibilities. Swimlanes may be used for several different purposes; for example, to show explicitly where actions are performed (in which object) or to show in which part of an organization the work is performed.

Synchronization   synchronization mechanisms are objects used to control the execution of concurrent threads, so that there is no conflicting usage of shared resources or overall ineffective resource usage.

Synchronous message   a nested flow of control, typically implemented as an operation call. The operation that handles the message is completed (including any further nested messages being sent as part of the handling) before the caller resumes execution.

Syntax   the rules that restrict how concepts (elements) may be combined with each other.

System   a set of items organized in some way; for example, information system, business system, or embedded system.

Table   the stereotyped component «table» represents a database table.

Tagged value   the explicit definition of a property as a name-value pair. In a tagged value, the name is referred to as the tag. Certain tags are predefined in the UML. In UML, property is used in a general sense for any value connected to an element, including attributes in classes, associations, and tagged values.

Template   *see* Parameterized class.

Thread   a process is a "heavyweight" thread of control; while a thread is a "lightweight" thread of control. The important difference between process and thread is that a process normally encapsulates all its internal structure and executes in its own memory space, while a thread executes in a memory space shared with other threads.

Time event passage of a designated period of time after a designated event (often the entry of a state) occurs.

Time expression an expression for a time event.

Trace a stereotyped dependency from one model element to another model element. The elements traced to each other may be in the same diagram or in different diagrams. The trace indicates that the source can be traced conceptually back to the target.

Transient a constraint that affects the life cycle of objects. Transient objects are created and destroyed in the same execution of a collaboration; that is, the constraint transient is a combination of the new and destroyed constraints.

Transition a relationship between two states that indicates that an object in the first state will perform certain specified actions and enter the second state when a specified event occurs and/or specified conditions are satisfied.

Type a description of a set of instances that share the same operations, attributes, relationships, and semantics. Primitive type, class, and use case are all types.

Use case a description of how a system can be used (from a external actor's point of view). Use cases show the functionality of a system, and are described in terms of external actors, use cases, and the system being modeled. A use case should yield an observable result of value to a particular actor.

Use-case diagram a use-case model is described as a use-case diagram, which contains elements for the system, the actors and the use cases, and displays the different relationships between these elements.

Use-case model describes a system's functional requirements in terms of use cases.

Uses a generalization relationship where one use case uses another use case, indicating that as part of the specialized use case, the behavior of the general use case will also be included.

Utility a stereotyped type that contains only class-scope operations and attributes. A utility is never instantiated.

Value an element of a type domain. The type domain specified for a certain type; for example, the number 42 is in the type domain for integer.

View shows different aspects of the system being modeled. A view is not a graph but an abstraction consisting of a number of diagrams (which are the actual graphs).

View element a projection of one or more model elements (also called notation).

Visibility an enumeration where the set of allowed values are public, protected, private, and implementation. The visibility specifies the allowed access to elements within types and packages.

Vote a constraint applied to a message. Vote constrains a collection of return messages. The vote constraint specifies that the return value is selected through a majority vote of all the return values in the collection.

References

ANSI X3H7 95. Object Model Feature Matrix, Doc. No. X3H7-93-007v10, ANSI, USA, 1995.

Astrakan 97. *The Astrakan Method*. (Sweden, Astrakan Strategic Development), 1997.

M. Awad, J. Kuusela, & J. Ziegler. *Object-Oriented Technology for Real-Time Systems*. (Upper Saddle River, NJ: Prentice Hall), 1996.

G. Booch. *Object-Oriented Analysis and Design with Applications*. (Redwood City, CA: Benjamin Cummings), 1994.

F. Buschmann, R. Meunier, H. Rohnert, P. Sommerlad, & M. Stal. *A System of Patterns: Pattern-Oriented Software Architecture*. (New York: John Wiley & Sons, Inc.), 1996.

The Cambridge Dictionary of Philosophy. (Cambridge: Press Syndicate of the University of Cambridge), 1995.

Catalysis v0.8 97. Desmond Francis D'Souza and Alan Cameron Wills, USA, 1997, in press. Component-Based Development Using Catalysis version Draft 0.8. 1997.

D. Coleman, P. Arnold, S. Bodoff, C. Dollin, H. Gilchrist, F. Hayes, & P. Jeremes. *Object-Oriented Development: The Fusion Method*. (Upper Saddle River, NJ: Prentice-Hall), 1994.

COMMA 96. COTAR. *Technical Report*, (Sydney, Australia: Center for Object Technology Application and Research, School of Computing Sciences), 1996.

H-E. Eriksson & M. Penker. *Objektorientering—Handbok och lexikon.* (Lund, Sweden: Studentlitteratur), 1996.

D. Falkenberg, W. Hesse, P. Lindgreen, B. Nilsson, J. L. Han Oei, C. Rolland, R. Stamper, F. Van Assche, A. Verrijn-Stuart, & K. Voss. "A Framework of Information System Concepts." *The FRISCO Report*, 1996.

E. Gamma, R. Helm, R. Johnson, & J. Vlissides. *Design Patterns.* (Reading, MA: Addison-Wesley), 1994.

A. Hutt. *Object-Oriented Analysis and Design: Description of Methods.* (New York: John Wiley & Sons, Inc.), 1994.

A. Hutt. *Object-Oriented Analysis and Design: Comparison of Methods.* (New York: John Wiley & Sons, Inc.), 1994.

I. Jacobson, M. Christerson, P. Jonsson, & G. Övergaard. *Object-Oriented Software Engineering.* (Reading, NY: Addison-Wesley), 1992.

N. Jayaratna. *Understanding and Evaluating Methodologies—NIMSAD.* (New York: McGraw-Hill), 1994.

P. Kruchten. "A Rational Development Process." White paper from Rational Software Corp. Santa Clara, CA 1996.

P. Kruchten. "The 4+1 View Model of Architecture," *IEEE Software*, IEEE, November 1995.

H. Leavitt. "The Volatile Organization: Everything Triggers Everything Else," *Managerial Psychology*, 1972.

B. Malmberg. *Readings in Modern Linguistics.* (Stockholmn, Sweden: Läromedelsförlagen), 1972.

G. Morgan. *Images of Organization.* (Thousand Oaks, CA: Sage Publications, Inc.), 1986.

B. Nilsson. "Towards a Framework of Information Systems Concepts." Keynote presentation, Conference ISCO3, 1995.

B. Nilsson. "Perspective on Modeling the Business and its IT Support," Presentation, Conference ER94, 1994.

B. Nilsson. "Vision 95," CaiSE91 Conference on Advanced Information Systems Engineering, 1991.

B. Nilsson. "On Models and Mappings in a Data Base Environment—A Holistic Approach to Data Modeling." Unpublished Dissertation, 1979.

OMG. *OA&D RFP Response*, (IBM Corporation and ObjectTime Limited USA), 1997.

OPEN Modeling Language Reference Manual 1.0. Open Consortium (Contact: David Firesmith, Knowledge Systems Corporation, Cary, NC), 1996.

M. Penker. "Report on NIMSAD," The Department of Computer Sciences, KTH—Royal Institute of Technology, Stockholmn, Sweden, 1996.

J. Rumbaugh, M. Blaha, W. Premerlani, F. Eddy, & F. Lorensen. *Object-Oriented Modeling and Design*. (Englewood Cliffs, NJ: Prentice-Hall), 1991.

B. Selic, G. Gullekson, & P. T. Ward, *Real-Time Object-Oriented Modeling*. (New York: John Wiley & Sons, Inc.), 1994.

G. Steneskog, Process Management, Stockholmn, Sweden: Liber), 1991.

D. Taylor. *Object-Oriented Technology: A Manager's Guide*. (Reading, MA: Addison-Wesley), 1991.

G. Booch, J. Rumbaugh, I. Jacobson, *Unified Modeling Language Semantics and Notation Guide* 1.0. (San Jose, CA: Rational Software Corporation), 1997.

H. Wilars. "Amplification of Business Cognition through Modeling Techniques." IEA Congress, 1991.

Index

Page references in boldface indicate illustrations.